ALSO IN THE
POSITIVE DISCIPLINE SERIES

NEW MILFORD PUBLIC LIBRARY

P9-CRZ-797

DISCARDED

Positive Discipline: The First Three Years
Jane Nelsen, Cheryl Erwin, and R̶

Positive Discipline for Preschoolers,
Revised 2nd Edition
Jane Nelsen, Cheryl Erwin, and Roslyn Duffy

Positive Discipline A–Z
Revised 2nd Edition
Jane Nelsen, Lynn Lott, and H. Stephen Glenn

Positive Discipline in the Classroom
Revised 3rd Edition
Jane Nelsen, Lynn Lott, and H. Stephen Glenn

Positive Discipline: A Teacher's A–Z Guide
Jane Nelsen, Roslyn Duffy, Linda Escobar,
Kate Ortolano, and Debbie Owen-Sohocki

Positive Discipline for Single Parents
Jane Nelsen, Cheryl Erwin, and Carol Delzer

Positive Discipline for Blended Families
Jane Nelsen, Cheryl Erwin, and H. Stephen Glenn

Positive Discipline for Parenting in Recovery
Jane Nelsen, Riki Intner, and Lynn Lott

Positive Time-Out: And Over 50 Ways to Avoid Power
Struggles in Homes and Schools
Jane Nelsen

OCT 2008

To my children, who continue to teach me there is always more to learn, and that learning from mistakes is a lifelong process
—Jane

. . .

To Casey and Corey, my first teens
—Lynn

DISCARD

Positive Discipline for Teenagers

Empowering Your Teens and Yourself
Through Kind and Firm Parenting

REVISED 2nd EDITION

Jane Nelsen, Ed.D.

Lynn Lott, M.A.

PRIMA PUBLISHING
3000 Lava Ridge Court • Roseville, California 95661
(800) 632-8676 • www.primalifestyles.com

NEW MILFORD PUBLIC LIBRARY
24 MAIN STREET
NEW MILFORD, CT 06776

© 2000 by Jane Nelsen, Lynn Lott

All rights reserved. No part of this book may be reproduced or transmitted in any form or by any means, electronic or mechanical, including photocopying, recording, or by any information storage or retrieval system, without written permission from Prima Publishing, except for the inclusion of quotations in review.

PRIMA PUBLISHING and colophon are registered trademarks of Prima Communications Inc., registered with the United States Patent and Trademark Office.

The case studies are based on actual events, but names have been omitted or changed to protect the privacy of the people involved.

All products mentioned in this book are trademarks of their respective companies.

Illustrations by Paula Gray

Library of Congress Cataloging-in-Publication Data

Nelsen, Jane.
   Positive discipline for teenagers / Jane Nelsen, Lynn Lott—2nd ed.
      p. cm. — (The positive discipline series)
   Includes bibliographical references and index.
   ISBN 0-7615-2181-X
   1. Parent and teenager. 2. Interpersonal conflict. 3. Adolescent psychology. I. Lott, Lynn.
II. Title.

HQ799.15.N45 2000
649'.125—dc21

99-059674
CIP

00 01 02 03 DD 10 9 8 7 6 5 4 3 2 1
Printed in the United States of America

HOW TO ORDER

Single copies may be ordered from Prima Publishing, 3000 Lava Ridge Court, Roseville CA 95661; telephone (800) 632-8676. Quantity discounts are also available. On your letterhead, include information concerning the intended use of the books and the number of books you wish to purchase.

Visit us online at www.primalifestyles.com

CONTENTS

FOREWORD

SOME SAY WE are born twice: first our mothers do the labor; second we do the labor during our adolescence. The second time is often harder on our mothers and us. The developmental state called *adolescence* has been noted as a time of great stress and turmoil—for those passing through it and for those who raise and educate adolescents. In terms of human development, individuals are born with no established identity. In the first five years, we accumulate data about ourselves. During the next five years, we refine this data and learn to behave in ways that reflect this sense of self. From ten to twelve years of age, we form beliefs about the world and ourselves. These beliefs govern our actions (morals and ethics). But just when we know who we are and what we believe, along comes puberty and "everything we know about life and ourselves is swept away in a rush of surging hormones, and we have to start over."

During adolescence, bodies change—or don't change—dramatically. Either can be quite traumatic. In any group of twelve year olds, there is up to six years' difference (in either direction) between minds and bodies. Teens are subject to feelings and impulses they don't understand and have never encountered before. They must separate from their parents and rediscover themselves as people in their own right. What they need most is supportive contact with more mature people who make them feel listened to, understood, and affirmed as unique and significant people. They need room to test and validate themselves as people. They need patience and stability from those around them and opportunities to develop.

Unfortunately, in America, as all these changes begin, we choose this moment in the educational system to take teens out of relationships with primary teachers they know and trust, a stable group where they feel secure, and an educational model they understand. They become part of a constantly rotating group of educational migrants, moving from teacher to teacher on an hourly basis. Today, extended family and long-term family friends, which were once adolescents' most critical socialization resources, are often unavailable. Similarly, opportunities for practical experience in life and the workplace are no longer provided.

The idea of *teenager* is a stereotype that says that the most significant thing about a young person between 13 and 19 years of age is the 1 in his or her age. We do not discriminate among the worth, significance, and needs of a prepubescent 13 year old and a 19-year-old man or woman. This is particularly problematic when we realize that the major task of adolescence is to break out of a stereotype (child) and achieve the status of individual. It is essential that we begin to perceive and refer to adolescents as *young people* to encourage them and allow for the individuation process.

In *Positive Discipline for Teenagers,* the authors have drawn on their extensive experience as counselors and workshop leaders to create a sensitive and practical resource for understanding and working with young people. The developmental insights are solid and helpful, and the anecdotal material drawn from workshops and case studies gives warmth to the discussion. The emphasis on firmness with dignity and respect highlights essential principles in teaching young people the nature of authority and helping to develop their own capacities of self-discipline, judgment, and responsibility. When coupled with the idea that "mistakes are wonderful opportunities to learn," we find a rich and powerful set of tools for encouraging self-actualization and building self-esteem in young people.

As a former director of the National Drug Abuse Training Center, I am encouraged by this book's treatment of drug and alcohol abuse. It is often difficult to recognize patterns of use and abuse and the stages young people go through as they are exposed to drugs and alcohol. Using and developing sound judgment without being judgmental has always been difficult, and the processes outlined here help focus and simplify the task. The intervention guidelines are very sound and reflect our best understanding of the process to date. The emphasis on maintaining the relationship may be troublesome to those of authoritarian orientation. It might be helpful to consider this: What good is a strong parental position if the child is alienated from the parent or is not converted to it?

Overall, *Positive Discipline for Teenagers* will join the authors' previous works as an important and useful resource for working with and understanding young people and ourselves.

—*H. Stephen Glenn*

ACKNOWLEDGMENTS

From Lynn

I'D LIKE TO acknowledge the following for their help and inspiration in the reworking of *Positive Discipline for Teenagers:* My mom, Shirley Barobs, for her stories from the juvenile panel in Phoenix where she volunteers; Ingeborg Heinje, for her teen stories and endless support; my stepsons, Steve and Dave Penny, my niece, Alissa, and my nephews, Joe, Dan, and Cole, who continued my education about teens and provided me with endless material; family therapist Marti Baerg, for her tireless efforts using our materials to encourage discouraged parents of teens; and Hal, who never runs out of energy helping me find and share my voice.

From Jane

YEARS AGO, I thought that if my children were raised on Positive Discipline, they would be perfect teenagers. I forgot about the normal individuation process. So, when my teens started rebelling, I panicked, threw all my philosophies and confidence out the window, and tried the control route. Of course, everything deteriorated. Fortunately, I attended a workshop on teens, conducted by Lynn Lott at a North American Society of Adlerian Psychology convention, and found my sanity as well as some encouragement. I knew I needed more. At that time, Lynn and I were only acquaintances through our Adlerian connections. I announced to her, "We have to write a book together on teens, because I know you can help me, and if I can get over my fears and apply Adlerian principles with my teens, we can share it with others." Lynn resisted and said she was too busy. But her husband Hal and I encouraged her until she gave in. The first edition took two years to write—it took that long to process all the suggestions with my teens and with other parents in our "Empowering

Teens and Yourself in the Process" workshops. We didn't want to suggest anything that didn't pass the test of practical application for positive results.

Thank you, Lynn. My relationship with all seven of my adult children is the best.

From Both of Us

BECAUSE WE ARE empirical scientists, we wanted to test every activity and every strategy with real parents. We are very grateful to all the parents of teens who attended our workshops and came to us for counseling. They demonstrated how difficult it can be to get past their fears and to let go of the pilot's seat of their teen's lives so they could take their proper place in the copilot's seat. They also demonstrated the rewarding results when they did. This book could not have been written without them.

And, this book would not have the form and polish without the help of Tara Mead, our project editor, and Jamie Miller, our acquisitions editor. And of course, this book would not have the lively feel without the illustrations of Paula Gray.

We are especially pleased by the feedback from teens who have read this book and have recommended it to their parents and teachers, even though we stress "holding teens accountable." Our guess is that they appreciate being treated with dignity and respect while learning the skills they need to become successful adults.

INTRODUCTION

REMEMBER WHEN YOUR teen was a baby just learning to walk? What a milestone. You didn't want to miss any of it, and you were very supportive and encouraging. You would take her little hands in yours and start walking along with her—but you knew you had to let go in order for her to walk by herself. You also knew she might fall when you let go, but you had faith that this was just part of the process.

So, you let go, and she took a few wobbly steps and fell. What did you do? You probably encouraged, "Look what you did! You took a few steps. You can do it. Let's try again." You were both having a great time. When she got tired of the game and didn't want to practice walking anymore, you backed off and waited awhile. You knew she would master walking in time, and you were having a ball supporting her in the process.

Meanwhile, you prepared her environment. You childproofed your home. You covered sharp corners and removed breakable objects that could hurt your child. You created a safe space in which she could expand her skills. We call this *bridge building*, and we think of you as a *bridge builder*. When your children are small and helpless, you build bridges that have sides close together, so your children have safety with room to move about, experiment, learn, and grow. As your children get older and more skilled, you move the "sides of their bridges" farther apart so they have more room to move about freely while continuing to be safe.

Are You Building Appropriate Bridges for Your Teen?

NOW YOU HAVE a teen who is learning to be an adult. Where are the sides of the bridge today? Are you closing them in because of your fears? Are you expanding them to support her process? Do you know you have to let go before she can ever master adulthood? Do you know that when you do let go, she will stumble and fall? When she falls or makes a mistake, do you understand that this is just part of the growing process? (Didn't you stumble and fall and make mistakes?) Do you encourage and cheer and show your faith in her to make it? Do you offer guidance and teach skills in respectful ways that invite listening and provide practice—whoever said that practice means perfect? Practice is part of the developmental growth process.

Do You Understand the Developmental Growth Process?

ADOLESCENCE IS AN important part of the individuation process. During this time, teens try to find out who they are and separate from their parents. The problem is that most parents tend to do many things during this time that make situations worse instead of better. This book will help you educate, challenge, and support teens in an atmosphere of mutual respect that affirms your self-worth as well as the self-worth of your children. It is also a time when you can explore your own unresolved teen issues.

Every chapter in this book has such valuable information that it was difficult to decide which chapters should be at the beginning. We thought all of the chapters warranted at least first or second status. Therefore, read the chapters in any order that appeals to you, because all of them will help you retrain yourself so you can "parent" your teen more effectively—and with perspective.

Have You Lost Your Perspective and Your Sense of Humor?

WE HOPE THAT you are operating in a kind, firm, and encouraging way. We know that going through the teen years can be like going through a war zone for both you and your teens and that it is easy for kindness and firmness to fall away and be replaced by less encouraging parenting methods. It is easy to lose your sense of awe along with your sense of humor—remember how cute and adorable you thought your teen was when he stumbled as a baby—and your loving ways when you look at your teen and ask yourself, "What have I created? Who is this person? How did this happen? What do I do now?"

There are many challenges and difficulties facing you as the parent of a teenager. Do you think that your teenager should be perfect by now, after all the years you have spent raising her? Actually, she is perfect—perfect in her individuation (rebellion) process, although that's probably not what you had in mind. Maybe you have forgotten about or weren't aware of the individuation process, so you are panicking. You may be taking her rebellious behavior personally and thinking you are a failure. If everything seems out of control, perhaps you are questioning what you have been doing. Perhaps you are thinking, "Maybe I should be more controlling. Control would keep my teenager from being so obnoxious and will save her from making mistakes that could drastically affect the rest of her life—if she lives!" You may not like to hear this, but control does not work with teens.

Do You Have the Illusion That Control Is Effective with Teens?

ALTHOUGH CONTROL SOMETIMES provides the illusion of success on a short-term basis, children who are raised with both choices and responsibility are more comfortable individuating under their parents' noses instead of going underground. And you don't want your children to go underground, because then they lose out on the best support and help they can get during these years—yours! This book will help you find answers and principles that work instead of throwing in the towel or giving up on your child or yourself. Working with your teenager can become an opportunity to learn or relearn the meaning of mutual respect and help you sort out the differences between your issues and hers. When you learn to parent with kindness and firmness instead of control, you'll truly see what a fascinating individual your teen is.

How Will Your Teen React to Your New Parenting Skills?

IF YOU HAVE parented your child with an iron fist up to this point, your teen will love you for giving her more room, but she may misunderstand what having more freedom and choices truly means. In that case it will be up to you to help her understand the responsibility that goes with choices. This book will show you many ways to get that message across successfully.

If you have spoiled and overprotected your children, your teen won't be thrilled to start taking more responsibility. She may be used to you doing everything for her. She may think that responsibility is your job. She may be unskilled and lazy and maybe even a little bit afraid. What if she really can't do what is needed? What if she looks stupid trying? What if it is stressful taking on more? Be prepared for when your teen tries to convince you that it is your job as the parent to continue doing for her what she could learn to do for herself. Be ready for her anger at you as you hold her accountable for her behavior. Once she finishes her "temper tantrum," you will be amazed at how easily she takes to being more responsible.

Have You Forgotten That You Count, Too?

ONE OF THE biggest changes we hope you will make as you read this book is to put yourself back in the picture. If you are reading this book, we know that you believe kids count, but have you remembered that you count, too? The more you consider your needs along with your teenager's, the quicker you will be able to feel better about both your teen and yourself.

Does Your Teen Have the Same Needs as Other Teens?

WE USE THE word *teen* loosely in our book to refer to a wide variety of young people. As you read the examples, keep in mind who you are dealing with in your family. Is your teen mature for her age? Is she a late bloomer? Some of our stories, activities, and suggestions are more appropriate for the teen who needs the sides of the bridge to be wider, while others are for the new teen who is beginning to test her wings. Because you are the *bridge builder,* it is important that you work with your teen to create the right amount of space as it is needed.

Are You Working *with* Your Teen?

NOTICE THAT WE say work *with* your teen. It's perfectly fine to start from wherever you are. However, instead of trying to fix, manage, or control everything yourself, it's time to create a dialogue and a method for involving your teen in the process of growing up. Your job is to prepare your teen for life. Perhaps you wish you had started when she was younger. That would have been nice, but if you didn't, it is time to start now. Remember to take small steps and work on your new skills one at a time until you feel more comfortable with them. You'll find parenting so much easier when you do this. This book will show you how!

How Do You Know When Your Child Becomes a Teen?

WHEN SALLY BECAME a teenager, her mother thought Sally had become a different person. But Sally was really the same person she had always been—she just looked different. She dressed differently, had different friends, became a rock fan, and started playing the guitar. Underneath, she was still Sally, but now she had taken on a new role: Sally "the rocker." I asked Sally's mother, "When Sally was little, was she interested in superheroes? Did she ask you to sew a 'W' on her leotard for when she played Wonder Woman? Did you think it was cute? Could you think of her that way now? Imagine that she's put on the suit of a rocker. That's what is going on; she's trying on an identity, but the identity is not who Sally really is." How different is your role now from the roles you played as a teen? Remember, even though living with your adolescent child may seem to last forever, adolescence is just a brief part of the growing process. It is by no means the final destination.

When Did You Realize You Had a Teen?

DID YOU REALIZE you had a teen the day you found out just how "dumb" you were and that you didn't know anything? Was it when you noticed that one day your child did not want to be seen with you and the next he was cuddling up to you, holding your hand, or asking you to take him somewhere?

Was it when she started speaking your name in four syllables if you did something she didn't like, such as reaching out to give her a hug (even though she had just hugged you)? You've heard it, haven't you? "Maaa-a-ah-mmm" or "Daaa-a-ah-ddd!"

You know you have a teenager when you hear yourself complaining, "She has no purpose. He won't help. She only cares about her friends. He is so self-centered. Her room is a mess. I can't trust him. This is out of control. I can't stand her hair, clothes, makeup, or music. He wastes his money. She resents me and idolizes rock stars. He is on drugs and treats me like dirt. She is moody and irresponsible."

Another sign that you have an adolescent is when you hear him complaining, "My parents treat me like a kid. They think I'm having sex all the time. They butt in. They hate my friends. They give advice. They try to live my life for me. They are never satisfied. All they do is ask questions and control my life. Why can't they just leave me alone?"

THE TRANSFORMATION

The door to the jetway closed as the last passenger arrived and still there was no sign of my fourteen-year-old nephew who had flown out to go snowboarding with me. He had been flying by himself since he was eight to spend winter vacations with us, so I figured everything would be fine, but still, where was he? In a few minutes, the door opened and out came—*whom!?* The person who emerged no longer looked like a boy. He had turned into a young man, with hair carefully combed in the latest style, standing up perfectly on top of his head instead of extending in twenty different directions. His shirtsleeves covered his hands, and his hip-hugger pants were carefully rolled at the bottom to expose tennis shoes with tongues neatly folded over the laces. This outfit wasn't the usual hand-me-down from his cousins, but was chosen with care to present a certain image. When I asked where he had been, he rolled his eyes and looked at me like I was the dumbest creature on the planet and said, "I was putting on my mousse." It was then that I knew my nephew was now a full-fledged adolescent!

The Dream Teen and the Normal Teen

IN OUR WORKSHOP on parenting teenagers, we asked one group to draw a "normal" teen, or how most parents see their teens. The composite teen was messy and self-centered, listened to loud music, defied authority, preferred friends to family, decorated room with posters, valued cars and an independent lifestyle, conformed to the clothing styles of peers (no matter how gross), smoked, and drank alcohol. Comments from the group included:

"Well this is an exaggeration. All teens aren't like this."
"But, it sure does depict the rebelliousness because most of them are a lot like this."
"It helps to be reminded that my teen would not be normal if he cleaned his room."
"Come to think about it, I was like that once."

This last comment was a nice reminder to the group that we all continue to grow and change beyond adolescence.

Another group was asked to draw a "dream" teen, or how most parents think they want their teens to be. The composite teen was voted prom queen or king, kept agreements ("I promise to be there on time, as always."), volunteered to help, loved to talk to parents ("Let me tell you everything about my life."), ate only healthy food, didn't watch television, was very athletic, earned two scholarships (one athletic and one academic), scored high on the SATs, lined up a summer job by January, supplied his or her own money for hair or makeup and saved the rest for college and a car, respected everyone (including siblings), was respectfully assertive, and was an A student. Comments from the group included:

> It helps to be reminded that my teen would not be normal if he cleaned his room.

"A teen like this wouldn't have any friends. No one could stand him."
"I have friends who have a teen like this and I can't stand her."
"My teen *is* like this, although she seems pretty stressed most of the time."

This exercise reveals that although you may fantasize about having an ideal teen, you instinctively know that such a creature is rarely found. Even though the reality of living with a "normal" teen can be quite painful, it will be easier if you can come to a deeper understanding of what is happening during adolescence.

Parents often see "the good kid" as the standard. You may not have thought about this, but these teens need help, too. They've often sold out to become pleasers and approval junkies. Their parents use them as the standard and say to siblings, "Why can't you be more like your brother or sister? At least I have one that doesn't give me any trouble." The good kid may feel significant only if he or she is getting this kind of praise. Many of these teens fall apart when they make their first big mistake. Some cannot handle the competition of finding that they are not the only special student in college. Unable to handle this pressure, some even commit suicide because they don't think they can stay on top.

Someone once said that the teen years were created so parents would find it easier to let go when their children turned twenty. At times this statement seems like an understatement. Some teens can be very hard to love. They make promises that they forget to keep. They think they know everything and continually tell you how stupid you are. They hate to clean their rooms, they listen to music you can't stand, and they exaggerate everything. They even talk funny. Sometimes they talk so fast, only another teenager can understand what they're saying. Other teens seem to withdraw into a shell. They don't put you down, they just clam up or revert to one-word sentences such as, "Yeah" or "Nah." Occasionally you may hear three words, "I don't know."

Often, parents look at their teens and feel a sense of failure. You may wonder how you could have created such a monster. You may wonder if there is any hope for one last chance to teach them lessons and to mold them into decent human beings. You may feel desperate and hopeless, angry and aggravated.

If you could simply relax and remember that these are the years when your children are experimenting in an attempt to find out what they think, you could enjoy them more. If you gave up trying to teach them and instead learned to be curious and amazed, you could appreciate their struggle. If you could relax, you could trust that who they are now is in no way a reflection on you or indicative of who they will be when they grow up. With these new attitudes, you could focus on long-range parenting and learn to be a guide and facilitator who your teen could trust.

Take a Trip Down Memory Lane

THINK BACK TO your teen years. Do you remember what your world was like? What were your issues? What did you think about all day? Take time to make a list of what was important to you. You might even want to talk to people who were teens during different decades (the 1990s, 1980s, 1970s, and so forth). Ask them what was important to them as teens, what they were like, and how they were parented. Compare your information with the following issues, mentioned by teens today:

TEEN ISSUES

Am I going to get invited to the dance?

What should I wear?

How can I find time for studying?

How can I be popular, or at least included?

How can I get a car?

What should I do about drinking, drugs, and sex?

What is happening to my body? Will my breasts/penis be as big as the other kids'?

Will other kids think I'm cool?

How can I get my parents off my back?

Should I go to college?

What is there to do? (I'm bored!)

What are other kids saying about me behind my back?

How can I ever please my parents? (All they care about is grades and chores.)

Notice that these issues do not include anything about clean rooms, a clean house, doing chores, spending time with family, being considerate, or being nice to brothers and sisters. Parents often think that their teens are doing or not doing certain things because they want to hurt their parents or that their teens are being disrespectful of their wishes. As you can see from your list and the list above, teenagers usually aren't thinking much about their parents. Parents will be much happier if they accept and respect the fact that, for instance, chores are not a priority for teens. That doesn't mean they shouldn't do them. It does mean you'll have better results if you acknowledge to your children, "I can understand that chores aren't a priority for you, but they need to be done anyway. Let's work on a plan to make chores as easy as possible."

What Is Happening During Adolescence?

IF YOU THINK that how your children behave as teenagers is who they will be for the rest of their lives, you probably feel a fair amount of anxiety. Although it may seem otherwise, your teens have not grown up to be terrible people, because they are not grown up yet. They are individuating; their behavior is only temporary. It will last for as long as it takes for them to find out who they are and how they can move from childhood to adulthood.

Many life tasks are inherent in child growth and development. These tasks may be physical, intellectual, emotional, social, psychological, or spiritual. As young people move through adolescence, from childhood to adulthood, their primary task is individuation.

Although it may seem otherwise, your teens have not grown up to be terrible people, because they are not grown up yet. They are individuating; their behavior is only temporary.

CHARACTERISTICS OF INDIVIDUATION

1. Adolescents have a need to find out who they are.

2. Individuation usually looks like rebellion to parents.

3. Adolescents go through huge physical and emotional changes.

4. Peer relationships take precedence over family relationships.

5. Teens explore and exercise personal power and autonomy.

6. Teens have a great need for privacy.

7. Parents become an embarrassment to their teens.

8. Teens see themselves as omnipotent and all knowing.

Adolescents Have a Need to Find Out Who They Are

Teens want to know how they are different from their families, how they feel and what they think about things, and what their own values are. This process of separation from the family in preparation for an independent adulthood is called individuation.

Individuation Usually Looks Like Rebellion to Parents

Although most parents worry when their teenagers rebel, it would be more appropriate to worry if they didn't. Teenagers must begin their separation from their families, and rebellion gives them the ability to do this. At first, teens may rebel by challenging what is important to their families (family values) or zeroing in on what their parents want and then doing exactly the opposite. Later, they may rebel in other ways—but at first individuation is primarily a reaction against their parents, and doing the opposite is the simplest, most natural way of being different. If teens are not allowed to rebel, they may do it in their twenties, thirties, or fifties. Even worse, they may become approval junkies— afraid to take risks or to feel comfortable with who they are.

Adolescents Go Through Huge Physical and Emotional Changes

Whether they like it or not, adolescents are maturing physically and sexually, undergoing biological processes that are essentially out of their control. In addition to the tumultuous, contradictory feelings these major changes cause, adolescents may feel anxiety regarding their rate of change—they may feel their physical maturation is too quick or too slow in relation to that of their peers. (Most parents would prefer their children to mature slowly, but nature has its own patterns.)

The physical maturation process, with its sudden and powerful hormonal changes, causes mood swings. Without premeditation, teens are delightful one minute and biting your head off the next. In addition, some teens are in such a rapid rate of physical growth that they experience real "growing pains," where their bodies actually hurt.

Peer Relationships Take Precedence Over Family Relationships

Teens need to work out their relationships with peers to find out if and how they fit in. Friendships take the place of time spent with family. Although peer relationships help teens in their task of separation, parents often interpret it as rejection or rebellion. Have patience. If you avoid power struggles and criticism, your teen will become one of your best friends in his or her twenties.

Teens Explore and Exercise Personal Power and Autonomy

Teens have a strong desire to find out what they are capable of—they need to test their power and importance in the world. This means that they want to decide what they can do for themselves without being directed and ordered. Parents often take this as a challenge to their own power, thus creating power struggles. Some teens find personal power so intimidating that they *want* others, usually their peers, to tell them what to do, which can be a dangerous consequence of overly controlling parents. This is not a very easy choice— rebellion or compliance—but it's often the only choice teens see when they don't have the opportunity to exercise their own personal power and autonomy. For parents, the key is learning to support teen rebellion in respectful ways that teach important life skills, which is the focus of this book.

Teens Have a Great Need for Privacy

Because their rate of development moves so fast and is out of their control, it can be embarrassing for teens to have their families watching and knowing. As teens try to figure out what's important to them, they may engage in activities without parental approval before deciding for themselves that they might not want to do the activities after all. To escape getting in trouble or to avoid disappointing you, teens will figure out how to test activities that you may not approve of without your knowledge.

Your teen's need for privacy can be very scary for you. You may worry that you are not being a responsible parent if you don't know everything your teen is doing. You may fear that your teen might build bombs (or engage in some other disastrous activity) if you are not vigilant. We have news for you: If your teens are going to engage in these activities, they will do it in spite of your vigilance. They will just go underground so they have less chance of getting caught.

The best prevention for possible disaster is to build kind and firm relationships with your teens—let them know that they are unconditionally important to you and provide opportunities for them to learn important life skills. They will then be able to think for themselves and figure out what is important to them. Accomplishing this goal is the aim of this book.

Parents Become an Embarrassment to Their Teens

During the teenage years, teens tend to put their parents down and try to show parents how "stupid" they are. Sometimes teens act embarrassed around their parents and families in public or may even refuse to be seen with them. The affection that may have been a normal part of family life may suddenly become taboo. We will remind you many times that this is a temporary condition, unless you make an issue of it that builds resentment for the future.

Teens See Themselves as Omnipotent and All Knowing

Parents who try to tell teens how to dress or eat or what they can or can't do just don't seem to understand that teens *never* get sick, *don't* get cold, *don't* need sleep, and can *live forever* on junk food or no food at all. Many parents wonder how their children even survive these years, but the facts are that most teens do. To some it may seem that the

The best prevention for possible disaster is to build kind and firm relationships with your teens—let them know that they are unconditionally important to you and provide opportunities for them to learn important life skills.

methods we advocate are permissive and increase the chances of drastic consequences. The opposite is true.

Not Permissiveness

OFTEN, WE GET a very strong reaction from parents who read this list of teenage characteristics. The comments of these parents are very similar, "You can't just stop being a parent and let kids go off on their own to *individuate*." That last word is said with a great deal of sarcasm.

We do not advocate permissiveness, because that kind of parenting deprives young people of the opportunities to learn life skills, to develop their own potential, to be self-reliant and responsible, and to learn from their mistakes. To do all of this, they need guidance (kind and firm parenting as described in chapter 3), but not external controls, which only increase rebellion. Throughout this book, we show you how to help guide your teens in new, positive ways.

The Many Faces of Individuation

BY APPRECIATING THE individual nature of each child and providing the nurturing that helps that child become the best of who he or she is, you raise the self-worth of everyone involved. You can learn acceptance from nature: It is clear that a cactus needs nurturing different from an orchid, and a rose cannot be a petunia, no matter what you might do to change it. Imagine someone giving you a cactus to take care of for the rest of your life. How would you feel about the plant you received? Would it be your favorite plant? If you received a cactus but wanted a rose, could you do anything to turn your cactus into a rose? What would it take to nurture the plant you had received?

Similarly, parenting teens is an acceptance process. Instead of trying to mold your teen to fit your perception of how he or she should be, focus on who your teen is. Let go. By doing so, your teens will be more able to discover their uniqueness and potential. And, as with the plants, when you nurture your teens instead of trying to change them, parenting becomes less difficult.

All Individuation (or Rebellion) Does Not Look the Same

Individuation may take as many different forms of behavior as there are different teens. But there *are* some general behaviors that most teenagers exhibit, such as not wanting to be with their families, not wanting to clean their rooms, and listening to music parents hate. Some rebel mildly or passively; some, severely and aggressively.

The most difficult type of rebellion for parents to deal with—and the most typical—is the kind directed against what parents value most. If you're a math teacher, it is possible that your teenager will fail in math. If piano lessons are important to you, prepare for a fight when your teen decides to quit the piano and take up the guitar. If being active in your church is what you value, your teen will probably stop going to church. For us as therapists, it is difficult to watch other teenagers flock to our doors, while our own children think "shrinks are stupid" and refuse to share anything important with us. It can be especially hard when your child who once told you "everything" now sneaks off to concerts or other "forbidden" (by you, of course) places rather than face your disapproval or disappointment.

Don't Fan the Flames of Rebellion

Keep in mind that the types of teenage rebellion are usually temporary (one to five years). However, if you do not understand that rebellion is part of adolescence and you instead make it an issue, the rebellion may extend into adulthood. Individuation often becomes all-out rebellion when you invalidate the normal growth process in any of the following ways:

YOU FAN THE FLAMES OF REBELLION WHEN YOU . . .

1. Don't understand, respect, or support the individuation process.

2. Take the individuation process personally: "How could she do this to me?"

3. Feel guilty: "This wouldn't be happening if I had been a better parent."

4. Get scared about the mistakes your teen makes as he or she tries different behaviors and different values.

5. Try to stunt your teen's individuation through shaming, control, punishment, overprotection, or neglect.

6. Think that what your teen is doing is what he or she has become and who he or she will be, *forever.*

7. Don't respect that your teen is different from you and may choose a lifestyle you would not enjoy or approve of.

In other words, if you could eliminate all of the above behaviors, individuation might not escalate into open rebellion—but we don't know many parents who can do this. It's also true that teenagers sometimes think they *have* to rebel to individuate, even when parents are supportive of teen individuation.

Don't Take Your Teen's Behavior Personally

We find that of all the ways parents fan the flames of rebellion, this is the most common. When you believe your children are against you and treating you badly for some personal reason, you feel a need to show them that they can't get away with that kind of behavior. You end up escalating problems so that you are in a war of hurt feelings. Your teenagers don't do what they do simply to hurt you. The truth is that teenagers usually aren't even thinking about parents when they do things. When you take your teen's behavior personally, you are reacting to your children as if you were a child. You can save yourself much grief when you see that, rather than doing something to you or against you, your teen is an individual who is going through a process of individuation that is unique to him or her.

Remember that teen concerns are very different from yours. Teenagers think things like, "How will I get enough money to party? How am I going to get my studying done? What will I do if my friend won't talk to me after school? What am I going to do about drugs, drinking, and sex?" You are thinking things like, "She is getting even with me by not doing her chores. How can he be so irresponsible and inconsiderate? How can I motivate her to get better grades? Why won't my fourteen-year-old son take a shower without me nagging him to do so?" We suggest thinking about whether you are understanding the world of your teenager, respecting his or her individuation process, and having faith in your teen's ultimate goodness. We hope you will step back and focus on knowing your teen better.

Get Into Your Teen's World

To be on your teenager's side, you have to know who your teenager is. You can't be supportive unless you get into your teen's world and understand what is important to him or her, which will be hard, if not impossible, to do if you spend too much time focusing on your own perceptions and remembering a world that is long past. Times change. Norms and values are different today from when you were a teenager.

> You can save yourself much grief when you see that, rather than doing something to you or against you, your teen is an individual who is going through a process of individuation that is unique to him or her.

Things that were unacceptable when you were young may be perfectly acceptable for teenagers today. A good example is pierced ears. When some of you were growing up, if a boy had his ears pierced, it meant he was a punk, a hippie, or even gay. Unless a boy wanted to be perceived that way, he wouldn't get his ears pierced—it was only acceptable for girls or women. Now it's different. Body piercing is popular and pierced or multipierced ears, for both men and women, are respectable fashion statements. The difference between what you find acceptable and what your teen feels is acceptable can create stressful issues for both of you. We found an extreme example of changing times when we read a book written on adolescence in 1890. One of the greatest concerns for teens of that day was to avoid being seen eating in public! Imagine how the author of the book written in 1890 would feel after reading the following scenarios. Notice how different each teen is. Try to figure out how you could be supportive of each.

When Tammi was fourteen, she couldn't understand why she did some of the things she did. She loved her parents and didn't want to hurt their feelings, yet she went to the beach with her friends even though she knew her parents didn't want her to. Tammi felt guilty—in addition to disobeying her parents, she lied by telling them she was going to a friend's house. She knew her parents wouldn't mind that. Tammi's behavior wasn't easy for her parents either, because they feared that she was making potentially life-threatening decisions.

Macey's parents met in junior high school, went steady in high school, got engaged in college, and married upon graduation. When their thirteen-year-old, well-developed daughter announced that it was time for her to start having sex, they were considerably shocked. Macey explained, with great sincerity, that sex is different from making love. She told her parents that sex was merely an activity, like bowling, and she was ready for the experience. She wanted to get some practice and learn how to do it properly. That way she would be prepared whenever she met Mr. Right and she wouldn't make love without bungling.

Thirteen-year-old Philippe was trying to figure out how to make friends after transferring from his private elementary school to the public junior high. His favorite activities were playing computer games, practicing the drums, skateboarding in the summer, and snowboarding in the winter. Philippe looked like a ten year old and was as naive as Macey was precocious. His parents were worried because when they were his age they had been extremely social. They thought he might be suffering from some kind of personality disorder.

Fifteen-year-old Max had discovered pot, partying, and girls. His idea of a good time was cutting school and going to his friend's house to get loaded, listen to music, and then hang out in front of the local coffeehouse. His parents knew nothing about his activities, as he had a friend in the school's attendance office who covered for Max. His parents were completely baffled by his slipping grades. Max explained that the teachers didn't like him and were picking on him.

Sixteen-year-old Chrissy handled her own checkbook, worked part time, was in the school orchestra, ran errands for her parents using the family car, and spent most of her spare time doing homework, practicing her flute, and volunteering at the local hospital in the candy striper program. Her parents were proud of her, but they were also afraid she was growing up too fast and not enjoying her youth.

Eighteen-year-old Marcus refused to leave his room. He had dropped out of school at seventeen because it had been "a waste of time." He spent every minute he could at his computer. He had friends around the world with whom he communicated regularly, and he was seen as the local computer genius, always available to help someone with any computer problem. Because Marcus' dad had quit school early to join the service and had never gone back to graduate, he blamed himself for Marcus' lack of interest in school.

How would you figure out what each of these teens needs? If Tammi, Macey, Philippe, Max, Chrissy, or Marcus were your teen, would you feel that you were a failure because he or she didn't conform to society's norms? Would you compare him or her with your other children or with the neighbors' kids? Do you think there is one right way to do things—how it was done when you were a kid or how it should be done according to the current pop psychology? Understanding that all teens individuate differently and on their own schedule could help you and your teens live through this stage with more ease—and even some enjoyment. The following tips will help, too.

Tips for "Growing" a Teen

LET'S REVIEW WHAT is important to your teen and how you can deal with your teen's issues while being firm and kind, and respecting your teen and yourself. Four of your teen's most important needs are the need for privacy, the need for social connectedness, the need for freedom to examine a new point of view, and the need for space to make choices that may end up as mistakes.

Your Teen's Need for Privacy

As mentioned above, teens have a tremendous need for privacy, which parents often don't recognize. An important part of teenagers' maturation is finding out where they stand in relation to the various issues and values that life presents. They need privacy in which to experiment so that they won't make you or themselves feel as if they are bad for experimenting.

If your teenagers want to do something that runs counter to your attitudes and values, they try to do it so you won't find out. This protects them from experiencing your disapproval and protects you from feeling disappointment. Usually, teens return to the values they were taught at home, but they must be able to do this on their own—not because you want them to but because they have adopted the value for themselves. In reality, values are formed by age five and are the last thing to change. Thus your adolescent is experimenting, not going off the deep end. Whatever your family values are, they are a very deep part of your child, and you'll most likely see those values re-emerge once your teen works his or her way through adolescence.

If you have a hard time allowing your teen to have privacy and if you demand that your teen tells all, you may end up with a teen who excels at lying to you. Teens often lie because they love you and they want to protect you. They want to be able to do what they do without hurting your feelings. Other times, they lie to protect themselves—from your harsh opinions and possibly harsh actions.

WHAT TEENS SAY ABOUT LYING

"I lie to go to parties because my mom won't even negotiate with me if there aren't some parents there."

"I'm pretty honest with my mom because she treats me like I'm older than I am, and she teaches me how to be a responsible drinker."

"I lied when I was a freshman and sophomore. Then I decided I didn't want to lie to them. I told them, 'cuz I don't want to lie, and now I tell them everything. I've been through lots with my mom."

"I don't share things they wouldn't want to hear. They only want to hear good stuff, so I make up things, like, 'There was this girl at the party who was so retarded who got drunk.' (The girl is really me.)"

"I would feel lower about myself if I told the truth because my mother wouldn't understand, because of how she was raised."

"Telling the truth depends on your parents: some you can tell and others would chain us to our beds. Their idea of doing something bad was that they snuck out and tipped the cow over. They just wouldn't understand what we do."

When you understand your teen's motivation for lying, you can be much more effective in creating an atmosphere in which your teen feels safe to tell you the truth—most of the time. How many of you would tell the truth if you knew you would receive blame, shame, or pain from your confidant? How many of you would tell the truth if that would mean you couldn't do something you really wanted to do—that your confidant would "rain on your parade"? Would you tell the truth to be sure your confidant would protect you from learning from your own mistakes?

On the other hand, would you tell the truth if your confidant had faith in you to make your own mistakes while helping you explore possibilities? Would you tell the truth if you knew that your confidant would be supportive and encouraging even if you made mistakes? Doesn't it make sense to stop doing *to* your teens what wouldn't work for you, and start doing things *with* your teens what would work for you? One definition of mutual respect is to encourage others as we would like to be encouraged.

HOW TO RESPECT TEENS' NEEDS FOR PRIVACY

1. Schedule special time to be with your teens to strengthen the relationship and really get to know who they are (see chapter 7).

2. Make it clear that when your teens do come to you, they won't get criticism, judgment, or disapproval, but instead will get a friendly, supportive ear.

3. When your teens do get into trouble from the choices they make, use friendly curiosity questions, instead of lectures, to help them explore the consequences of behavior.

4. Kindly and firmly allow teens to be accountable for their choices without adding more punishment.

Respecting privacy doesn't mean abandonment. If your teen makes mistakes, you can still help out and work with your teen to correct those mistakes. We have worked with many families who have spent special time helping their teens figure out how to budget to pay for their own traffic tickets or insurance deductibles on accidents rather than rescuing their children or adding more unrelated punishment. When a teen earns minimum wage and is suddenly faced with a $500 deductible payment over time, reality is the best teacher. On a smaller scale, when your teen forgets to throw his favorite shirt in the laundry or spends all her money on a pair of designer jeans and has nothing left for other necessities, stand back and let him or her figure out what to do. This is the kind and firm way to teach your children about life.

Your Teen's Need for Social Connectedness

There are times when teens need something different from what is important to you. This often occurs when the issues of friendships and connecting with other teens arise—whether it centers on use of the telephone, e-mail, the Internet, the mall, the local hangout spot, or teen parties. Your teens will want to connect with people who they feel comfortable with and who they perceive to be like them or like they want to be.

Most parents try to be good parents by following the conventional wisdom that says they should always know who their teens' friends are, where they are, and whether a parent is around. Some teens will have no problem with parents meeting their friends, knowing their friends' parents, making sure an adult is around when kids get together, and telling parents where they are going and who they are going to be with. This information sharing could seem acceptable when your teens are younger, but then it might change as they get older.

Even if parents are extremely accepting and open minded about their teen's choices, teens find attempts to question where they are going, who is going to be there, and whether there is a parent at home a real pain and will even feel insulted as parents pry, question, lecture, or dig. Teens don't want adults choosing their friends or judging the ones they have. They don't want parents telling them that certain people or situations are dangerous for them, because often their experience of the situation doesn't seem dangerous at all.

Teens resent having parents tell them who they can hang out with and who they can't. They hate it when they are told that their friends are a bad influence, even if it is true. Teens usually go underground when parents try to control where they spend their time. If you don't believe this, ask your teen. However, this isn't to say that you shouldn't have opinions and policies. But you need to understand your teen's needs as well as your own. You also need to make sure that you participate in dialogues instead of monologues.

Consider the example of using the phone and computer. It can be very scary for many adolescents to interact with their peers face to face, so the telephone and email provide comfortable ways for them to get to know each other. During their conversations, they can check out various ideas, attitudes, and feelings—and because they are in the process of maturing, they have a lot to check out! Teenagers need a great deal of telephone or computer time, which you may find difficult to accept. Trying to control how long they talk or with whom they talk while they are on the phone usually results in ugly battles. On the other hand, when you respect their needs, they are more likely to negotiate phone time that is respectful to everyone.

We have all heard the horror stories about what is happening on the Internet. Yes, there are spooky adults out there who are pretending to be teenagers communicating with real teens. We heard about one adult who offered to buy an airplane ticket for a teen (who thought the adult was a teen) to come for a visit. The parents found out and somehow caught the adult, who was turned over to the police. However, it is sad when parents live their lives based on fears of the dangerous exceptions. It is much better to help children prepare for dangerous situations rather than fear them. We recommend conversations that allow for all involved to state their needs and opinions without being put down or told they are wrong or stupid. (Chapter 8 provides more information about how to do this at family meetings or one-on-one with your teen.) Having conversations with teens in which they tell you how they would handle potentially dangerous situations and how they would research to learn what is dangerous and what is not can be very helpful—much more helpful than telling them what is dangerous and what is not.

> It is sad when parents live their lives based on fears of the dangerous exceptions. It is much better to help children prepare for dangerous situations rather than fear them.

As you work out an agreement with your teen, consider the following solutions to teen communications: regulate the use of the family line, put in a second phone line, let your teens earn money to pay for a private line, set up a dedicated line for the computer, or use separate voice mails for your phone line. Although it is not your responsibility to pay for your teen's long-distance charges, it is up to you to communicate that information respectfully and to help your teen find a way to stay in contact with long-distance friends within his or her budget.

If your teens balk about you meeting their friends, you will gain more ground by asking curiosity questions instead of giving orders. Examples of such questions include, "Tell me more," "How is it a problem for you if I know where you are going or who you will be with?" and "How will you protect yourself if you get into trouble?"

Your Teen's Need for Freedom to Examine a New Point of View

Raymond got a call from juvenile hall telling him that his son James had been picked up for vandalism. In his parenting group, Raymond shared how he had panicked, gone crazy, and then catastrophized (made a huge mountain out of a molehill): "'I'm a failure as a father. My son is amoral, will end up a criminal, and will spend the rest of his life in prison.' I was so angry. I told James he could stay in juvenile hall and rot for all I cared. Then I went to the other extreme and bailed him out—but not without a price. The price was a class A guilt trip: 'How could you do this to me? I'm a failure. You're a failure. I have a criminal for a son.'"

Imagine yourself in Raymond's position. Has there been a time when your teen did something that seemed so awful to you that you jumped down his or her throat before finding out what he or she was thinking and what had happened from his or her point of view? There probably isn't a parent who hasn't reacted that way, but you can retrain yourself to help your teen think through a situation without your judgments and thus give him or her the space needed to figure out if he or she will want to do things differently in the future.

Look at the same scenario with a different reaction. This time Raymond used six firm and kind parenting tools.

SIX KIND AND FIRM PARENTING TOOLS

1. Show your unconditional love. (Let your teen know you are on his or her side.)

2. Remember to empathize.

3. Talk *with* your teenager—not *to*, *at*, or *for* him or her. (It is okay to share your feelings using "I" messages.)

4. Use what and how questions to help your teenager explore the consequences of his or her choices. (This is very different from imposing a consequence.)

5. Increase a sense of understanding by sharing a time when you had had a similar experience.

6. Decide, with dignity and respect, what you will do. (State what *you* will do instead of what you are going to try to make your teenager do.)

As Raymond drove James home from juvenile hall he remembered to empathize (1) and said, "What a bummer! I'd be pretty upset if that happened to me. Were you scared? How did they treat you? How did you feel?" Then he listened, without speaking, to what James had to say.

After driving in silence for a while, Raymond mentioned that he had decided to pick James up (2) because this was the first time James had been in juvenile hall. Raymond told James, "I'm not sure what happened, but I know you're not a criminal. You may have made a poor choice, but you are still a good person and a worthwhile human being. Want to tell me what happened?" (3) This is a tricky skill for most parents. It means forgoing lectures, judgments, guilt trips, and assumptions. It means really wanting to know and understand your teen's perspective, even though it may be very different from your own. Most importantly, it means asking your teenager if he would like to discuss the experience with you and stifling yourself if he says no. And he *will* say no if you lecture, judge, lay on a guilt trip, or assume you know what he thinks or should think.

When James agreed to talk with his dad, Raymond began asking what and how questions (4) that were completely void of judgment but that expressed a sincere desire to understand James's point of view: "What happened? What were you thinking of? What were you trying to accomplish? How was it for you? What was the most important thing you learned from this experience? How do you think you might handle this kind of thing in the future?"

After James answered the questions, Raymond decided to tell his son the following story: "I can remember a time when I was twelve years old. The police came to our house (we didn't have a juvenile hall in the small town where I was raised) because some friends of mine and I had thrown rocks through the windows of a neighbor's warehouse. I was just having fun with my friends. It didn't even occur to me that it would cost a lot of money to replace those windows. I felt so ashamed of myself and embarrassed for my parents. I knew I wasn't a bad kid. I had just done a stupid thing."

Still trying to understand James' point of view, Raymond talked with his son some more to draw him out: "I wonder if you had any feelings similar to mine. I wonder if you were just going along with the crowd, or if you had other motives. I wonder if you didn't think about the other person like I didn't. I wonder if you felt embarrassed like I did, or just angry about getting caught. I would really like to know if you feel like sharing with me."

Your Teen's Need for Space to Make Mistakes

Because Raymond wanted James to think about how he would handle a similar situation if it happened again (6), he said, "James, I don't know what you learned from this situation or how you would handle it differently in the future, but I'd like you to know that this was scary for me. I felt like bailing you out this time, but I know I'd feel resentful if I bailed you out again. I'd like you to know that if you make choices that lead you to juvenile hall again, I'll respect your right to experience the consequences. I'll support you in other ways. I'll visit you, and I'll always love you. However, it will be up to you to work things out with the juvenile justice system."

The above scenario illustrates parental support, which helps to teach life skills, rather than punishment. Usually when children make mistakes, parents punish them. When parents punish instead of support their teens, they are only thinking of their own perceptions and points of view. Parents are not considering the world and the perceptions of their teens. Most likely they have forgotten what life was like when they were teens. When they do remember, they often don't understand and can't relate to how different life is for teens today. In addition, by punishing teens, parents miss many opportunities to teach teens how to deal with something that they'll encounter all their lives—they *will* make mistakes.

You must remember that once a mistake has been made, it cannot be undone. Your teen might be able to learn from it or might be able to fix it, but your teen cannot undo it. However, the process of learning and fixing can be so valuable that situations and relationships can be even *better* because of the mistake. When you focus on the mistake rather than on what can be learned from it, you miss great opportunities to learn and grow.

We Are Not Advocating Permissiveness!

ARE WE REPEATING ourselves? You bet, because the reaction of many parents who read about the six tips for growing a teen believe we are suggesting permissiveness because we don't advocate control and punishment. On the contrary, however; our lessons teach you how to become a firm and kind parent. Being a firm and kind parent takes much more time and effort than taking the easy way out, which would be to do *to* or *for* children instead of *with* them. It also takes time to get to know your teens and to teach them to think for themselves and to help them learn from their mistakes instead of being punished for them.

Know Your Teen

We get so annoyed when we see the bumper stickers that ask, "Do you know *where* your teen is?" This message can instill fear and guilt in parents and provoke them to become controlling and punitive. It would be so much nicer to see the message, "Do you know *who* your teen is?" When you know your teens and have helped them develop good character and useful life skills, you don't need to worry about where they are.

The greatest gift you can give your teens is your faith in them. Although teens need much more, such as the skills we teach in this book, your unconditional love and faith is a good foundation.

KIND AND FIRM PARENTING TOOLS TO REMEMBER

1. If you are arguing, scolding, lecturing, and shaming with no success, you might have a child who has just become a teen. Put on your "Isn't this interesting?" hat and sit back to watch for the signs.

2. Find out what your teen's issues are instead of assuming they are the same as the ones you had when you were a teen. Times change.

3. Remind yourself that your teen is growing up, not a grown up.

4. Look at what you might be doing to feed the flames of rebellion instead of honoring the individuation process. Review the characteristics of individuation (pages 7–8).

5. Make an effort to get into your teen's world and honor the individuality of your teen's trip through adolescence.

6. Balance the need for privacy with special time and with kind and firm support.

7. Practice the tips for "growing" teens instead of resorting to punishment and control.

Practical Application Activity

We suggest that your relationship with your teenager is valuable enough to spend a short amount of time each week writing in a journal the answers to the activity following each chapter. Doing so will help you increase your awareness or practice a new behavior. You may feel encouraged by discovering how much innate wisdom you have, given a little guidance in the right direction. By taking time to write your answers in a journal, you will more easily gain insights, learn from your mistakes, expand your perspective, and tap into that innate wisdom of yours.

When you realize that the things your teens do and say are statements about them and not about you, you can stop blaming yourself for their behavior or taking it personally. Your children are separate people from you, and the mistakes and successes they make are theirs to learn from and to own.

1. To help you realize that your children are separate from you, pick one of their behaviors that really bugs you or choose from the following list:

    Cutting classes

    Spending time in room

    Refusing to go on family vacation

    Trading outfits you gave as gifts

    Moodiness

    Forgetting to do chores

    Not wanting to sit with you at a movie theater

    Not wanting to go to college

2. Read the following two attitudes:

    A. Taking it personally means I tell myself that my child's behavior has something to do with my failures or successes. For example, I'm a terrible parent; I'm a good parent; What will others think?; How could he do this after all I have done for him?; She must hate me, or she wouldn't behave this way.

    B. Not taking it personally means I tell myself that my child's behavior has to do with him or her, not me. For example, This is important to him; She needs to find out for herself; He is exploring what life and values mean to him; This is not important to her; I have faith that he can learn whatever he needs to learn from his mistakes and challenges; I wonder what this means to her.

3. Return to the behavior that bugs you and write out how you would act with attitude A. Then write how you would act with attitude B.

4. Talk with your teen about what you have learned by doing this activity.

MY PLAN FOR THE WEEK

This week I will focus on

_____

_____

I will work on changing my attitude by thinking

_____

_____

_____

I will change my behavior by doing

_____

_____

_____

2

Whose Side
Are You On?

TEENS TODAY WANT to be pilots of their own life planes. They want their parents to love them, support them, and accept them but leave them alone to pursue their lives. Because teens don't think that their parents can love them and leave them alone, teens act as if they want to kick their parents off of their planes.

Parents want to stay in the pilot's seat of their teens' life planes. They are scared that their teens will get in trouble, get hurt, or fail. With this fear in mind, they often become ineffective parents and invite more rebellion—more motivation for teens to want to kick their parents off of the plane.

Your task as a kind and firm parent is to move over to the copilot's seat to be available for support and guidance when necessary while encouraging your teens to be skilled and responsible pilots. We call this letting go without abandoning. To be an effective copilot, you must know your teens and have faith in them.

Connie wanted to learn to become a copilot, to find a way to be on her son's side without taking over his life. Connie joined a parent study group to learn more about kind and firm parenting. In this group she soon discovered why her efforts to pilot her son's plane were failing miserably. She discovered the importance of getting into the world of her teenage son, Brad, of understanding her son's life tasks, and of supporting Brad through the rebellious stage of his growth in ways that would develop confidence and life skills. However, when Connie learned that Brad had been skipping school, she forgot all her new resolutions, tried to jump back into the pilot's seat, and began using her old control style. She cornered Brad in his room and lectured him about his irresponsible behavior.

Brad responded by telling his mom to get off his back, which hooked Connie into escalating her lecture into a heated scolding about Brad's disrespect for his elders.

Brad retorted, "I don't see you being respectful to me."

Connie was now so angry, she felt like hitting her son for speaking to her that way. Instead, flashing back to her parenting group, she realized what was happening and changed her approach. "Son, do you know I'm on your side?"

Brad retorted, "You could have fooled me." Then, with tears stinging his eyes he said, "How can I think you're on my side when you're always putting me down?"

Connie put her arm around her son and, fighting tears of her own, said, "I see your point. I'm so sorry." Connie had become sensitive enough to know this was not the time to say any more; instead, she would follow up later when they both felt calmer.

How could Brad know that his mom was on his side when he was being bombarded with lectures and scolded about his deficiencies? Fortunately, Connie had learned enough to catch herself behaving ineffectively and was able to change her approach. As she left her son's room, she said, "Why don't we talk about this later when we're both in a better mood?"

Old Habits Are Hard to Change

OF COURSE, AS a parent, you *are* on your children's side, but often they won't perceive you as being on their side. In fact, too often your behavior could fool any astute observer. In the name of their children's best interests, many parents lose sight of who their teens are, what being on their side means, and what will really help teens develop the character and life skills they need to be successful in life. It is easy to forget whose side you are on when you allow your fears, judgments, and expectations to take over. It's only natural at those times to return to whatever parenting style has become the most familiar. (See chapter 3 for detailed information about the parenting styles that are mentioned briefly in this chapter.)

> As a parent, you *are* on your children's side, but often they won't perceive you as being on their side. In fact, too often your behavior could fool any astute observer.

Although you want your children to do well, how do you communicate that you are on their side? Different parents use different methods for "communicating" with their children. Although the methods may seem like the right reactions, they often evoke the wrong responses. When a controlling parent criticizes, scolds, lectures, corrects, uses put downs, and expresses his or her disappointment, young people do not feel supported or loved. In the name of "for their own good," controlling parents might do everything they can in an attempt to make their teens meet the parents' expectations. For these parents, being on their teens' side is conditional; and, of course, their teens pick up on this condition immediately. Teens know that the only way their parents will be "on their side" is when the teens do exactly what their parents want.

Permissive parents, on the other hand, may allow their teens too much freedom without requiring responsibility. They may indulge their teens, buying them cars and too many clothes without any contribution from their kids. Permissive parents constantly intervene to save their children from the consequences of their behavior and bail them out of situations that could be useful learning opportunities. This is not a healthy way to be on a teen's side, and it does not help a child do well.

Nor do children feel you are on their side if you neglect them. Neglect takes many forms, from drug addiction to workaholism to giving up because parenting is too hard or too inconvenient or because you believe you have nothing to offer your children.

Even though your teens want a relationship with you and need you in their lives, it may not always be in the ways you think are best or the ways you fall back on when scared. To increase your influence with your teens and give them the space they need to safely individuate and grow, you need to have a positive relationship with them. We offer six easy tips for turning around your relationships with your teens and convincing them you are for them and not against them. As you strengthen and improve your relationships, you will find that the rest of the material in this book will be easier to apply. Most of our suggestions will not be effective if you don't have a good relationship. If you feel your relationship regressing to old patterns, review these six tips and try again.

TIPS FOR TURNING AROUND YOUR RELATIONSHIP WITH YOUR TEEN

1. Get into your teen's shoes and empathize.

2. Listen and be curious.

3. Stop worrying about what others think—do what is best for your teen.

4. Replace humiliation with respect.

5. Make sure the message of love gets through.

6. Practice respectful involvement.

Get Into Your Teen's Shoes and Empathize

You get a call from the school saying your teen has cut two classes today and has gotten a detention. Your blood starts to boil. You can't wait until your child comes home so you can let her know how angry you are and how unacceptable her behavior is. Your teen, completely unperturbed by the events at school, decides to stay after school to hang out with friends and arrives home late for dinner. As she walks in the door, you start yelling from the kitchen, "You are in so much trouble. Get in here this minute. Where have you been? What has gotten into you?"

Imagine yourself in the shoes of your teenager. How would you feel if you were treated the way you just treated her? Would you feel inspired and encouraged to do better? Would you feel confident about your capabilities to explore the world and to decide for yourself (sometimes through mistakes) what makes sense to you? Would you know your parent is giving you the guidance and character training you need in ways that are encouraging instead of discouraging? Would you believe that your parent was "for you" or "against you"? We hope that when you are in a situation like this, you will set aside your tirade and first find out from your teen what her impressions are. Teens will listen to you *after* they have been listened to.

Connie was caught up in the familiar trap of thinking she knew what was best for Brad. She tried to express that she knew best by using humiliating lectures and angry reprimands. When she became aware that she was acting as though she were against her son, Connie decided to use the skills she had learned in her parenting group to improve her relationship with Brad. Connie's first step was to find a way to get into his shoes and empathize. She approached Brad in a spirit of support rather than aggression. She asked if Brad would like to drop out of school, as at seventeen years old he didn't legally have to attend. Suspicious of this new approach, Brad asked, "And do what?"

Connie was honest. "That's a good question. I don't know. Maybe just do what you're doing—sleep in, work in the afternoon, spend time with your friends in the evening."

For the first time in a long while, Brad dropped his defensiveness and seemed willing to share his thoughts with his mom. "I don't really want to drop out, but I would like to go to a continuation school."

Connie wondered out loud, "Why?" Teens are usually very suspicious of the "why" question, because they sense that parents don't really want to know but instead want the "right" answer.

Brad could sense that his mother really wanted to know, so he explained that he didn't want to be a high school dropout. In continuation school he could take the classes he'd failed in his regular school. If he remained where he was, he'd have to take those courses during the summer, and he didn't want to ruin his summer. In addition, since continuation school allows students to progress at their own speed, Brad felt that he could do much better than simply catch up.

Listen and Be Curious

This action step shows that you are on your teen's side, which then allows you to make positive changes with your teens. Think of a time when you didn't listen or show any curiosity. What kind of results did you get? Now, imagine that situation, and picture yourself listening and being curious. Listening without comment or trying to fix the problem is best.

Brad's mom did an excellent job of listening and showing curiosity and understanding when she asked her son about his reasons for wanting to go to continuation school instead of dropping out of school altogether.

Being curious is different from the usual twenty questions that most parents ask. The purpose of curiosity questions is to help teens process their thinking and the consequences of their choices rather than to get information you can use against them later or to bring them around to your way of thinking. Don't ask questions unless you really are curious about your teen's point of

> Listening without comment or trying to fix the problem is best.

view or unless you are feeling calm and want to take the time to listen. If your teen gets punished after giving honest information, curiosity won't work. Helping teens explore the consequences of their choices is much different from imposing your own consequence on them. The former invites learning; the latter invites rebellion.

Stop Worrying About What Others Will Think— Do What Is Best for Your Teen

Once committed to being on Brad's side and supporting his idea, Connie decided to suspend her fears about what other people might think. She also put aside her stereotype of teens who go to continuation schools as those who can't make it in regular schools. Instead, she looked at the benefits. She told Brad that she believed he would do extremely well when allowed to progress at his own speed in an atmosphere of mutual respect. (Many continuation school staffs treat teens more respectfully than regular school staffs.) Connie agreed to call both schools to find out what could be done about a transfer. In her next study group, Connie learned that it would have been even more effective to make the calls *with* Brad rather than *for* him, but she was making huge progress in her efforts to become a kind and firm parent.

Later, Connie told her parent study group,

I have no idea how this will turn out. I know I felt closer to my son, because I got into his world and supported him in living his life as he sees it. I got out of the power struggle that was making us both feel like losers, so we could look for solutions that would make us both feel like winners.

I took a look at my own issues about being a "good" parent. Whenever I try to make him do what I think is best, I become a lecturing, moralizing, controlling mother—and he rebels. But when I try to support Brad in being who he is through kind and firm parenting, he's willing to talk to me and look for solutions. Whenever I worry about what others think (usually people whose opinion I don't really respect anyway), I create distance from my son. It is so rewarding to remember whose side I'm on and to act accordingly.

The more you change yourself instead of trying to change your teens, the more you invite your teens to be responsible, capable, and caring. Clearly, Brad cared about his education, but his solution was different from what his mother might have recommended.

If you worry what others think, ask yourself, "For what purpose do I worry?" Do you want everyone to think you are a great parent? Is impressing others more important to you than your relationship with your child? What is your worst fear about what others might think? Remind yourself of your long-term goal for your child. Determine how you can shift your focus to what is in the best interest of your teen, instead of worrying about the judgments of others.

> Whenever I try to make him do what I think is best, I become a lecturing, moralizing, controlling mother—and he rebels. But when I try to support Brad in being who he is through kind and firm parenting, he's willing to talk to me and look for solutions.

Replace Humiliation with Respect

Connie had learned the difference between supporting her son and thwarting him. She learned that humiliating Brad did not bring her son closer or give the impression that she was on her son's side. Instead, Connie invited cooperation by respectfully using her awareness and newfound parenting skills.

A group of high school girls gave the following suggestions to adults who wanted to replace humiliation with respect in order to invite closeness and cooperation with their teens. Review the list and share it with your teen. Ask what he or she would add to or subtract from the list.

ADVICE ON RESPECT FROM
TEENS TO PARENTS

"Sometimes I hate talking to my parents because they make everything into a big deal. Some things are little, and we don't need to talk about them forever."

"Friendly is better. It's okay for you to teach us stuff, but be more like a big sister or brother or a friend."

"Never accuse us of doing something; ask instead."

"If we do something wrong, don't yell, because our first response is to rebel when we are yelled at. Yelling or trying to scare us doesn't work. You sound stupid and it makes us mad. Instead, really talk to us and be honest."

Make Sure the Message of Love Gets Through

Lorna, a mother from Connie's parent study group, shared her success with this step. Lorna's daughter, Mara, did not come home one night. Although Lorna was both angry and afraid that Mara might be involved in drugs, she remembered from her parenting group that mistakes can be opportunities to learn. Lorna also remembered that parents create distance by scolding and lecturing. Instead of focusing on her fear and anger, which would make her daughter feel that she was against her rather than on her side, she decided to focus on love.

When Mara came home the next morning, Lorna said, "I'm glad you're okay. I was worried about you. Before you say anything, I want you to know that I love you, and I'm on your side." Mara seemed genuinely apologetic and said, "I'm really sorry, Mom. I was watching television at Stephie's and fell asleep." Lorna said, "I can see how that could happen, but I would have appreciated a call as soon as you woke up—even if it was in the middle of the night, so I would have known you were okay." Mara gave her a hug and repeated, "I'm sorry, Mom."

Enjoying the closeness she felt with her daughter and feeling more comfortable with her new skills, she continued, "I can see that you might not want to call after you've made a mistake if you think I'm going to scold you like I usually do. I want you to know I'm going to try not to do that any more. No matter how many times you make a mistake, you can still call me, and I'll be on your side, not against you."

Some of the other members of the class were suspicious of Mara's story and started "yes, but-ting:" "But, you let her get away with staying out all night." "But, do you believe she really just fell asleep?" Lorna was not phased because she deeply understood the concept of making sure the message of love gets through to change her relationship with her daughter:

> Mara had already "gotten" away with it. She had stayed out all night. Punishing her wouldn't change that. I used to think that punishment might scare her into not doing it again. Instead, she just got better at trying to hide what she did. I also suspected that falling asleep may not have been the truth—or at least not the whole truth. The third degree about that wouldn't help or change anything. I truly believe things will change when she knows I love her, have faith in her, and when I create an environment where it is safe for her to think for herself, instead of for or against me. I think it will take time to change the patterns I helped create when I parented from my fear instead of from my love, but that is what I'm going to do. Besides, after I established the foundation of love, I was able to talk with Mara, share my feelings, and work on an agreement.

The other members of the group were very touched by Lorna's wisdom and conviction. It forced them to look at their own fear-based behavior—and the unsatisfactory results they were getting.

Think of a time when you were really worried or scared about your children. Did you lecture and scold your teen instead of letting them know how worried you were? Instead, remember to start with the message of love and state how you are feeling. Most teens really don't like upsetting their parents. If

> **M**ost teens really don't like upsetting their parents. If you calmly say how you feel, they *will* hear you, even if it seems like they couldn't care less at the moment.

you calmly say how you feel, they *will* hear you, even if it seems like they couldn't care less at the moment. Watch for changes in your teen's behavior in the next twenty-four hours. Usually you don't have to wait that long to see an act of kindness or friendship on his or her part.

Practice Respectful Involvement

Lorna could see that she had now created enough closeness to work *with* Mara on an agreement. In the past, she would have told her what to do and threatened her with some punishment or loss of privilege if she didn't comply. Instead, replacing demands with involvement, she asked, "Could we work on an agreement about you calling me if you're going to be late?"

Mara said, "What if it's really late and you're asleep?"

Lorna said, "Even if I'm asleep, I'm not sleeping well when I don't know if you're okay. You can call me anytime."

Mara understood. "I hadn't thought about you worrying about me. I always just thought about you being mad at me. You don't need to worry about me, Mom, but I *will* call you whenever I'm going to be late."

That night when she got home, Mara went to her parents' bedroom and hugged them goodnight—something she hadn't done in months.

Later, Lorna told her parenting group, "What a difference! Before, I never thought how Mara would feel about my anger with her whenever she was inconsiderate. I'd just yell and accuse her—and she'd feel that I was against her. This time, I let her see how much I love her, and we were able to come to an agreement. I still don't know if she was telling the truth about falling asleep on her friend's couch—but the way I used to act didn't encourage the truth at all. It created a big chasm in our relationship instead. This feels so much better to me. Mara's independence still scares me, but at least we have a basis for communication and some consideration this way."

Many parents share the "yes, but" concerns of Lorna's parenting group and believe that what Lorna did was too permissive; that her approach let Mara "get away" with disrespectful behavior; and that Lorna should have found out if

Mara was lying or doing drugs. When we examine these concerns more care-fully, we can see that any other approach would not solve anything; it would only make matters worse. If Mara's mom became a controlling parent, Mara would only get more rebellious and secretive. She couldn't force her to tell the truth (through controlling behavior), but she could create an environment in which she feels safe to tell the truth. Permissiveness would not teach Mara any skills for mutual respect. By being kind and firm, Mara's mom modeled respect. Lorna was wise enough to create closeness and trust before engaging Mara in the process of working together on an agreement—one that Mara would be more likely to keep because of the respectful manner in which she was treated.

You may think you are working things out with your teens when you tell them what you want and when they seem to agree. However, there are many kinds of agreements. Your teens may actually do what you ask because they think they must; they also could be agreeing to get you off their backs now so that later they can sneak out and do what they want. Although teens may agree, they may hold a grudge and then find ways to get even later. You are left wondering why your teen is so angry or disrespectful, when what is really hap-pening is that your teens believe you aren't on their side. While appearing to agree, they may simply be counting the days, hours, and minutes until they can get away and do what they want.

The agreements we encourage are ones in which you practice respectful in-volvement. You can practice respectful involvement by saying to your teen, "I can't agree with that, but I'm willing to keep working on this until we find something we could try out for a week and see what we can learn from it." It's often necessary to say to a teen, "I prefer to continue this discussion until we figure something out we both like. But if that isn't possible, for now, we'll stick with things the way they are."

If you make a plan, try it out for a short time to see if the situation im-proves, and your teen is accountable for his or her behavior (see chapter 6).

Being on Your Own Side Usually Helps Your Teens

IF SOMEONE ASKED you, "Are you on your teenager's side?" the odds are good that you would say, "Of course I am!" (even if your actions might indicate otherwise). But are you on your own side? You might say, "Of course I'm on my side. You know what they say, 'If you don't take care of yourself, no one else will.'" Yet very few parents practice self-respect. They don't seem to realize they have a right to a life separate from their children and that they don't have to dedicate every action to their teens. Being on your own side means you consider your needs as much as you consider those of your teen. When your fears become the basis of your thoughts and actions, then actions become the dance of the "mischief shuffle," a dance that ignores self-respect and self-care.

The Mischief Shuffle

The mischief shuffle consists of the mischief you create with thoughts and the actions that get in the way of your long-term parenting goals and your self-respect. This shuffle not only keeps you from being on your teen's side, but also keeps you from taking care of yourself with dignity and respect. Some of the most common characteristics of this dance help you justify short-term parenting techniques (such as control or permissiveness).

MISCHIEF SHUFFLE STEPS THAT KEEP YOU FROM BEING ON YOUR OWN SIDE

1. Trying to fix everything that goes wrong, rather than allowing teens to grow by fixing their own mistakes. This attitude also distracts you from fixing your own mistakes while you busy yourself rescuing your teen; to be on your own side, you need to learn from your mistakes.

2. Worrying about what others might think, which makes looking good more important than finding out what is best for your teens and for yourself. You cannot be on your own side when you are busy trying to please others who aren't really involved.

3. Trying to protect teens from all pain, which also protects them from learning and growing into capable adults. Being on your

own side means facing some of your own pain, forgiving yourself, and allowing yourself to grow.

4. Being afraid of your teen's anger, which means giving up, giving in, or doing whatever it takes to avoid the wrath of your
teen. This teaches teenagers that anger is bad and should be
avoided or that it can be used to manipulate others. Instead,
show that anger is a valid feeling and can be handled appro-
priately. Being on your own side will make your teens angry at
times, especially when you say no when you believe it's right
for you.

5. Believing that you are selfish if you aren't self-sacrificing, which
means you're never allowed to enjoy yourself. Being on your
own side means finding your own balance between doing
things for yourself and doing things for or with your children.

When you stop dancing the mischief shuffle and focus instead on your long-term parenting goals, you'll find that you actually have a lot of power to influence your teens. You'll find that taking care of yourself and being on your own side is one of the best ways to influence your teens and thus be on their side at the same time. With this realization, you can decide what you want to say no to, to express and honor your own limits, to listen without having to fix or judge, to ask for help, to be your "own person," and to give up guilt and manipulation.

Being on your own side means understanding your own individuality, just as you understand the individuality of your teenagers, and supporting your own growth with dignity and respect, just as you support your teen's growth with dignity and

> Being on your own side means understanding your own individuality, just as you understand the individuality of your teenagers, and supporting your own growth with dignity and respect, just as you support your teen's growth with dignity and respect.

respect. Your teens will give you many opportunities to work on taking care of yourself. The following examples illustrate how two parents practiced self-love and self-respect.

How I Learned to Say No and Mean It: Notes from a Parent of a Teen

For Christmas, either I take my kids on a shopping spree and let them buy what they want, or they give me a list and I buy them what I can afford from it. Last year, my daughter chose the shopping spree. She had purchased several low-cost items but then decided she wanted a sixty-dollar bottle of perfume. Normally, I'd explain to my daughter why such expensive perfume is inappropriate for a teenager, and I'd justify this by saying I wouldn't buy it for myself, although I earn my own living. I'd probably get into a moral and ethical lecture about the price of perfume, which my daughter would neither understand nor care about, and we'd end up having a big fight. Although I wouldn't buy the perfume then, I'd feel so bad that I'd go back and buy it later. Then I would feel worse, not only because I had given in but also because I wasn't standing up for what I believed.

But this time I simply said, "No, I'm not going to buy the perfume." I didn't explain or lecture. My daughter got incredibly angry, said something insulting under her breath, and announced, "I'm going upstairs," adding that she would meet me later.

Although I acted cool, I was so flustered that I left my credit card at the perfume counter and went upstairs to do some more shopping. By the time I found my daughter, she was over her anger and on to the next thing that she wanted me to buy. (It's hard for me to remember how quickly kids get over their upsets while I stew for a long time.)

Realizing I had forgotten my credit card, I went downstairs to get it. The salesperson said, "Was your daughter really angry?"

I said, "Yes."

The salesperson seemed very concerned and asked "Well, was that okay?" (Parents aren't the only ones who have difficulties with anger.)

I said, "Sure. My daughter was angry because I was unwilling to spend sixty dollars on perfume for her. I could explain to her until the cows come home, and, at this age, she wouldn't get it. But you and I understand, don't we?"

The salesperson nodded. She added that she'd noticed I also hadn't purchased the forty-dollar perfume I was interested in for myself, and that, like her, I would probably wait for the holiday, hoping someone would buy it for me. Neither of us had grown up buying expensive things like that. I told her it was good to talk with someone who understood, especially since I couldn't have this discussion with my daughter.

I learned a lot from that experience. I saw how much less traumatic it was for my daughter to hear "no" than it was for me to say it. Although she got over her anger quickly, I remained upset much longer (out of fear of her anger, fear of her dislike, fear that I might not be a good mother, and fear of standing up for my beliefs). However, I realized how satisfying it was to discuss this with someone who understood my position.

I also learned that it's much easier and more effective to decide what I'm willing to do and be firm about it. I learned that lectures and moralizing can create defensiveness and resistance rather than understanding and agreement. Although my daughter might enjoy hearing about my "deprivation mentality" some other time, she won't be open to it when I'm trying to do the right thing to teach her a lesson.

I realized that her mumbled insult was not meant to manipulate me, but simply to express how frustrated she was. (Frequently, feelings are intense for teenagers.) Too often I take everything she does personally or feel I have to let her know that she can't talk to me that way.

Teens handle their anger differently than adults do and differently today than was acceptable for my generation. (If I had mumbled an insult to my dad, he would have washed my mouth out with soap.) I realized it wasn't my job to soothe her feelings or appease her or quickly fix the situation. I was able to allow the situation to get worse before it got better. I didn't ignore the insult, but I realized that discussing my feelings and wants during the conflict would be like asking a volcano to stop spewing. Later I said to my daughter, "Look, I know you were angry and I understand that, but I wish you'd find another way of expressing it rather than insulting me. It's really disrespectful and hurts my feelings." And she said, "I know, Mom, and I'm sorry."

How I Learned to Expect Give and Take: Notes from a Parent of a Teen

During a family vacation at Lake Tahoe, we had done everything the kids liked to do. We rented jet-skis, played golf with them, and rented movies of their choice. But when we adults wanted to go for a ride around the lake, the kids had a fit and complained, "Oh, this sucks! This is so boring."

I was ready to start listing everything we had done for them when Grandma simply looked at them and said in her quiet, no-nonsense voice, "Have you ever heard the expression, 'give and take?'" The kids quieted down immediately and said, "Oh, okay. I guess it won't be so bad."

The next day I got a chance to try out Grandma's solution. The kids and I had been driving around looking for a store that sold baseball cards, listening to their music. After almost an hour of hard rock, I started getting a headache, so I changed the station to listen to music I liked. They got hysterical, berating me and treating me like a criminal. Before, I would've lectured them and explained how wounded I was. This time I just said, "Have you ever heard of the concept of give and take?" They knew. They got it right away.

Change Requires Practice

EVEN THOUGH YOU may be working on being on your teen's side or being on your own side, it takes time to change old habits. One of the parents who has been using the methods in this book wrote the following:

When I was using my best skills of curiosity, respectful involvement, making sure the message of love got through, and replacing humiliation with respect, my 14-year-old daughter looked at me and said, "Mom, I need more space. This is my life, and you need to let me make my own decisions."

I became defensive and said, "Well, you didn't tell me that I was interfering," to which she replied, "That is because you didn't allow that space." I thought about it for a minute and realized she was right. I had wormed my way over to the pilot's seat once more, and she wasn't having any of it. I thanked her for her courage to let me know and that she can point out to me when I am overstepping her boundaries so I can learn.

Even when you decide you want to be the copilot instead of the pilot, and even when you want to be on your teen's side, you will most likely find yourself slipping into old habits based on old fears. Making changes may feel as awkward as the wobbly experience you had when first learning to ride a bike. Keep practicing. You'll get it.

And remember that you are an important person, too. We find that parents think they should give up their needs and their lives until the kids are gone. If you parent that way, your teens will probably think the world revolves around them, maybe more than they already do. When you respect yourself and show your teens that you have needs and wants and a life to live, too, your teens will thrive.

KIND AND FIRM PARENTING TOOLS TO REMEMBER

1. Move over to the copilot's seat so you can have a positive influence on your teens without trying to run their lives.

2. Remember that making changes takes time and you will probably slip back to your familiar parenting style when you are scared. Keep practicing.

3. Use the six tips for turning around your relationship with your teen (see page 35) to create a base of love and respect.

4. Ask your teen what advice he or she would give about any ways you may inadvertently be using humiliation instead of respectful communications.

5. Remember to talk *with* your teens first before making decisions about their lives or taking actions that will affect them.

6. When you find yourself doing the mischief shuffle, decide if you'd like to try a new dance that would help you be more on your own side.

7. Whenever you practice, you get better, so practice, practice, practice.

Practical Application Activity

When your teen thinks you are on his or her side, the impulse to act out in extreme ways is greatly reduced. This activity can help you be aware of ways you are not on your teen's side and how to remedy that.

1. Recall a situation in which you treated your teen disrespectfully. In your journal, describe the situation.

2. Imagine that you are a teenager. What would it be like to have a parent who acts like you in the situation? How would you feel? What would you decide? Would you think your parent was on your side?

3. What can you learn from this activity? What could you do differently as the parent in that situation? Imagine how the situation would occur, and describe it in your journal.

4. Ask your teen whose side he or she thinks you're on. Using the six tips for turning around your relationship, choose what you could do differently so your teen would know you were on his or her side.

MY PLAN FOR THE WEEK

This week I will focus on _____

_____

I will work on changing my attitude by thinking _____

_____

I will change my behavior by doing _____

_____

3

What Is Your Parenting Style?

PARENTING STYLES CAN be encouraging or discouraging. In this chapter we discuss four parenting styles, three that are discouraging (short-term parenting) and one that is encouraging for both teens and parents (long-term parenting). In *The Prophet,* Kahlil Gibran beautifully illustrates the foundation for the parenting style that we advocate:

> *Your children are not your children.*
> *They are the sons and daughters of Life's longing for itself.*
> *They come through you but not from you,*
> *And though they are with you yet they belong not to you.*
> *You may give them your love but not your thoughts,*
> *For they have their own thoughts.*
> *You may house their bodies but not their souls,*
> *For their souls dwell in the house of tomorrow, which you cannot visit,*
>   *not even in your dreams.*
> *You may strive to be like them, but seek not to make them like you.*
> *For life goes not backward nor tarries with yesterday.*

Although the beauty and simplicity of Gibran's poem are inspiring, most parents do not know how to apply this poem to their own lives. Relax. As you read this book, you will acquire many ideas about how to be a very active, supportive parent who is neither permissive nor controlling. We include many

As you read this book, you will acquire many ideas about how to be a very active, supportive parent who is neither permissive nor controlling.

suggestions on "what you can do" in the areas that concern most parents of teens. Everything we teach is based on respect—respect for teenagers and for parents.

The Common Methods of Parenting Teens

MANY PARENTS THINK it's their responsibility—part of their jobs as parents—to control their teenagers. (This is a theme you will hear us repeat many times because it is such a huge mistake.) Parents seem to believe that if they don't make their teens do things for "their own good," then they are being permissive parents. Most parents use some form of punishment as their primary method of control. With teenagers, the most common punishments are grounding, withdrawing privileges, taking away allowances, using physical and emotional abuse, and withdrawing love and approval.

We know many parents won't want to hear this, but any form of control or punishment is very disrespectful to teenagers and extremely ineffective for the goals of long-term parenting. It is sometimes appropriate to withdraw privileges from children under twelve or thirteen when the withdrawal relates to the misbehavior, is respectfully enforced, and seems reasonable, by advance agreement, to both parent and child. However, by the time children reach adolescence and see themselves as adults, they won't see grounding or removal of privileges as respectful or reasonable. Instead, you may create the following long-term results.

LONG-TERM RESULTS OF CONTROL AND PUNISHMENT

1. Alienation

2. Permanent apron strings

3. Late bloomers

Alienation

When children of controlling parents become adults, they often cannot stand to have a relationship with their parents because they feel smothered, judged, and obliterated for being who they are. Their parents are very hurt by this, especially because they were trying to do what they thought was good for their children. It's hard for these parents to understand why their children now have such anger and resentment or why they simply withhold closeness.

Permanent Apron Strings

Other children never escape the control of their parents. Their whole lives revolve around doing what they think their mother or father would want. They often grow up to become approval junkies who find other people to continue the job of controlling them. This can be devastating to marriages, parenting, friendships, and jobs.

Late Bloomers

Some children who were raised in a controlling environment later get into therapy, where they find support in learning to grow—support their parents never offered. These children lack the skills needed to make their own choices and decisions. It takes a while to convince late bloomers that it's okay to be separate people from their parents and to give up their mistaken perceptions of what they need to do to get approval in life.

Any parenting style that does not empower teens to become capable adults is short-term parenting. Successful long-term parenting, however, empowers children with the life skills they need for success—to become happy, contributing members of society. The purpose of this book is to teach long-term parenting—the kind and firm parenting style.

Parenting Styles

Short-Term Parenting	Long-Term Parenting
Controlling/Punitive/Rewarding	Kind and firm
Permissive/Overprotective/Rescuing	
Neglectful/Giving up on being a parent	

Perhaps like many parents, you go back and forth from one short-term style to another. You probably even have moments of kind and firm parenting. As you read this book and try out the ideas, you'll find yourself decreasing the amount of time spent in short-term parenting and increasing the time spent in long-term parenting. You will understand why you do what you do. You will learn what works and what doesn't work when empowering teenagers. First, figure out which of the styles is your present method of operation most of the time.

Controlling/Punitive/Rewarding Parenting

Trying to gain control through punishment, lectures, or rewards makes parents feel that they have done their job. However, this kind of parent usually provides opportunities for children to learn:

1. Might makes right.
2. "I have to give up myself to be loved by you."
3. Avoid contribution unless there are external rewards.
4. Manipulate for bigger rewards.
5. Rebel or comply.

Although this is the most popular form of short-term parenting, parents need to look at who is learning to be responsible. It is the parent's *responsibility* to "catch" their children being "bad" so they can dish out the punishments and lectures. It is the parent's *responsibility* to "catch" their children being "good" to dish out the rewards. What responsibilities are teens learning? Perhaps teens' only responsibility is not to get caught.

If all power is taken away from teenagers, they will never have the opportunity to learn responsibility—or to make their own mistakes and learn from them. In addition, these teens will never have the opportunity to discover and set their own limits. Controlling parents provoke many teens to rebel continuously, making for little familial understanding or happiness. How can teens learn to be responsible if parents continue to take that role? One of the best ways to teach children to be responsible is to be consciously not responsible as a parent.

Example: A parent attending one of our workshops challenged us on the issue of giving up control. He explained that his fifteen-year-old daughter habitually came home later than the curfew he had set for her. The last time she came home an hour late, he grounded her for a week. When he was asked what he thought she learned from this, he said, "She learned that she can't get away with this behavior." When asked how he felt about this, he said, "I feel good. It's not my job to be her buddy. It's my job to be her parent."

Further exploration revealed that even though when this father had been a teen he had hated it when his parents grounded him, he now believed as a

> How can teens learn to be responsible if parents continue to take that role? One of the best ways to teach children to be responsible is to be consciously not responsible as a parent.

parent that it was his job to set rules and restrictions and to punish children when they disobeyed. He felt a sense of accomplishment that he had done his job, although he admitted that grounding did not solve the problem. His daughter continued to come home late, and he continued to ground her. Later, he realized that he still hates his father and that being grounded hadn't done him any good. He said, "Come to think of it, I acted like my daughter and continued to defy my father as long as I lived at home. I didn't keep curfew until I left home and felt like getting home early so I could get a good night's sleep. And I still don't want to have anything to do with my father. Good grief, I don't want that kind of relationship with my daughter. Okay. I'm ready to learn alternatives."

Permissive/Overprotective/Rescuing Parenting

Many parents don't want to give up their controlling, punitive style because they think the only alternative is permissiveness. Permissive parenting usually includes overprotection and rescuing. This kind of parent provides opportunities for children to learn the following:

1. Expect undue service from others.
2. Love means "getting others to take care of me."
3. Care more about things than about people.
4. "I can't handle being upset or feeling disappointment."
5. "I'm not capable."

The permissive style of parenting seems to make parents feel that they've done their job because they protect or rescue their children from pain or suffering. However, this short-term parenting robs teenagers of learning the life skills of self-reliance and resiliency. Instead of learning that they can survive pain and disappointment, and even learn from it, children grow up extremely self-centered, convinced that the world and their parents owe them something and that they are entitled to whatever they want. Thus, permissiveness is not a good parenting style for helping teenagers become adults with good character and life skills.

Example 1: Coretta was a permissive parent who gave in every time her daughter, Jesse, wanted a toy or candy in the store. After all, Coretta wanted to protect Jesse from any suffering. When Jesse was late with a school assignment, Coretta was quick to rescue her by dropping all her own plans and rushing to the library or the store to get whatever was required so she could *help* Jesse complete the assignment.

By the time Jesse reached the eighth grade, Coretta and Jesse had a well-established process. Jesse decided that her popularity depended on being the best-dressed girl in her school. She demanded more and more clothes. If her mother said no, Jesse would plead with tears in her eyes and would threaten to quit school if she didn't get what she wanted. Coretta would give in. Imagine the kind of character and skills Jesse was developing.

When Jesse went to college, she continued her materialistic lifestyle by using credit cards. It wasn't long before she was far in debt. In desperation, she found ways to defraud her employer at her part-time job to get extra money. Jesse was caught, fired, and about to go bankrupt. So, she went crying to her mother, who bailed her out again. Because Coretta did not see how she had contributed to the problem

> Permissiveness is not a good parenting style for helping teenagers become adults with good character and life skills.

in the first place by being a permissive/overprotective/rescuing mother, she continued to make matters worse.

Jesse would have been empowered if her mother had allowed her to experience the consequences of her choices. (Note: We did not say that Coretta should *impose* consequences.) Coretta would not have had to be mean about it, and lecturing would not have helped. The most encouraging thing she could have done would have been to show empathy, clearly set limits of how much she was willing to spend, and help Jesse brainstorm for ways of taking financial responsibility. Although this would not be easy for either of them, it would be empowering to both.

Example 2: Gina and her ex-husband Tony shared custody of their college-aged son. They lived about 100 miles apart. Early one morning, Gina called Tony and asked him to rush to her house with a picture that their son Chris needed for a project that was due the next day. She explained that Chris had inadvertently left the drawing at Tony's house when he had visited. If Tony didn't deliver the drawing immediately, Chris would get a poor grade. Tony refused, saying in a firm and friendly manner, "I'm not willing to rescue Chris. I'm sure he knew earlier in the semester what he needed for this project. He's chosen to be irresponsible. I don't know why you're on the phone with me doing Chris's work. If he has a problem and needs some help, he can give me a call. I'll be glad to bring the picture next weekend when I come down. In the meantime, I'm sure Chris can figure out another solution."

Although Chris was a freshman in college, his mother still tried to manage his homework. As long as Gina continued to take care of him, Chris would never learn to be on his own. If this had been the first time that Chris had forgotten something, it would have been fine for Tony to do a favor. However, Chris had made a habit of leaving everything until the last minute, because he was sure his mother wouldn't let him down if he messed up.

Tony later shared with his parent study group that it had been hard for him to stay out of his ex's plan to rescue Chris. However, he recently learned that his own habitual procrastination and frequent inability to finish projects were the result of his mom rescuing him as a child. He told his group, "My mom typed my papers. I never learned to write because I would wait until the last minute and plagiarize. I never learned to spell because my mother corrected all my spelling. I have an opportunity to help Chris do better by not spoiling him, and I intend to take it."

Permissiveness, overprotection, and rescuing may make you appear to be a saint—your teens may even love it. But these parenting styles don't help your teens learn to fly on their own. Many adults are angry with their own parents for not allowing them to learn the skills they need to succeed in marriages, jobs, and life in general. When you avoid overprotection and rescuing, your teens may momentarily think you don't care; they may even accuse you of not loving them. But this doesn't last—they know better in the long run.

Think of some areas in which you may be overprotecting and rescuing, and thus robbing your children of the opportunity to develop self-reliance and the belief that they are capable. Choose some specific areas in which you can use kindness and firmness to stop this pattern. The firmness simply requires that you stop being so permissive. The kindness may require time for training your teens or expressing your faith in them to handle the situations.

Neglectful Parenting/ Giving Up on Being a Parent

Neglect and giving up on parenting are other forms of short-term parenting. The neglectful parent provides opportunities for children to learn:

1. "I'm not important and probably unlovable."
2. The only choices are to give up or to find a way to belong somewhere (either in constructive or destructive ways).
3. "It's my fault my parent doesn't pay attention to me, so I have to be a certain way and improve myself so that I will be worthy of my parent's love. I have to prove I am lovable."

Although it can take many forms—some quite severe (for instance, substance abuse, depression, workaholism, or complete indifference to a child's physical, emotional, or mental welfare)—many forms of neglect, such as aloofness, emotional unavailability, and lack of communication, occur because of ignorance or misguided beliefs. Sometimes neglect is the result of despair—the belief that no matter what you do, you cannot make it work, so it's better to do nothing at all.

Example 1: One mother complained that her husband refused to parent her son and daughter from a previous marriage. He expected her to handle all discipline, but criticized her parenting methods. Although he complained vehemently about his stepchildren's behavior, he refused to deal directly with them. As a result, the children felt unloved and unimportant and lacked respect for this grown-up who had lived with them since they were preschool age. The stepfather was unable to see his behavior as neglectful: he provided for the family's economic welfare, advised the mother on raising her children, and coparented his younger biological child.

Fortunately the stepfather received some counseling. When he realized that, in fact, he *had* been neglecting his stepchildren, he told them so, saying he'd made a mistake. He told them that he loved them and that they were important to him. He found ways to spend quality time with each of them. Instead of turning his back on what happened with these children (and later complaining to their mother), he involved himself in their lives by sharing his feelings and ideas directly with them and listening to theirs.

Giving up is another common form of neglect. Instead of controlling, parents simply try to ignore their child's behavior, hoping fervently that it will go away by itself. It usually doesn't. No matter how often teenagers say they want to be left alone, in reality they need and want *some* guidance. They still need a copilot. Even though they act as if they would like to throw you out of the plane, they feel abandoned if you go. Also, even if it seems that they don't hear a word you say, they do, although it might take days, weeks, or years for them to show you in ways that you will notice.

Example 2: One mother could see that her controlling behavior was increasing rebelliousness in her son without teaching him life skills. She made the mistake of giving up control and not replacing it with any other method. Instead of moving to the copilot seat, she got off the plane, and it veered out of control. Whereas before her son had been staying out late, he now stayed out all night. Instead of punishing him the way she used to, she wavered between doing nothing and buying him things to show she loved him. Although she tried to get him to talk to her about his feelings, he refused. She blamed herself and her ignorance. She felt that if she only knew what to do, things would get better. But because she couldn't figure out what to do, she did nothing except feel frustrated and inadequate.

> No matter how often teenagers say they want to be left alone, in reality they need and want some guidance. They still need a copilot. Even though they act as if they would like to throw you out of the plane, they feel abandoned if you go.

Eventually, this mother quit blaming herself and quit trying to buy her son's love. Instead, she purposely decided to do nothing. There is a difference between doing nothing out of frustration and doing nothing on purpose. The former conveys the message: "We're both failures, and it's mostly your fault. How could you do this to me?" The latter conveys the message: "I respect you and have faith in you. I also have respect for and faith in myself. I'm here if you need me, but I won't force my judgments and criticisms on you. I'll tell you how I feel without demanding that you tell me how you feel."

This mother decided to love her son no matter what he did, and she told him, "I hope someday you'll talk to me about whatever is going on with you instead of being so disrespectful to me." She told him she had faith in him to learn from his own experiences.

To many parents, having faith in their children and controlling their own behavior instead of their teen's behavior seems like doing "nothing." But in this case, *nothing* doesn't really mean "nothing." Instead, it means "stop doing the things that don't work." Sometimes all a copilot can do is offer love and faith. And even though this may not achieve the desired short-term goals, the payoff in the long run is tremendous, for both parent and teen. For example, when the mother in this example stopped being controlling or neglectful, she was surprised to find that her son began to be more respectful. She learned that example really is the best teacher.

Kind and Firm Parenting

Kind and firm parenting is the essence of this book. In every chapter we present skills for being a kind and firm parent that go beyond the overview discussion in this chapter. The kind and firm parent provides opportunities for children to learn the following:

1. Freedom comes with responsibility.
2. Mutual respect is practiced here.
3. "I can learn valuable life skills, such as problem solving, communication, and respect for others."
4. Mistakes are opportunities to learn.
5. Family members have their own lives to live, and I am part of the universe, not the center.
6. My parents will hold me accountable through exploring the consequences of my choices in an atmosphere void of blame, shame, and pain.

Kind and firm parenting means being more interested in long-term results and goals rather than immediate short-term fixes. One of the first issues parents need to overcome if they want to move toward long-term parenting is an aversion to mistakes. Although it's human to make many mistakes during the growing process (and indeed we continue to make mistakes throughout life), we often equate mistakes with failure rather than with opportunities to learn (see chapter 5). The following story provides an example of how Rhonda avoided the temptation to rescue her daughter and instead used kind and firm parenting to support her daughter in learning life skills.

Example: Rhonda's daughter Betsy had set up an appointment with her teacher because she was upset about the way he had handled a situation in the classroom. Betsy asked her mother to come with her to the meeting. Because Rhonda was more concerned about the long-term goals of her daughter than about the situation at hand, she agreed, but said, "I'll be there with you for support, but I know that you will do a fine job of expressing your feelings to your teacher."

Rhonda stood next to Betsy as she stumbled all over her words, even though Betsy had had no trouble stating her opinions when the two had practiced in the car on the way to school. Rhonda then thanked the teacher for his time and later told Betsy

> Kind and firm parenting means being more interested in long-term results and goals rather than immediate short-term fixes.

how proud she had been when Betsy talked about her thoughts and feelings with her teacher. Rhonda didn't mention a word about Betsy's nervousness.

Rhonda's long-term goal is to help her daughter build courage. She knows that, as the years go by, Betsy will need to stand up for herself and state her opinions in situations that could be troublesome or abusive. If Betsy practices speaking for herself while her mother stands quietly by her side, the day will come when Betsy will have the confidence to take on situations by herself.

Changing Parenting Styles Can Be Uncomfortable

THE MORE UNCOMFORTABLE you feel, the better you are doing. You may feel comfortable punishing, rescuing, or overprotecting because you are used to it and believe that it is right. But what are you and your teen learning from this experience? On the other hand, you will probably feel very uncomfortable saying, "No, you can't have money for skiing" or "I'm uncomfortable about you coming home so late last night, and I want to talk with you about it." Betsy's mom had been very uncomfortable watching her daughter's struggle and had been tempted many times to jump in and rescue her daughter from an awkward situation. But she didn't jump in, because her desire to build courage in Betsy was stronger than her need to relieve Betsy's feelings at the moment.

Kind and firm parenting may feel uncomfortable to you because you may not experience the immediate results that often occur with short-term parenting. Sometimes it may feel as if you are letting your teen get away with something. When your actions relate to your long-term goals, it requires a leap of faith and a deep understanding of the long-term results to feel confident that you're doing a good job of parenting. We have worked with countless parents who have not had the chance to see the results of their efforts until a year or two down the road. Talk about faith!

You may have heard the story about the little boy who was watching a butterfly struggle to break out of a cocoon. Feeling sorry for the butterfly, the boy opened the cocoon and set the butterfly free. But after flying only a few yards, the butterfly fell to the ground and died. The little boy hadn't realized that the butterfly needed to struggle to gain the strength that would allow it to fly and live. Similarly, long-term parenting gives teens the strength and skills to leave home and make it on their own.

When Kind and Firm Parenting Looks Like Control, But Isn't

SOME SITUATIONS REQUIRE a firmness that may seem like the controlling style of parenting. However, there is a difference. The difference is in the parent's foundation of respectful attitudes, use of kindness, and letting teens know they can use self-control as soon as they are ready.

For example, thirteen-year-old Kirk was addicted to his computer. He spent every waking hour when not in school sitting in front of his computer, playing games or surfing the Internet (an activity that many adults find just as addicting). Kirk's parents tried working on solutions with him, but nothing worked. His parents finally became very firm, yet still kind. During summer vacation, they told Kirk that from then on he would not be able to use the computer between noon and 6:00 P.M. Kirk's mom told him that they would eat lunch together and would then spend an hour doing something together, such as

visiting the zoo or the library or playing a board game. They could decide on this activity together. From 2:00 to 6:00 P.M., it would be up to Kirk to decide what he wanted to do with his time—but the computer was off-limits. Kirk complained and whined. At first he sat listlessly in a chair, not doing anything; but soon he was going through his room looking for something new to do. He even decided to read the books his teacher had recommended for summer read-ing. After a week, he stopped pouting and engaged in small talk with his mom over toasted cheese sand-wiches he prepared for lunch.

This example illustrates that it is the parent's job to be firm as well as kind. Had Kirk been able to work out a solution on his own, his parents would have been happy to let him. What wasn't okay was to let the problem continue.

One reason many parents have difficulty chang-ing from short-term to long-range parenting is be-cause of their concern that this means giving up their parental roles and control. It helps when they remember the "firm" part of the kind and firm equation. It takes courage to turn control over to teens while still being "the parent." However, turn-ing over control is the only way teens can learn to be successful adults.

One reason many parents have difficulty changing from short-term to long-range parenting is because of their concern that this means giving up their parental roles and control. It helps when they remember the "firm" part of the kind and firm equation.

Support Teens in Their Process of Becoming Adults

ALTHOUGH TEENAGERS NEED to learn successful grown-up skills (see chapter 11), support in learning these skills is not what they usually get from their parents. Children can't learn self-control when their instincts cause them to rebel against or comply with overly controlling parents. They need the freedom to practice these skills. They also need a different kind of guidance than younger children need.

To become a self-actualized human being capable of reaching his or her full potential, every adolescent must go through individuation. Individuation is the time in life when teens still need a bridge with safety railings, but the railings must be much further apart to support their individuation process. However, instead of giving teens more space, too many parents try to bring the railings of the bridge closer together because of their fears for their children. These parents are unwilling to have faith that their teens will grow and learn from their mistakes. By keeping the bridge rails too close together, the parents are prohibiting their teens from practicing the skills necessary for successful adulthood.

WHAT TEENS SAY ABOUT FREEDOM AND TRUST

"We want a chance to be responsible and trusted. . . . We have a conscience."

"Parents should know us by now. Just give us the general idea and then trust that we won't do dumb stuff, instead of talking about every last thing."

"There's a point when you have to start trusting your kid. We have to practice being our own judge of what's right and wrong. How will we learn when we leave, if we don't start now while we are still living at home with you where it is safe?"

"Remember that the majority of what we've learned is from you, so now trust your parenting."

During your teenage years, many of you were not encouraged to become fully functioning human beings and to develop your unique potentials. Instead, you became approval junkies or rebels. You therefore have many unresolved issues. It's almost impossible to deal effectively with teenagers if you have unresolved teenage issues of your own. In this book, especially in chapter 13, you'll learn to discover and resolve your own issues so that you may support your teenagers more effectively through long-term parenting.

Beware of Short-Term Solutions: A Summary

Short-term parents limit the adolescent growth process—finding immediate solutions that *seem to* control teen's behavior without considering long-term results or goals. We say "seem to" because short-term parenting *can* get results, but only briefly. Grounding, nagging, helping too much, or removing privileges can give temporary relief from a problem behavior. A nagged or grounded teenager may do his or her homework for a while, but at what price? If the long-term results are rebellion, lack of personal responsibility, and low self-esteem, then we must *beware of what works*. Rewards often motivate children to do what their parents want for a while, but at what price? If the long-term results are demands for bigger and better rewards or refusal to do the task because "doing their own thing" is more important than any reward, then we must *beware of what works*.

A parent who uses punishment or other forms of control may think he or she has been effective in eliminating certain behaviors. But the fact is that the child has only been forced "underground." If that parent consciously gives up control, however, he or she will discover that nothing but the illusion of control has really been given up. In neglect, the other extreme of short-term parenting, parents stick their heads in the sand and hope the problem will go away. They do not even consider teaching life skills for long-range results. If you are feeling defensive, ask yourself, "What are my long-term goals—to control behavior or to teach life skills?" The next question is, "Is what I'm doing achieving my goals?"

> If you are feeling defensive, ask yourself, "What are my long-term goals—to control behavior or to teach life skills?" The next question is, "Is what I'm doing achieving my goals?"

Many parents share that their long-term goals for their children include one or more of the following: courage, responsibility, cooperation, self-esteem, self-respect, respect for others, success, and a sense of humor. We have found, however, that most parents haven't given much thought to what exactly constitutes these characteristics. Definitions of these characteristics, and how to help children develop them, are provided in chapter 11.

Button, Button, Who Has the Button?

IF MOST PARENTS really do have these long-term goals in mind for their children, why would they use short-term parenting methods? Often they do so because of a lack of skills. Sometimes the do it because they are following their own parents' methods or are rebelling against the way they were brought up. Other times it is because they are coming from fear instead of faith or because their "buttons" get pushed.

Parents have buttons, and children know what they are and know how to push them. When these buttons are pushed, parents often revert to their reptilian brains and "lose it." (Reptiles often eat their young.) Although humans are more civilized than reptiles, while in their reptilian brain, parents seem to forget everything they "know," including anything about long-range parenting. While in the reptilian brain, the only option is fight or flight. When buttons are pushed, parents usually go on a rampage that puts their teen into his or her reptilian brain, where the only option is fight or flight as well. And into the war zone they go. Power struggles between adults and teens seem to be epidemic.

Take Some Positive Time-Out for Cooling Off

We hope that the analogy about the reptilian brain will help you recognize what you do when your buttons are pushed. When you sense a fight-or-flight situation, take some time-out for yourself until you feel better. Wait until you once again have access to your cortex and rational behavior before dealing with a situation. After all, if we expect children to behave rationally, wouldn't it be nice (and effective) if we learned to do so first?

The first thing to do is to forgive yourself. Remember that mistakes are wonderful opportunities to learn. What an exceptional example to give your children, who have many mistakes ahead of them in their lifetimes. In chapter 5, you will learn how to use mistakes as opportunities to come up with a plan to do better.

The second thing to remember is that it is unlikely that you will ever be a perfect parent; nor will your children ever be perfect children. Reacting and forgetting good parenting tools can happen to anyone, anytime, which is one reason to learn the valuable skill of taking some positive time-out as soon as you catch yourself losing it. We will *all* continue to make mistakes throughout our lives, even when we know better. Taking positive time-out to manage your behavior allows you to crawl out of your reptilian brain back into your rational brain, where you can think clearly and calmly. From this state of mind, you will use kind and firm parenting skills to encourage and empower your teen.

> Parents have buttons, and children know what they are and know how to push them. When these buttons are pushed, parents often revert to their reptilian brains and "lose it." (Reptiles often eat their young.)

Have the Courage to Allow Your Teen to Develop Courage

IF YOU ASK teens whether they want their parents to stop grounding them, they may say, "No. I don't want that kind of responsibility for my life. It's way too scary." Teens often want their parents to take responsibility for them through overprotection or over-control. Overprotective parents free teens to do what they want and to blame the consequences on their parents. It also protects teens from the risks of trying, failing, and learning.

Our goal is to help parents develop the courage and the skills for kind and firm parenting so that their children can develop the courage it takes to be a responsible adult. The growing process can be an enriching experience for both parents and teens.

KIND AND FIRM PARENTING SKILLS TO REMEMBER

1. Use long-term parenting, instead of control or permissiveness, to help your teens become more responsible, self-reliant, and capable.

2. When tempted to control, ask yourself, "Will this work in the long run?" If not, use kind and firm parenting instead.

3. Although it may be more comfortable for you to micromanage your child's life, it doesn't get the job of "growing adults" done. Allow your teen to manage him- or herself.

4. Help your teens balance freedom with responsibility by giving them more room to learn from their mistakes.

5. Focus on the big picture and remind yourself that parenting out of fear stunts growth.

6. You don't have to parent perfectly. Take time to cool off so you have the chance to help your children learn and grow.

Practical Application Activity

1. Think of a recent time when you were more interested in the short-term goal of controlling your teenager (a time when you were probably acting from your reptilian brain). Describe the situation in your journal.

2. Think of how you could handle the same situation in a more rational way that would help your teen learn some skills to prepare him or her for adulthood. Write it down. This will help you be prepared for the next encounter.

3. Are there some ways in which you are being too permissive with your teen? If so, explain in your journal.

4. Think of skills to use that would start the weaning process to help your teen become self-reliant. Write them down.

5. Think of a time when you rescued your teen so that he or she would not have to experience the consequences of his or her choices. Describe it in detail.

6. What will you do the next time you are tempted to rescue your teen? How can you kindly and firmly teach your teen some important life skills?

7. Try to think of a situation in which you may be neglecting your teen out of frustration or inadequacy (or due to workaholism, substance abuse, depression, or any other reason). Describe in your journal the effect this is having on your teen.

8. What are you willing to do differently to improve your relationship with your teen and with yourself? Write down specific actions you will take.

MY PLAN FOR THE WEEK

This week I will focus on

_____

_____

I will work on changing my attitude by thinking

_____

_____

_____

I will change my behavior by doing

_____

_____

_____

4

Why Is It So Difficult to Change Your Parenting Style?

WHAT IF YOU grew up learning one language in a culture and someone suggested you start speaking a new, completely foreign language? Naturally you'd be resistant to making such a change; but even if you decided to learn the new language, it would still take time. Spending time around people who spoke the new language would make it easier to learn. If you were around people who only spoke the old language, it would be very difficult to remember and practice your new skills.

Changing your parenting style is almost the same as learning a completely new language. Right now you live in a culture in which the language spoken is what we call the *conventional wisdom.* And in our society, the conventional wisdom is to punish and control. Almost everyone around you follows the conventional wisdom, whether it fits the needs of the situation or not. Very few people have a picture of what firm, kind, positive-discipline parenting is like. When you practice a new way of parenting, you stick out like a sore thumb, and many people judge you and think you are "flaky." Even your teens might ask you to stop trying to help them to be responsible and just ground them like normal parents do, so they can get on with their lives and do what they want.

When you parent according to the conventional wisdom, you are in the controlling parent role. The more rigid your role, the less responsible your teen needs to be. The more you parent as a person and let go of the role, the more responsive your teen will be.

Do the "Three-Step" to Change Your Parenting Style

IF YOU WANT to change your parenting style (and because you are reading this book, we are sure you do), we suggest doing the "three step." The first step in changing your parenting style is to understand why it is a good idea. You may have to read this chapter many times to understand this, and even then it can be very difficult to change old patterns.

The second step is to learn effective parenting skills to replace the old patterns. This step is not as easy as it may sound. Getting rid of old patterns and applying new parenting skills requires a paradigm shift—you really have to see yourself and your teens in a new and different light.

The third step is to acknowledge that letting go of control can be scary. This became evident to us during our parenting lectures and during counseling sessions with parents of teens. We would spend hours helping parents understand why the old methods don't work, teaching new parenting skills, and talking about how control is an illusion. During the lecture or counseling session, heads would be nodding in agreement, yet someone would eventually ask, "But, what do I do about _____?" Inwardly, we would groan and think, "Can't they see that we've gone over at least six parenting tools that would be very effective for that situation?" Of course, we wouldn't say this out loud, but the question would always cause us to ponder, "Why don't they get it?" Eventually, we came up with a possible answer: Many parents are asking the wrong questions. As long as they are asking these questions, kind and firm parenting will not work for them.

The Wrong (Short-Term) Questions

1. How do I make my teen "mind" me?
2. How do I make my teen understand "no"?
3. How do I get my teen to listen to me?
4. How do I get my teen to cooperate and do what I say?
5. How do I make this problem go away?
6. What is the punishment/consequence for this situation?

These questions may seem perfectly legitimate to you. If so, you are still in short-term parenting mentality. You will shift to long-term parenting mentality when the following questions become your point of reference.

The Right (Long-Term) Questions

1. How do I help my teen become capable?

2. How do I get into my teen's world and support his or her developmental process?

3. How do I help my teen feel belonging and significance?

4. How do I help my teen learn social and life (cooperation) skills, such as problem-solving skills and the ability to identify feelings and communicate about those feelings in words (also known as developing a feeling vocabulary)?

5. How can my teen and I use this problem as an opportunity to learn from our mistakes? How can we learn to try again instead of give up when we make mistakes?

Change Your Parenting Style by Asking the "Right" Questions

Do the "right" questions represent what you truly want? The interesting thing about these questions is that when they are answered there will be no need for the "wrong" questions. When teens are respectfully involved in the problem-solving process, they may not "mind you" (which wouldn't really be healthy anyway), but they will be more likely to cooperate. As we have said before, teens are more likely to listen when they feel listened to and when you use the skills that invite listening.

> When teens are respectfully involved in the problem-solving process, they may not "mind you" (which wouldn't really be healthy anyway), but they will be more likely to cooperate.

Problems and mistakes are ongoing, unavoidable parts of life. Instead of struggling against problems as if they were stumbling blocks, what an empowering gift it would be for you and your teen to see them as opportunities to learn. Likewise, everyone makes mistakes, and everyone can use those mistakes as chances to solve problems and gather information, instead of viewing themselves as failures. Once you realize this, you'll be amazed at how much time and energy many parents waste in trying to save their children from making mistakes. (The issue of mistakes is so important that we have dedicated chapter 5 to this topic.)

Will Children Raised with Positive Discipline Still Rebel?

MANY PARENTS HAVE developed the mistaken belief that if they use positive-discipline principles with their young children, their children won't make mistakes as teenagers. On the contrary, children who were raised democratically and respectfully are often more self-confident about risking, rebelling, and learning.

Let's assume you've been using the firm and kind model of parenting since your children were young. You've used problem-solving skills in family meetings, and your children have become very responsible and cooperative. You have a great relationship with them and are convinced they can go through adolescence smoothly. Not true. A teenager has to be a teenager. There is no technique in the world that can tame hormones. And when those hormones start jumping around, your children will begin their adolescent developmental tasks.

Don't panic. Your child's teen years are not the time to question everything you've been doing as a parent or to think, "What if this democratic stuff doesn't work?" You may tell yourself that you should have given more lectures on morality, spent more time helping your children set goals for themselves, and taken more control so your kids wouldn't be so inconsiderate and disrespectful now. You may wonder if you should tighten the reins before it's too late. This is not an easy time for any parent, but we can guarantee that things would not be better, nor would they get better, through punishment and control.

It may help to know that children raised under the positive-discipline model often feel freer to rebel under their parents' noses instead of going underground. They may even use many of the messages you gave them to fuel their rebellion, such as, "But I thought you told me you wanted me to think for myself and listen to my inner voice," and "Why are you so upset? You always taught me that mistakes are opportunities to learn. We can fix the dented fender."

Gloria thought she had done an excellent job teaching her children about good nutrition. They discussed nutrition during family meetings, and the kids helped with the shopping and made their own nutritious lunches. But when her kids became teenagers, they seemed to throw everything they knew about nutrition out the window and went for junk food. Gloria's children seemed to rebel against all the skills she taught them about healthy eating—at least for a while.

Gloria shared with her parent study group,

I didn't want to be nagging about nutrition and wasting energy doing something that wasn't going to work when I turned my back. My kids had the knowledge, and I trusted they would return to good food when they were done rebelling. Instead of destroying my relationship with my kids by yelling about potato chips, I thought there were other places where they would really need me. It wasn't always easy. I felt like a failure when they started eating junk food. At times I thought, "Oh, they haven't learned anything. I tried so hard. It's obvious that all my parenting skills are worthless!" I felt disappointed, disillusioned, unhappy, scared, and worried. It was very uncomfortable, but I kept my long-term goals in sight. It was a rational process. If I had acted on my feelings, I would've driven my kids and myself nuts. Thank goodness for all I've learned! I maintained faith in them and in myself. Now that they're grown-ups, my son is a health-food nut and my daughter eats well because she's very conscious of her body.

You may be thinking, "I don't worry about little things like nutrition. I worry about sex, drugs, and failure in school." The area of concern is not the point. Effective methods for dealing with concerns are similar no matter what degree of importance you give them. Being a good parent does not mean saving your children from all pain, from all mistakes, from life. If you could manage to save them from all these things, they wouldn't be able to function as adults in the real world.

Being a good parent does not mean saving your children from all pain, from all mistakes, from life. If you could manage to save them from all these things, they wouldn't be able to function as adults in the real world.

Be Prepared for Your Teen's Resistance to You Changing

PARENTS ARE NOT the only ones who resist change. Often, your teens don't want you to let go. Even when they've complained and rebelled against your control, they may be afraid when you give it up. If you have been an extremely controlling parent, go slowly, because your teens don't have practice at taking on responsibility. It will be easy for them to misunderstand that freedom and responsibility go hand in hand. Teens who have been over-controlled welcome your smallest steps to let go. On the other hand, if your children have been spoiled and rescued and you suddenly stop bailing them out, they will resent you and will want you to go back to your old ways. They may criticize you for not doing "your job."

Susan tried to control her son, Kent, by attaching strings to his having his own car. She made a list of arbitrary rules without discussing any of them with her son. She informed Kent he could use his car as long as he got A's and B's on his report card, had a job, came home on time, and didn't drink. Kent rebelled, got a few D's and an F, came home late, and drank anyway. Although he kept his job, the other areas were a constant battleground. When Susan took Kent's car away from him, he only got more rebellious.

> Making rules for teens without their input is futile. When rules are arbitrary, they belong to kings. You may be acting like a king or a queen, and that doesn't cut it with your teens.

It took an outspoken member of her parent study group to help Susan see the folly of her efforts. "You had a whole bunch of rules that Kent might have agreed with if you discussed them together first, but without his input, they seemed ridiculous to Kent. When someone makes a rule, I'm either going to comply without thinking it through for myself—which isn't helpful to me—or I'm going to rebel—which isn't helpful to anybody. Making rules for teens without their input is futile. When rules are arbitrary, they belong to kings. You may be acting like a king or a queen, and that doesn't cut it with your teens."

Susan had to admit that giving her son a car with strings attached did not produce the results she wanted. She also realized that she had been a permissive parent to give him a car in the first place without allowing him to earn it, or at least most of it, through his own efforts. In an attempt to prevent problems with his car use, she adopted a controlling parenting style. Although it was too late to undo those mistakes, she could move forward and take the opportunity for herself and her son to learn from the mistake. Her first step was to give up punishment, since it wasn't working anyway, and to try something different.

Inform Your Teen When You Change Your Parenting Style

WHEN YOU DECIDE to use firm and kind parenting and to change your relationship with your teen, give notice. You'll be changing your role dramatically, and your teen needs to know what to expect. Giving up punishment is a major change, so be sure to explain this to your teen. Acknowledge that you made a mistake, that punishment doesn't work, and that you plan to change. Given that you've probably made a lot of pronouncements in the past that you didn't follow through on, your teen will most likely watch to see if you really *do* anything different.

Because Susan didn't know how to tell Kent she was changing, she volunteered to participate in a role-play with a member of her parent study group. The following dialogue is a transcription of that role-play. The dialogue in parentheses represents what each person later shared about what he or she was thinking and feeling in the role, rather than what he or she thought a teenager would actually say.

SUSAN: Kent, I made a mistake when I took the car away from you.

KENT: What was the mistake? Do you think you made a mistake buying the car? I don't think that was a mistake.

SUSAN: I think it would have been better if I had helped you figure out how you could buy a car, or at least be part of the financial responsibility. But that's not what I want to talk about right now. The mistake I'm referring to are all the strings I've attached to the idea of you having the car—which just shows how much I've been trying to control your life.

KENT (I'm trying to not drop dead here. I'm hoping this is as good as it seems.)

SUSAN: I've been doing this in the name of "for your own good."

KENT: Oh, don't be so hard on yourself, Mom.

SUSAN: Thanks. It's probably going to be hard for me, but I want to learn not to do that.

KENT: It's okay. I don't mind.

SUSAN: What don't you mind?

KENT (I'm starting to get scared. What if I make a mistake? As long as you control me, I can blame you. But if you let go and I make a mistake, it's my fault. Then I'm a bad person. I don't know how to handle this. You go ahead and take control. Being grounded is a very small price to pay for the benefits of not being responsible.): It's okay. You have to try to control me. You're a parent.

SUSAN: But I don't feel good about it anymore. I don't want to do it anymore. I want to relieve you of having to live up to my expectations so that you can get on with figuring out what is right for you. I'm willing to help you sort that out if you'd like my help.

KENT: So what does this mean exactly?

SUSAN: It means that I'm removing the strings from the car, and we'll start from scratch to make agreements we both can live with.

KENT: But I might have an accident.

SUSAN: I'm scared about that, too. What we need to discuss is what to do if you have an accident, not what punishment will happen.

KENT (I'm feeling really nervous about this. If you don't tell me not to drink, I might go ahead and drink and drive!): Maybe we should say that if I drink and drive, I can't use the car for a week.

SUSAN: That seems like a possibility. We could try it out this week and re-evaluate your suggestion at the end of the week. You do know that if you drink and drive and get caught in this state, you will lose your license for quite some time. I think it might be till you are 18. Perhaps you'd like to review your driver's manual to find out what the consequences are. I like the idea of you starting to think about what you are doing and take responsibility. As I back off and stop micro-managing your life, I expect you will have many more opportunities to think about your behavior.

KENT (This is feeling like a miracle. I'm afraid you got hit over the head or something.): Okay, Mom.

Susan said what she did in the role-play felt much better than her usual attempts control and her tirades when control didn't work. She felt that she had gained enough skill and courage to try this exercise with Kent.

The following week she shared with her group that she could hardly believe how similar the real thing was to the role-play.

When I told Kent I wanted to remove the strings from the car he said, "But what if I have an accident?"

I told him that I'd be glad to talk to him about things he could do to minimize the chances of an accident.

I got off track for awhile, going right back into my good-mother bit by talking about what I thought he should do. But then I caught myself and went back to being curious about Kent's world. "You're afraid you might have an accident if I remove the strings? What do you mean by that?"

Kent said, "Well, it's your job to get me to do the right thing. Moms are supposed to ground their kids."

I remembered to be curious. "You mean you want me to keep trying to control you, because if I don't you might get into more trouble and even an accident?"

Kent grinned sheepishly and said, "Yeah."

I continued, "So you hate my nagging, but you also feel like I might be helping you if I do it?" Kent agreed. "And you're afraid of what you might do if I stop nagging you?" Again Kent agreed.

Finally, I asked, "Would you like to know how I feel about that?" Warily, Kent said, "I guess." So I told him. "It scares me, too. For a long time, I've felt that it was my job to control you to keep you from getting into trouble. Now I know it's not my job. I do know it's important for both of us to grow beyond that, and I'm scared because I'm not sure how to do it. But you know what? I have faith in you and in myself to figure it out, even though it's scary."

Kent said, "Maybe we should keep some of those rules you made just for awhile. I don't think it's okay for me to drink and drive, but I don't think it's fair for you to take away the car if I don't come home on time. And if I get behind in school because I'm spending too much time goofing off, maybe we could have a deal that I just use the car for work and school during the week."

You may be thinking that this sounds like a fairy tale, but when you back off and leave some space for your teens to have input, they often want to follow exactly the points you've been making. The difference is that now the points are *their* ideas.

Don't Let Your Teen Use Your Need to Control as a Crutch

JANET, ANOTHER MOTHER in the same parent study group, had a son, Stan, who had been jailed twice for stealing. When Janet told Stan she would no longer get him out of juvenile hall, he panicked, saying angrily, "That sucks!"

Janet asked him, "Are you saying you want me to let you have the freedom to choose to steal, but if you get caught you don't want me to let you have the freedom to experience the consequences of your choice?" Stan, who was as creative as Kent, said with a sheepish grin, "Yeah."

Janet said, "I love you, and I will no longer rescue you. If you go to jail, I will bring you cookies, but I won't bail you out. I have faith in you to figure out how to stay out of jail—or to learn what you need to learn if you do have that experience."

Teenagers are often afraid; their lack of confidence leads them to look for a crutch. Parents can provide this crutch if they don't allow their teens to experience the consequences of their choices and their behavior. Stan was a good example of this. He wanted his mother to save him from the consequences of his choices. His behavior said, "I want to be as bad as I can be and to do everything I want to do and never have to think about the consequences. If anything goes wrong, I want to know you will be the responsible one and bail me out." This role is perfect for a mother who wants to be a "good" parent. But actually she's being an ineffective parent by buffering him. His behavior and the subsequent consequences will only get worse, not to mention that his self-confidence to handle life will start to slip.

If you ask them, many kids will say they want their parents to protect them. They want to be grounded and monitored. But what kind of people will their parents create? People who don't grow up until they are forty or fifty years old, if at all. People who spend too much money, can't pay their bills on time, can't hold jobs, become addicts, become materialistic because they were buffered all the time.

> Teenagers are often afraid; their lack of confidence leads them to look for a crutch. Parents can provide this crutch if they don't allow their teens to experience the consequences of their choices and their behavior.

Don't Buffer and Then Abandon Your Teen

MANY PARENTS BUFFER teens until they can't stand it anymore, then they abandon. These parents kick their teens out of the house, telling them not to come back until they learn to "behave." This puts kids in a real dilemma. Teens are being asked to learn how to behave without any support system to teach them the necessary skills. Supporting teens means allowing them to learn from their mistakes in a safe environment in which they can explore the consequences of their choices instead of being judged and criticized. What teens learn will eventually allow them to control their own lives. Of course, it's easy to support teens when they're making decisions that you like. It's much more difficult when their decisions seem to be poor choices for their future. In the following example, notice how Shelly's parents practiced their new parenting style and what the results were.

Shelly was flunking several classes. She was refusing to do homework assignments, because she thought they were busy work and that her teachers were "stupid" to insist that kids do homework even if they could pass the tests without it.

Shelly's parents listened to her ideas about homework and asked her if she could do the homework anyway, because it might be even more "stupid" to miss out on going to college because of her poor grades. Shelly insisted that she would not work for teachers who didn't respect kids, and she didn't care if she lost credits, because she could always make them up.

When Shelly's teacher called to ask her parents to talk about Shelly's poor performance, her mother said that she had faith in Shelly to work this out and that she would pass the message on to Shelly. Later, Shelly's mom told her, "You've decided how you want to handle these classes. We wish you could make a different choice because we think it would be better for you in the long run, but we honor your right to decide what is right for you. We have faith that if college is important, you'll find a way to make up the credits. We appreciate your willingness to share what is happening in school with us. We also feel this is between you and your teacher. It's up to you to talk to your teacher first, but if the two of you can't work this out, we will be happy to come in with you to see your teacher. If you haven't worked this out with your teacher by next week, we'll call to set up an appointment so we can all go in."

Shelly made an appointment the next day to talk to her teacher. She explained her feelings about homework to the teacher and also said that her parents were unhappy with her choices but believed it was up to her to make her life work and that schoolwork was her responsibility. Shelly said that her parents would come in if necessary but would prefer that she work things out with the teacher if possible. The teacher responded that his policy on homework stood and that if Shelly chose not to turn in homework assignments, she would fail the class. Shelly told her teacher, "It's up to me to pass or fail. If I fail, it's not your fault, and it's not my parents' fault. I'm sorry we can't work this out, but I'm glad we could talk about it."

Have Faith in Yourself and Your Teens

SHELLY'S PARENTS DEMONSTRATED their faith in her, and it paid off. Shelly eventually went to college and was very resourceful in figuring out how to get good grades while working to earn most of her college money. In the next example, you can see how Billy's parents may have saved his life by having faith in their son from an early age.

At camp, nine-year-old Billy got too close to the edge of a fifty-foot waterfall and fell. Campers at the top of the waterfall watched aghast as Billy fell headfirst. But as he fell he pushed himself off the side of the rock face, righted himself, and landed on his bottom in a small pool of water. He turned death into a stunt. When his father heard about Billy's fall, he said, "All I could think was, thank God for all those times when I didn't rush in and rescue him. I kept having faith in him, even when I was scared to death, so he had faith in himself. I gave him opportunities to figure out problems as he went along in-stead of doing it for him. The long-range results of not controlling and rescu-ing probably saved his life. Not that I saved his life, but he saved his life because I could give him those gifts." This kind of faith in our children can be carried into their teen years.

Many parents are afraid that their faith in their teens will not teach their kids values; instead, they try cramming their own values down their teens' throats. But, part of having faith is knowing that adolescence is the middle of a transition, rather than the end of a story. In the end, teens are likely to become adults whom parents will enjoy and admire. Remembering this can help par-ents maintain perspective while supporting teens in being who they are. One way to maintain perspective is to stop focusing on the ten kids who have over-dosed instead of on the ten thousand who haven't. Too many parents choose a controlling parenting style based on trying to prevent unrealistic odds.

Scott gave his parenting group an example of how easy it is to understand, in retrospect, the importance of keeping things in perspective and having faith in teens.

> My son Stewart graduated from a church university, is now married with two children, and has a successful business. When he tells me the things he did as a teenager—he even sold pot—I can't believe it! Now that those years are over, it's easy to see that it would have made sense to have faith in him all along. But I'm not so sure I would have maintained faith in him at the time if I'd known what was going on. How do you have faith when you're in the middle of a problem?

But when you are in the middle of a problem is when faith and perspective are the most valuable.

Changing Parenting Styles Doesn't Mean Changing Values

MODELING IS THE only way to teach values. Ever since your child was born, you've been teaching your values by modeling. As a matter of fact, most of your child's values were formed by the age of five. Even though it looks as though your teens are throwing away your values, they aren't. They are simply experimenting and finding out what works for them. If you try to cram your values down your teens' throats by lecturing and cajoling, they will resent it and rebel and may actually give up the deeper family values completely. If, instead, you continue to model your values, your teens will be able to observe your behavior without feeling forced to behave the same way. You may think your teens are not absorbing your values because they don't immediately accept them—there is a time lag. You may even fear that your changes are producing valueless youth. You may be tempted to relapse to forcing your teen into agreeing with your values, no matter what. But if you refrain and continue to model your values, as your teens get older, they will probably adopt many of those very values that you modeled.

Look at Your Motives for Perpetuating Control

THERE ARE AS many different issues behind the need to control as there are different parents, so we'll mention a few of the general categories and give a few examples.

MOTIVES FOR PERPETUATING CONTROL

1. **Fear of what others will think:** If you don't control your children, others will see you as a bad parent.

2. **Fear of loss:** If you don't control your children, your children will do permanent damage to themselves (for example, become pregnant, go to jail, drop out of school, not go to college, abuse drugs or other substances, die accidentally, commit suicide). Although it is true that these things happen to many teenagers, they happen to just as many teens (if not more) whose parents are controlling as to teens whose parents are not controlling.

3. **Fear of powerlessness:** If you aren't in control, then you don't have belonging and significance.

4. **Fear of inadequacy:** If you are not in control, you are inadequate.

5. **Overprotection:** If you don't control your children, your teens might get hurt emotionally by others.

6. **Ignorance:** You simply lack alternative parenting skills.

7. **Unresolved personal issues:** This usually underlies the need to control. When you feel strongly about something and attempt to control your teenager regarding that something, it's probably an issue of your own that remains unresolved.

Although we dedicate an entire chapter to helping you with your un-resolved teen issues (chapter 13), we want to show here how one mother, Marissa, was able to get past her need to control her daughter, Charise, once she understood her own unresolved personal issue.

During a counseling session, Charise asked her mother whether she could go to a party. Marissa was upset that her daughter had waited until the coun-seling session to ask, and many issues came up. Marissa was jealous and angry because she felt Charise thought the counselor was a better mother; she be-lieved that Charise and the counselor were ganging up on her; and she thought the counselor said what Charise wanted to hear.

Charise explained that she doesn't ask at home because her mother always says, "I'll have to think about it," and then doesn't get back to her. Marissa says she wants to think about it because she worries about what her religion wants her to do; she worries about her family being upset if she doesn't follow her re-ligion; and she worries about what neighbors and friends will think. In addi-tion, Marissa is afraid that her husband—who isn't the same religion as she is—will call her a hypocrite if she doesn't follow her religion's dictates.

Charise told her mother, "I feel put off when you say, 'I'll talk to you later.' I never know where I stand with you." Marissa finally said, "I'll let you go, but I have a lot of reservations." Helped by the counselor to get to the bottom of her reservations, Marissa eventually realized that her real issue was fear of someone breaking Charise's heart. Her own heart had been broken when she was eighteen. By understanding her long-suppressed fear, Marissa was able to begin supporting her daughter in living her own life, rather than trying to control her and protect her.

Fear of Saying No Can Stop You from Changing Your Parenting Style

ONE OF THE most difficult lessons for you to learn when you change your parenting style is to say no and mean it. Your fears or avoidance of saying no can drag you back to your old ways faster than anything else can. If your personality style is to be a *chronic pleaser,* you may be afraid to say no out of a fear of rejection. If your personality style is *control,* you may say no too often out of a fear of being weak and humiliated. This "no" is seldom based on a reasonable understanding of your teen's world or on your parental wisdom, and it creates rebellious teens or approval junkies with low self-confidence. If your parenting style is to constantly seek *significance,* you may be very unpredictable because "no" is based more on your need to be "right" than on the issue at hand and the direct consequences to your teen. If *comfort* is your personality style, you may not say no, even when it would be appropriate, simply to avoid the stress of following through with dignity and respect.

Saying No in a Kind and Firm Manner

As you learn to think first before opening your mouth, as you ponder the appropriateness of saying no and the consequences of having to follow through, and as you discover ways to make no sound more like yes, your ability to say no in a kind and firm manner will increase.

Take the teenager who wants to borrow five dollars on his way to the movies, whose friends are standing nearby as he makes his request. He needs the money because he spent his paycheck on a new computer game and now he doesn't want to miss out on a fun evening with his friends. Are you ready for what is going to follow if you say no? Think first, because although it is very appropriate for you to say no, you're going to be in for a scene if being kind and firm isn't how you handled things in the past.

We suggest that you pick your confrontations, especially when you are just getting started with your new kind and firm parenting. Don't confront a situation with firmness unless you're prepared to go the distance. In the example above, expect a guilt trip about how you are ruining his life. Don't be surprised by his display of disrespect toward you in front of his friends as he slams the door, muttering words you really don't want to hear about what kind of person you are. Don't bite, because by allowing him to experience the consequences of his choice, you may be helping him develop the self-discipline to budget his money in the future to make it last longer. On a bigger scale, he may begin to understand that the choices he makes affect *his* life and that he is responsible for his choices and their consequences.

In this situation, if you react by lecturing about responsibility, think about what your teen would learn. Turning a deaf ear to your lectures is a small price for your teen to pay to have his cake and eat it too.

Similarly, if you back down on saying no, not only do you rob your son of the opportunity to become a more capable person, you also allow him to feel successful at manipulating you and avoiding the consequences of his choices. He learns once more that you are willing to buy his approval, which is probably not the lesson you are hoping to teach.

If you sidetrack the real issue and react to his bad attitude, insisting that he treat you respectfully, and so forth, you won't provide him with a wonderful opportunity to take responsibility for his choices and learn from his mistakes. You might even escalate the situation into something ugly that you'd both regret later.

> Turning a deaf ear to your lectures is a small price for your teen to pay to have his cake and eat it too.

Instead of any of these suggestions, we suggest saying, "I'd really like to help you out. So at our next family meeting, when we're both more relaxed, why don't we talk about ways this could work?" Or you could say, "I'm really sorry you are in a bind, and I wish I could help you out, but not this time." Or, "If budgeting is a problem, I'd love to sit down with you and show you some of the tricks I've learned over the years. Let me know if you'd like my help." When your intention is truly to help your child take responsibility and learn from mistakes, your attitude will be one of caring and concern instead of shame and blame.

Think First

Teens complain about parents arbitrarily saying no all the time. But teens can be very demanding and persuasive when they insist they must have an answer immediately. They push you into a corner with all the intensity they can muster. It's easy to react with an immediate no and then feel the need to back down later.

To avoid the problem of reacting and then backing down, you can buy some time: In a kind but firm manner, tell your teen that you need to think for a few minutes before you answer. Many kids may resent this approach, because you have probably used it in the past to avoid dealing with issues. Therefore, to be respectful, you need to give a deadline for your decision. Then you need to follow through and give a decision by the promised deadline.

Sometimes You Need to *Sound* Like the "Old" Parent

Julian was an understanding father who talked most issues over with his adolescent son and daughter. He noticed that much of the time, his two teens made pretty good decisions, but every now and then they burned the candle at both ends, got completely exhausted, and stopped doing the work for which they were normally responsible. At those times, he'd say no if they asked to go out two nights in a row on a weekend. His teens called this his "too much fun theory," saying that parents must have a pact against teens to make sure they don't have too much fun. They hated hearing the no, but they knew their father was mostly reasonable, so they went along without too much of a fuss.

Another mother decided to change her parenting style in steps and created a rationale that pleased her and that seemed to work with her son. When her son got his new braces, instead of jumping in and taking over, she sat back and observed for several weeks. It didn't take long to notice that he wasn't doing any of the things he was supposed to do to care for his braces, as specified by the orthodontist. So, Mom sat him down and said, "I know this is your responsibility. I know I said it was between you and the orthodontist, but I've nagged you for so long to do things that I think we need some kind of transition instead of going cold turkey. I've decided to nag you for a month until I think you have created a new habit. Then I'll back off and see what happens. If you have created a good habit and can keep it up on your own, I'll back down and get out of your business." Her son looked at her with relief, but saved face by acting like he was doing her a favor and said with his teen attitude voice, "Oh, all right!"

Change Your Parenting Style to Learn and Grow with Your Teen

WHEN YOU CHANGE your parenting style, you'll begin to notice the part you had played in creating problems in your relationship with your teens. In the past, if your kids didn't want to talk to you, what had your part been? If they were rebelling beyond what was normal for their age, how might you have been inviting this?

No matter how you look at it, you'll find that it's not only your teenagers who need to grow up. It's crucial for you to continue your own growth process as well. It's too easy to see the faults in others and yet be blind to your own. One mother summed it up beautifully when she shared what she learned from another participant after a role-play in a teen workshop:

> *When working with Sharla, it was so easy for me to see how uptight, rigid, and controlling she was and how suffocating that must be to her daughter—and how miserable she makes things for herself. It was so easy for me to think, "Why can't she lighten up and let go and trust the basic goodness of her daughter? So what if her daughter fails in school? Maybe that's exactly what she needs to learn to become the flower she is meant to be."*
>
> *Then I realized how uptight, rigid, and controlling I am with my son, because I'm afraid he might be making some mistakes that could ruin his life. It had seemed to me that to lighten up, let go, and trust his basic goodness would be too permissive and irresponsible. Even though I know how devastating it was to me when my own mother was controlling with me, it's been easy for me to justify controlling my son because what he's doing is so much more dangerous than what I was doing. Now I see how easily I've justified hurting him deeply in my efforts to keep him from hurting himself.*
>
> *Having faith in my children's basic goodness is very difficult when I get uptight about how they seem to be growing—even though I have experienced the wonderful results of letting go and providing nothing more than nurturing.*

No matter how you look at it, you'll find that it's not only your teenagers who need to grow up. It's crucial for you to continue your own growth process as well.

You have heard it before, and we will say it many times because it seems so difficult for parents to absorb: You can't save your teens from all pain and all mistakes, but you can teach them skills and nurture the strength that will help them live through pain. Control and punishment do not teach your teenagers the skills they need. Kind and firm parenting does.

KIND AND FIRM PARENTING SKILLS TO REMEMBER

1. When you understand why it's a good idea to change your parenting style, when you replace outdated skills with more effective ones, and when you accept that it *is* scary to let go of control, you are on your way to accomplishing more of what you want with your teen.

2. Are you asking the wrong questions? Refresh yourself with the right ones.

3. When your teens want you to continue to micromanage them so they don't have to take responsibility, pat yourself on the back for being kind and firm and turning a losing pattern around.

4. Your teens need to know how you think, how you feel, and what you want. Don't hesitate to tell them, in a nonlecturing way.

5. The fact that your teens are moving in the opposite direction from your values doesn't mean they won't come back to those values at a later date. Don't panic and don't overreact during the lag time.

6. It's appropriate and necessary to say no when you are controlling your own limits and what you are willing to do. No is most effective when it is said infrequently, when you really mean it, and when you follow through with your action on what you said.

7. When you think that it is not enough to have faith in your teens, think about how you feel and how you behave when someone has faith in you.

Practical Application Activity

GIVE AND TAKE

In many families, either the parents "rule the roost" or the children "run the show." Learning the skills of give and take fosters consideration, equality, dignity, and respect for self and others.

1. Think of areas in which you think you have to do everything either your way or your kids' way:

   TV shows

   Movies

   Music

   Vacation

   Restaurants

   Meals

   Phone use

   Choice of clothing

   Borrowing or lending clothes

2. Describe a typical scene that shows the most common "your way or my way" situation in your home. Include:

   a. What you usually say or do.

   b. What your teen usually says or does.

   c. The results of this interaction.

3. Discuss with your teen what you wrote or present your situation at a family meeting. Work with your family or teen to come up with a give-and-take solution.

4. A week later, evaluate how the give-and-take solution worked.

MY PLAN FOR THE WEEK

This week I will focus on

_____

_____

I will work on changing my attitude by thinking

_____

_____

_____

I will change my behavior by doing

_____

_____

_____

5

Is It Really Possible to Learn from Mistakes?

Mistakes are a natural part of growing and learning. Consider an average toddler learning to walk. She doesn't begin with perfect balance and skill. She falls a lot. If she hurts herself, she may cry but she doesn't think, "Oh, dear, I failed again. What will people think? I'm so inadequate. I'd better not risk humiliating myself again. I can't get it right, so I must be a bad person. I give up."

When does this same toddler start feeling self-conscious about mistakes? When does she start hearing that mistakes mean she is failing and inadequate, rather than finding out that mistakes are part of the learning process? Her perceptions about mistakes are shaped in a large part by the messages she receives from adults.

Sometimes negative messages about mistakes are overt: "Bad girl. You shouldn't touch the vase." The truth is that she's not "bad" for touching the vase; she wouldn't be normal if she didn't want to touch it.

Sometimes the messages are more subtle. How much damage is done to budding self-confidence and the joy of learning when you send your children off to school or to play saying, "Be careful" or "Be good"? By saying these things, the negative connotation about mistakes is implied. Imagine the different message that would be conveyed by saying, "Enjoy your adventures today and see how much you can learn from your mistakes." This creates a climate of freedom in which to learn and grow without any loss of self-esteem from the numerous mistakes that will always be part of living. Children who are raised with that kind of encouragement can still feel good about themselves as they learn from their mistakes.

It is inevitable: Your children will make mistakes, and so will you. It will be hard to watch your children make mistakes, especially big ones. Your fear of making mistakes may even be the very cause of mistakes. Your efforts to over-protect or micromanage can turn a naturally curious and courageous kid into a fearful child or a rebellious, careless child who wants to prove that you are too worried about taking unnecessary risks. But remember, the freedom to make mistakes and learn from them is essential to individuation and growth. And, yes, it is really possible for your teens to learn from their mistakes, especially if you believe in the concept and practice your copilot skills.

> It is inevitable: Your children will make mistakes, and so will you.

Being a Cheerleader During Tough Times

IT'S NOT ALWAYS easy to figure out how to maintain that, "*Come on, you can do it! Hooray, that's wonderful!*" attitude when your teen is making one mistake after another. Do you run to write in the baby book the first night your son or daughter comes home drunk? How encouraging do you feel when you've just spent a bundle on braces and your teen won't wear a retainer? When your teen fails a class because she spent all her time on the phone instead of doing home-work, you probably don't feel like calling her grandparents to brag—even though when she was little and she dropped her food off the highchair for the dog to eat, you would call them right away. Back then, instead of scolding her for age-appropriate behavior, you probably put a big piece of plastic under her chair and, as soon as possible, rushed to the phone to tell everyone how cute she was. It doesn't seem as cute when your teen wants to spend every waking mo-ment talking to friends, even though this is also age-appropriate behavior.

Your job at this stage of your teenager's life is to help him or her learn from mistakes with encouragement and support rather than with hand-slapping and punishment. Although you may be tempted to move the "sides of the bridge" (see Introduction) closer together, doing so could inadvertently reverse the individuation process and create teens who feel they must rebel, comply, or remain helpless. As was mentioned in chapter 1, extremely rebellious teens put most of their energy into cover-ups, power struggles, and manipulation rather than into individuation and development of their full potential. Extremely compliant teens become approval junkies, whose main life task is trying to live up to the expectations of others—and never quite making it. Extremely helpless teens grow up to be extremely helpless adults. Some teens may even take desperate measures—such as suicide, drug abuse, dropping out, or running away—to ease the frustration or pain of not being able to do something that is natural and necessary to their development.

During the individuation process, kids want and *need* to figure things out for themselves—they can't have parents do it for them. Your teens are thinking, "The kind of help I want is to know you are there, you won't abandon me, and you love me. Other than that, I'd like to work this out myself. If I want to tell you something, I will; but I don't want you asking me what I'm feeling and what's going on."

Model How to Learn from Mistakes

IT'S IMPOSSIBLE TO grow and increase your awareness without discovering that many things you've done in the past were ineffective and were possibly even damaging to your children. Your teens aren't the only ones who can learn from mistakes. You can, too. Your teens do the best they can, given their experience, knowledge, support systems, and developmental process. And so do you. One of the best ways to teach children that mistakes are wonderful opportunities to learn is to practice this principle yourself. When you make mistakes, either you can feel inadequate, humiliated, and think you are a failure or you can look for the opportunities to learn. The Four Rs of Recovery from Mistakes can help you when your mistakes involve other people.

THE FOUR Rs OF RECOVERY FROM MISTAKES

1. Recognition
2. Responsibility
3. Reconciliation
4. Resolution

Recognition
Recognition means not seeing yourself as a failure because you made a mistake, but rather simply seeing that what you did was ineffective.

Responsibility
Responsibility means seeing what part you played in causing the mistake (without attaching blame to yourself or others) and being willing to do something about it.

Reconciliation
Reconciliation means telling the other people involved that you're sorry if you treated them disrespectfully or hurt them in any way.

Resolution
Resolution means working with the others involved to come up with a solution that is satisfactory to all. Once you've recognized your mistake, taken re-

sponsibility for it, and apologized, you have usually created an atmosphere conducive to resolving the problem.

Jane Practices the Four Rs of Recovery from Mistakes

One day my daughter was bugging me while I was at a salon having my hair done. She kept asking me for money, wondering how much longer I was going to be, and interrupting my conversation with the beautician every five minutes.

When we finally got home, I was so angry that I called her a spoiled brat. She retorted, "Well, don't tell me later that you're sorry!" (She was familiar with the Four Rs of Recovery from Mistakes.)

I was in my reptilian brain and said, "You don't have to worry, because I won't!"

She stormed off to her room and slammed the door. And then I realized that I'd made a mistake calling her a spoiled brat. (I had made many mistakes during this episode, but that was enough to start with.) I went to her room to apologize, but she was in her reptilian brain and wasn't ready to hear me. She was busy underlining passages in *Positive Discipline*.

When I tried to talk to her, she said, "You're a phony! You teach other parents to be respectful to their kids and then you call *me* a name."

She was right. I felt very guilty and quietly left the room. At first, I did not see my mistake as an opportunity to learn. Instead, I was thinking I should give up my career because I couldn't practice what I preached.

Within five minutes my daughter came to me, gave me a hug, and said, "I'm sorry."

I said, "Honey, I'm sorry, too. When I called you a spoiled brat, I was being a spoiled brat. I was so angry at you for the way you behaved at the beauty salon that I lost control of my behavior."

She said, "That's okay. I really *was* being a spoiled brat."

"Yeah," I said, "but I can see how I provoked your behavior by not being respectful to you."

She said, "Yes, but I did interrupt you and bug you."

And that is the way it so often goes when we're willing to take responsibility for our part in creating a problem: Our children learn from our example and take responsibility for their part. My daughter and I resolved the problem by deciding that next time we would make a plan before I went into the salon. I would tell her how long I'd be, she would decide what she wanted to do during that time, and we'd meet when we were both done.

I could have wallowed in guilt about not practicing what I preached. Instead, my daughter and I both learned a valuable lesson. So now I preach about the value of mistakes.

Don't Let Guilt Be a Barrier to Relationships

WHEN YOU FEEL guilty, you may create all kinds of mischief by trying to keep your kids from making the same mistakes you did. Or you may be so busy trying to hide your feelings of guilt that you also hide your feelings of love and enjoyment. Perhaps you try to make your children feel guilty to get them to behave "properly." If your children don't conform, you feel guilty about not being a good enough parent.

There are many forms for guilt to take, but they all get in the way of relationships. Forgiving yourself is essential to being on your own side; it allows you to get on with your life and have close relationships with your loved ones. When you get rid of guilt in your life, you won't feel the need to make your kids feel guilty. When you realize you are doing the best you can, you can stop taking your teenagers' behavior personally.

What Do Mistakes Mean to You?

BEFORE YOU CAN help your children learn the value of mistakes, you may have some work of your own to do. Many adults carry heavy, useless, childhood baggage about mistakes. Even though this baggage has not served adults effectively—and has hurt them a great deal—they pass it on to children as if it were a precious family heirloom.

Thomas Edison conveyed his understanding of the value of mistakes during an interview. When asked, "How did you feel about your 10,000 failures before you finally invented the light bulb?" Edison replied, "I didn't have any failures. I learned 10,000 things that didn't work. Each one of those discoveries gave me valuable information that eventually led to success."

Do you agree with Thomas Edison, or are you like many parents who, with good intentions, try to save their children from making mistakes? Do you want to protect your children from pain, disappointment, and embarrassment? Are you afraid your teenagers will make the kinds of mistakes that could "ruin" their lives? Do you argue, "But I can't let my child make a mistake that could really hurt him"? Of course, you have to use common sense. You don't want your children to learn from the mistake of overdosing on drugs. Yet, too many parents use the "need to protect" excuse and end up creating more damage than good.

> Many adults carry heavy, useless, childhood baggage about mistakes. Even though this baggage has not served adults effectively—and has hurt them a great deal—they pass it on to children as if it were a precious family heirloom.

Good intentions backfire when you inflict pain on your children through your disapproval. When you protect your children from the pain of mistakes, you end up robbing them of self-confidence, of a positive attitude about mistakes, and of skills that could be learned from making mistakes. When your teen was younger, you kept the "sides of the bridge" very close, watching your child's every move, creating a safe space in which your child could grow. But if you try to keep the bridge walls too close now that your child is a teenager, you will likely fail. No matter how good your intentions are, you can't watch your teen's every movement. And even if you could, you risk fanning the flames of rebellion or creating approval junkies and the disease of perfectionism.

Are you more concerned with your reputation than with the growth of your children? Are you afraid that your children's mistakes reflect on you? Do you hear yourself saying, "I'm so embarrassed about what you've done. What will people think?" We may never know what other people think, but we do know that your children feel conditionally loved in such a situation. Their self-confidence diminishes, and they're more likely than ever to compound their mistakes rather than to learn from them. However, if your children are more important than what other people think, you might ask, "What was that experience like for you?"

Many Decisions Are Not a Matter of Right or Wrong

SOMETIMES ADULTS ARE less concerned about their reputation and more concerned about the whole philosophical question of right and wrong. The comment, "I guess I'll just have to trust my son to make the right decisions" may seem like progress toward kind and firm parenting. But what a burden for both parent and teenager to feel that the "right" decision must always be made. How much more liberating to know that if the teen made the "wrong" decision, he could then do his best to correct it and learn from it.

Leslie, a participant in one of our workshops on empowering teenagers, volunteered to look at her fears about right and wrong decisions. The following dialogue shows what she learned.

FACILITATOR: How would you like to have a perfect teenager?

LESLIE: I wouldn't.

FACILITATOR: Well, most people would say they would. But let's go with you not wanting a perfect teenager. Why not?

LESLIE: Because I want my kids to be who they are.

FACILITATOR: You are an unusually supportive parent. Let's write that one down. We can learn something from this. Can our kids be who they are if they can never make a mistake? If they can never make a mistake, for whom are they living?

LESLIE: Well, I don't want my kids to be perfect, but I don't like it when they make mistakes.

FACILITATOR: So you have a conflict here. You want your kids to be who they are, which means you know they won't be perfect, but you don't want them to make mistakes.

LESLIE: No, they can make mistakes. There are just certain ones I don't want them to make.

FACILITATOR: So the key here is that they can make the mistakes that are okay with you, but you feel uncomfortable with the mistakes they make that are not okay with you. So you still have some issues with right and wrong and control. What happens when you feel good about your child making mistakes? Can you give us an example of a mistake your child made that you felt good about?

LESLIE: My daughter went to two dances with people she couldn't stand. She spent a lot of money on the dances for dresses and other stuff. The two guys were totally obnoxious. One of them threw up in her car from being so drunk. But she felt it was important to go to the dances. I thought it was a mistake to go with someone she didn't like at all. But she decided that's what she had to do. But before the last dance of her senior year, she told me, "I don't really want to waste any more money going to dances with people I don't like. Right now there's nobody I really like, so I'm not going to go to the dance."

FACILITATOR: What did you do to support her in making those choices?

LESLIE: I listened. I didn't interfere. I didn't tell her what I thought. I didn't lecture. I didn't judge and tell her it was stupid. I just stood back and watched to see what would happen.

FACILITATOR: What would you guess she felt from you?

LESLIE: Support. Freedom to explore. Safe. That her privacy was respected. She had room to blow it without anyone looking over her shoulder. She experienced unconditional love.

FACILITATOR: What do you think she learned from that?

LESLIE: She learned that it's better to do something because you enjoy it, not because you want to impress others. She learned it's better to respect yourself.

FACILITATOR: So, she learned all those things from her experience.

LESLIE: Yes, I think she did.

FACILITATOR: Do you think she would have learned all those things if you had tried to prevent her from making her mistakes? Would she have learned it from your lectures, overprotection, and so on?

LESLIE: No. I think she learned to trust her own judgment. If I had tried to control her or overprotect her, she probably would have learned that to get my approval she'd have to memorize all the things I have judgments about and make sure she doesn't share anything with me that goes against these judgments. She would have learned to hold back on those things. And, she would have falsely concluded that my approval of her is conditional, which it is not. But she wouldn't have known that.

FACILITATOR: Now give me an example of a time you did not want your child to make a mistake.

LESLIE: Hmmm. That's interesting. It's more the mistakes I'm afraid she might make.

FACILITATOR: How often is it true that we're more afraid of particular mistakes they *might* make?

LESLIE: It's really hard, because I have so much faith in her that even the things she's doing that I don't like, I think it's going to be okay.

FACILITATOR: Let's look at one you are afraid she might make.

LESLIE: I think she might make a mistake about college. I'm not even sure what the mistake will be, but she didn't get accepted to Harvard and that was really important to her. Kind of in the back of her mind is that if she really wants to be a professional singer, she shouldn't be going to college anyway at her age. She thinks she should be getting an agent and going for all that. I guess my fear is that this might be an excuse for her; that rather than go to another college, she might not go to college at all.

FACILITATOR: When you're afraid she might make a mistake, what kinds of things do you do?

LESLIE: I might tell her how I feel. It's interesting that in the other one I didn't tell her how I felt. I listened to how she felt. I wouldn't tell her what to do. I was much more respectful than that. But about this college thing, I'd tell her how I feel to help her make the "right" decision. I'd have the good intentions of just doing this to help her.

FACILITATOR: You would want to help her?

LESLIE: Yuk! I'm done. Gross! Now I can see how that would be a manipulation to get her to do what I think is best.

FACILITATOR: You can't be done! We've got to finish the process so everyone else can learn. If you want to help her by telling her how you feel, what does she learn from that?

LESLIE: Nothing! She'd feel a righteous indignation. She'd be angry with me, and it would give her rebellion steam. It'd be like throwing coals on her rebellion.

FACILITATOR: What would she learn from this?

LESLIE: Whatever she learned, it wouldn't have anything to do with college. That's for darn sure. She would learn that her mother is an obstacle. It would nip away at her confidence and her faith in herself to make decisions. And . . . I wouldn't want to do that. I would rather have her make mistakes and feel confident from what she learns.

FACILITATOR: What did you learn from going through this process?

LESLIE: I re-learned that whatever happens is going to be just fine. And that I'm happier when I'm listening than when I'm telling.

FACILITATOR: And how do you think she feels when you are listening instead of telling?

LESLIE: Sometimes I read all this stuff about talking about feelings and I feel guilty if I'm not being "real" with my kids, telling them how I feel or what I think. I use this stuff the wrong way, like I should be more open with my kids. But I've learned that that is mischief. There are times when my openness is appropriate, and there are times when it's manipulative. When I share my feelings inappropriately, when my kids aren't ready to hear them, I can see how they feel criticized and judged. It will be very helpful for me to be aware of the difference. In this case, it would be appropriate just to listen to her. Then I think she would feel validated and loved unconditionally. If she doesn't go to college, I'm sure it won't be the end of the world—and she can always decide to go later if she wants to.

Using Mistakes to Understand Consequences and Accountability

INSTEAD OF PERPETUATING feelings of judgment and guilt by focusing on the mistake itself, you will teach your children infinitely more if you help them evaluate their feelings about the result of their decision, understand what caused the result, and determine what they might do differently to achieve a different result next time. You can use this same process to evaluate your own mistakes.

Recently Becky, a parent at one of the teen workshops, asked:

What could I have done? I know I made a mistake. My fourteen-year-old son wanted to eat his dinner in front of the TV. I told him he couldn't; that he had to eat at the table with us. He became very angry and said, "That's so stupid! I hate always eating at the table."

I told him, "Don't get smart with me, young man. You'll sit at the table and be respectful or you won't go to your soccer practice." He sat at the table but refused to eat and was sullen and miserable. We were all miserable. Later, he left me a note saying, "I feel no love at all for you."

I know I did it all wrong. I can see that I certainly didn't use kind and firm parenting by threatening him with missing practice, but I don't know what else I could have done.

The facilitator responded:

Remember, mistakes are wonderful oppor-tunities to learn, so let's not think of this situation as "wrong." Instead, see it as an opportunity to discover what you really wanted to happen, what did happen, what caused it to happen, and what you could do differently next time.

> You will teach your children infinitely more if you help them evaluate their feelings about the result of their decision, under-stand what caused the result, and determine what they might do differently to achieve a different result next time.

Becky and the facilitator then went through the following questions to review the situation for a better solution.

FACILITATOR: Why did you want your son to sit at the table with the family?

BECKY: It's important to me. I like having my whole family together at dinnertime.

FACILITATOR: Do you think he got that message, especially that you would miss him if he wasn't there?

BECKY: Well, no.

FACILITATOR: Let's store that information for now. We'll come back to it when we get to suggestions. Why do you think he wanted to eat in front of the TV?

BECKY: I think he just wanted to see a program he was excited about.

FACILITATOR: Have you ever felt that way about something you wanted to watch?

BECKY: Yes. I can understand that.

FACILITATOR: Can you see how you skipped the issues that were important to you and your son and got into a power struggle that escalated into a revenge cycle?

BECKY: Yes. I felt bad after threatening to make him miss soccer practice, but I couldn't let him get away with talking to me like that. So I won the round, but he sure got back at me. I was very hurt and frustrated when I got his note.

FACILITATOR: Based on the issues we've brought to the surface, can you think of any principles and strategies we've discussed in the workshop that might apply to this situation?

BECKY: No. I feel really stuck. I can't imagine what logical consequence I could have used.

FACILITATOR: Great! If you can't think of one, it probably means a logical consequence is not appropriate in this case. As I've mentioned before, most of us are so enamored with the idea of consequences that we often try to apply them when they aren't appropriate. How about making sure the message of love gets through, sharing what you want, getting into his world to find out what he wants, and then working out a plan where you both win? Would you like to role-play all that to see what it feels like?

BECKY: Sure.

FACILITATOR: Okay. Would you like to play the son and I'll play the mom?

BECKY: Yes. That feels easier to me right now.

FACILITATOR: Start with what your son said in the beginning.

BECKY/SON: Mom, can I eat in the other room in front of the TV?

FACILITATOR/MOM: It's really important to me that we sit together as a family at dinnertime—I really miss you when you're not there. Is there something special about the TV program you want to watch?

BECKY/SON: Yeah. It's something I've been looking forward to seeing.

FACILITATOR/MOM: Well, I can understand that. There are times when I look forward to a certain program, too. Would it be okay with you if we tape your show on the VCR tonight and discuss this at our next family meeting so we can work out a plan to accomplish both our goals?

BECKY/SON: Sure. Thanks, Mom.

FACILITATOR: How are you feeling now as the son?

BECKY: I feel loved and respected and willing to work on a plan with you at the family meeting.

FACILITATOR: What would you like to work on at the family meeting?

BECKY: I'd like to set a time for dinner that's agreeable to everyone so they'll make a commitment to be there. I'd also like to discuss exceptions to the rule and how often exceptions would be reasonable to everyone concerned.

FACILITATOR: It sounds to me like you're now on a track that side-steps the power struggles and revenge cycles. This track is more likely to get everyone what he or she wants while teaching perceptions and skills that will be useful to your son.

The following is a list of the perceptions and skills that help parents to improve understanding and communication after making the kinds of mistakes that lead to power struggles, rebellion, and revenge:

**Correcting Mistakes That Lead to Power
Struggles, Rebellions, and Revenge**

1. Get back to the spirit of the rule rather than the letter of the rule. (The spirit of eating together was to enjoy togetherness and to share with loved ones. The letter of the rule was be there or else.)

2. Treat children the way you would like to be treated—with understanding, dignity, and respect. (How would you like it if someone threatened to deprive you of something simply because you wanted to watch a TV program?)

3. Share what is important to you and why. (Make sure the message of love and respect comes through.)

4. Find out what is important to your child and why.

5. Be willing to make exceptions to rules. (This is not the same as being permissive.)

6. Make an appointment (family meeting or some other time) to work on a plan to meet the needs and desires of all involved, without forming a pattern of exceptions.

To correct mistakes regarding communication, change your attitude of fear, anger, disrespect, and control to one of love and understanding. By doing so, you can remember your kind and firm parenting skills and demonstrate interest in your teen's point of view and faith in his or her basic goodness and abilities. When you find yourself involved in a conflict that creates distance between you and your teenager, ask yourself, "Am I acting from my fear and anger or from my love and faith?"

Crazy Ideas About Mistakes

WHERE DID PARENTS ever get the crazy idea that in order to make kids do better, they first have to make them feel worse? People cannot feel bad and learn anything positive at the same time. The best learning takes place when people feel good. If you berate your children for their mistakes, they will simply feel bad and be unable to learn from them. But if you can change your attitude and see mistakes as wonderful opportunities to learn, your kids might approach things differently in the future and have more faith in themselves.

Think of all the misery created in the world because of perfectionism! Illusionary fears about mistakes disable you and your teenagers. On the other hand, the ability to learn from mistakes is encouraging and enhances the parent-teen relationship. Mistakes are a small price to pay for the valuable lessons that can be learned. Give yourself and your child a break and remember that "Misteaks r wunderfull oppertuniteez 2 lern."

> Where did parents ever get the crazy idea that in order to make kids do better, they first have to make them feel worse?

KIND AND FIRM PARENTING SKILLS TO REMEMBER

1. Tell your teen often that mistakes are wonderful opportunities to learn.

2. Have faith in your teenager to make decisions and to learn from mistakes.

3. Help your teenagers explore the consequences of their choices through friendly what and how questions.

4. Teens are young people with feelings and should be treated with understanding, dignity, and respect.

5. Share what is important to you and why. (Make sure the message of love and respect comes through.)

6. Find out what is important to your child and why.

7. Be willing to make exceptions to rules. (This is not the same as being permissive.)

8. Instead of trying to parent on the fly, make a date or wait for the family meeting to work out a plan that all can live with.

Practical Application Activity

THE BAGGAGE FROM MISTAKES

What leftover baggage from the mistakes of your childhood do you have? The following activity will take you back and help you heal.

1. What are the messages you heard from your parents about mistakes—either stated or implied? List as many as you can think of.

2. What decisions did you make about yourself based on those messages? What do mistakes say about you?

3. Based on those decisions, what do you do either to avoid making mistakes or to keep others from knowing if you do?

4. What messages are you giving your teenagers about mistakes?

5. What do you think they are deciding about themselves when they make a mistake?

6. Based on those decisions, what kind of behaviors do you think your teenagers will do either to avoid making mistakes or to keep others from knowing if they have made mistakes?

7. What new decisions would you like to make about mistakes?

8. What kind of decisions about mistakes would you like to foster in your teenager?

9. Create a plan that includes specific things you will do to foster the kind of legacy you would like to leave your child about mistakes.

MY PLAN FOR THE WEEK

This week I will focus on

_____

_____

I will work on changing my attitude by thinking

_____

_____

_____

I will change my behavior by doing

_____

_____

6

How Do You Get Teens to Keep Their Agreements?

Follow-Through

THE IDEA OF giving up control and punishment can be a real stretch until you realize that there are kind and firm alternatives. We are not asking that you settle for broken agreements, unkept promises, and consequences that turn into punishment and revenge. Once you learn the art of follow-through, you will be able to help your teens learn skills, accept responsibility, and achieve real cooperation.

Follow-through is a surefire method (perhaps the only method) that really works at helping teens to keep their agreements. Follow-through is an excellent alternative to authoritarian methods or permissiveness. With follow-through, you can meet the needs of the situation while maintaining dignity and respect for all concerned. Follow-through is also a way to help teens learn the life skills they need in order to feel good about themselves while learning to be contributing members of society.

Before showing you how to follow through, however, we will try to convince you to stop using what doesn't work—logical consequences. Too many parents think that teens should experience a logical consequence when they don't keep their agreements. Not so.

Follow-through is a surefire method (perhaps the only method) that really works at helping teens to keep their agreements.

Because the use of logical consequences has become one of the more popular parenting methods today, it may be difficult to accept what we have to say about using them with teenagers. You probably won't like hearing that logical consequences are usually ineffective with teenagers, especially if you have learned how effective they can be with younger children. Even under the best of circumstances, using consequences effectively is a fine art, because it's so easy to cross the line between consequences and punishment. Most parents try to disguise punishment by calling it a logical consequence—but teens see through the disguise. Because the main life tasks for teens evolve around power, they see the use of logical consequences as a method to control them. Once you realize how teens view logical consequences, you will see that the concept of follow-through is more applicable.

What Is Follow-Through?

FOLLOW-THROUGH IS A respectful, four-step approach to parenting teens that teaches cooperation, life skills, and responsibility in spite of resistance. The key is that follow-through involves *you*, because *you are the only one who does the follow-through*. The result is that your teen also follows through, but rarely without your participation.

The Four Steps for Effective Follow-Through

1. Have a friendly discussion *with* your teen to gather information about what is happening regarding the problem. (Listen.)

2. Brainstorm solutions *with* your teen, and choose one that both you and your teen can agree to. (We call this "Let's Make a Deal!") Finding a solution you both like may take some negotiating, because your favorite solution may be different from your teen's favorite.

3. Agree on a date and time deadline. (You will find out later why this is imperative.)

4. At the deadline, simply follow through on the agreement by holding your teen accountable with dignity and respect.

Before we provide examples of effective follow-through, we first present the traps. The concept of follow-through is simple unless parents make the mistake of falling into one or all of the following four traps.

Four Traps That Defeat Follow-Through

1. Thinking that teens think the way you think

2. Wanting teens to change personalities instead of behaviors

3. Not getting specific agreements in advance or making agreements you haven't thought through

4. Not maintaining dignity and respect for yourself and your teen

Thinking That Teens Think the Way You Think

This means thinking that your way is the only right way to think. It means you want your teens to have the same priorities you have. You want them to be excited about keeping their agreements and to do the things that are important to you. (Is it news to you that they don't care what the neighbors think about their "droppings" left around the house and that cleaning up their dirty dishes after they've made a snack is nowhere on their list of priorities? This doesn't mean they shouldn't do these things. It just means they aren't priorities for your teens.)

Wanting Teens to Change Personalities Instead of Behaviors

This means that you criticize, judge, and engage in name-calling, instead of focusing on the task or issue at hand. ("How can you live like such a pig? What kind of irresponsible person are you? No one will ever want to hire you," instead of, "Our agreement was that you would clean up after you made a snack.")

Not Getting Specific Agreements in Advance or Making Agreements You Haven't Thought Through

This means trying to control things that you can't control or things that are logistically impossible to follow through on. (How can you know if your teen has done his homework just because he tells you he has? How can you follow through if you have a commitment to be somewhere else at the time when you need to be with your teen to follow through?)

Not Maintaining Dignity and Respect for Yourself and Your Teen

This happens when you get sidetracked into warnings and criticisms or when you allow your teen to sidetrack you with excuses, arguments, manipulations, and displays of anger.

But Does It Really Work?

IN OUR WORKSHOPS, to help parents learn the art of follow-through and to show them that it really does work, we often ask for a volunteer to role-play a teen who has not kept an agreement to do a task. We then ask the volunteer to pretend we have already gone through the Four Steps for Effective Follow-Through. The deadline has arrived, but the task is not done. We then role-play follow-through by using the Four Hints for Effective Follow-Through.

Four Hints for Effective Follow-Through

1. Keep comments simple, concise, and friendly. ("I notice you didn't do your task. Would you please do that now?")

2. In response to objections, ask, "What was our agreement?"

3. In response to further objections, shut your mouth and use nonverbal communication. (Point to your watch after every argument. Smile knowingly. Give a hug and point to your watch again.) It helps to understand the concept of "less is more." The less you say, the more effective you will be. The more you say, the more ammunition you give your kids for an argument—which they will win every time.

4. When your teen concedes (sometimes with great annoyance), say, "Thank you for keeping our agreement."

One thing we ask of the volunteer role-playing the teen is to be in the present moment. By this we mean the volunteer should respond to what is being done now rather than responding in ways that a teen would react to disrespectful methods. When the volunteer does this, it is amazing how quickly the "teen" comes to agreement (after a little resistance).

Many parents object and say, "My teen would not give in that quickly." We disagree and show them why by referring to the Four Traps That Defeat Follow-Through and asking the volunteer teen the following questions:

1. At any time, did you feel criticized or judged?

2. At any time, did you feel we did not maintain dignity and respect— for you, for ourselves, and for what needed to be done?

3. How much difference did it make knowing that you had agreed to a specific deadline?

The volunteer always says "No" to the first two questions and responds that the specific deadline made it difficult to argue for delays. The volunteer also shares that it is very effective when we stop talking and give the "look" (Hint 3 for Effective Follow-Through) with a smile that says, "Nice try, but you and I both know better."

Other parents object to follow-through because they don't think they should have to remind kids to keep their agreements. They want their kids to be "responsible" without reminders. We have four questions for these parents:

1. When you don't take time to remind them with dignity and respect, do you spend time scolding, lecturing, and punishing or doing the job for them?

2. Have you noticed how responsible your kids are about keeping agreements that are important to them?

3. Do you really think mowing the lawn and other chores are important to your kids? (Even though chores aren't a high priority for teens, it is important that they do them.)

4. Do you remember, without reminders, to complete everything that you have promised to do—especially when it is something you don't want to do?

Although follow-through takes energy, it is much more fun and productive than scolding, lecturing, and punishing.

Follow-Through in Real Life

WHEN YOU CHANGE your behavior, your teens will change theirs. You will be amazed at the results when you follow the Four Steps and avoid the Four Traps. When kids have made a deal that includes a deadline (to the minute), they are left with a feeling of fairness and responsibility when they are held accountable.

Thirteen-year-old Cory was not washing his clothes or changing the sheets on his bed as he'd agreed to do. Cory's mom, Jamie, said, "I'd like to talk with you about your laundry. Let's meet after dinner." When they sat down, Jamie asked Cory what his issues were about doing his laundry. She found out that he wasn't really sure how to run the machine and was afraid he would break it. Jamie shared *her* issues, which were that she didn't like to see him wearing dirty clothes to school and sleeping on dirty sheets.

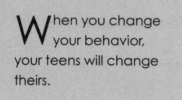

When you change your behavior, your teens will change theirs.

Cory said he was willing to do his laundry but he needed help with the machine. Jamie agreed: "I'd like you to choose a day this week to meet me in the laundry room at 6:00 P.M. for a lesson. I'd also like you to choose which day of the week you'll set aside for doing your laundry and changing your sheets. With a family as large as ours, it would be best if we each have our own laundry day. I'll check back with you in an hour to see which day you've chosen."

An hour later, Cory said he guessed that Tuesday would be all right for the laundry lesson and would also be okay for his laundry day. Jamie said, "Fine. I'll see you at 6:00 on Tuesday in the laundry room."

But on Tuesday, when Jamie went to the laundry room at the agreed-upon time, Cory wasn't there. Jamie found Cory parked in front of the TV and said, "Do you remember your decision about the best time for a laundry lesson?"

Cory said, "Aw, Mom, I don't want to do it now. I'm watching this."

Jamie was very friendly but very persistent, "You agreed to do it at 6:00 tonight."

Cory responded, "I'll do it later, Mom."

Jamie simply stood in front of him with a friendly but expectant look in her eye. Cory finally said, "Oh, all right! This is so stupid!"

Instead of responding to the dig, Jamie simply said, "Thank you for keeping your agreement."

Every Tuesday, Cory and his mother went through a similar routine. Jamie would say, "Remember the day you chose to do your laundry and change your sheets?" No matter what kind of arguments or put-downs Cory came up with, Jamie would simply follow through in a friendly manner while avoiding lectures and insults. She knew it would be absolutely abnormal for Cory to be excited about washing his clothes and changing his sheets. But it was important to her that he help around the house and also that he be equipped with these skills. She saved them both a lot of hassles by simply getting an agreement and then following through.

Jamie gave up the notion that Cory would remember to do this job without being reminded. At thirteen, she realized Cory was thinking more about how to buy a new skateboard or how to tell his dad that he got a poor grade on his report card rather than about his laundry. She decided that follow-through once a week, as long as it didn't turn into a power struggle, was worth it. (She was pleasantly surprised when Cory eventually started remembering to take care of his laundry without being reminded.)

This example illustrates how Jamie decided to act as if Cory intended to keep his agreement. Every Tuesday, she found him and simply reminded him of his agreement. Typical of a kid his age, his actions didn't match his good intentions. However, that didn't matter because Jamie was in charge of her own behavior, not Cory's.

Jamie took care of herself. She decided what her limits were and what she would do about them—not what she would make Cory do. She showed respect for her son and kept the lines of communication open by being curious about his views and by sharing her feelings. She and Cory worked out an agreement that *they both felt good about.* Jamie then kept it simple by following through in a firm, kind, matter-of-fact way.

THE MAGIC KEY

The magic key that many parents miss about follow-through is that *parents* are the ones who need to follow through, not teens. Follow-through does not work if you are not there to hold your teens accountable by expecting them keep the agreement and respect agreed-upon deadlines. When parents follow through by showing up at the agreed-upon deadline, finding their teen, and insisting in a calm and quiet way that the agreement must be kept, the end result is that the teen will follow through too. We call this a magic key, because it makes everything else work, and it is simple, even if it isn't obvious to most parents.

The Many Ways to Follow Through

LEARNING TO FOLLOW through is an important life skill for parents. An attitude of respect is the primary ingredient. It is also important to use as few words as possible to help stay focused on the task at hand rather than on personalities. Notice how the parents in the following examples use the magic key to make sure that the task gets done. Try practicing the skill of follow-through by using one of the methods described below.

Use One Word

The one-word method gets results while maintaining dignity and respect—an excellent model for your kids to follow when they get through individuating.

Andrew had agreed to mow the lawn by 4:00 P.M. each Friday. The first Friday after this agreement was reached, Andrew followed through and mowed the lawn. The second Friday, he forgot. At 4:05 P.M., Martin, Andrew's dad, found Andrew washing his car and respectfully said, "Lawn."

Andrew said, "I'm in the middle of washing my car now, Dad. I'll do it later."

Andrew's dad maintained a respectful attitude and said, "Agreement."

Andrew said, "I know, but it won't hurt to do it a little later."

Martin repeated, "Agreement."

In total disgust, Andrew turned off the water and went to get the lawn mower, mumbling under his breath, "I can't believe you can't wait a few minutes!"

Most parents have experienced the results of waiting a few minutes. Next time, it's a few more minutes, and then a few more, and then other manipulative postponement techniques are used. By not getting into huge discussions and by following through with dignity and respect, Martin taught Andrew to keep his agreement even if he didn't like it.

Parents often object that their kids would not respond as quickly as Andrew did to the one-word method. These parents are basing their belief on the stereotypical responses they get from their teens when faced with punitive methods of parenting. How would you respond if you forgot to keep an agreement and someone grounded you, took away your car, phone, or TV privileges, withdrew love, withheld money, or used physical or emotional abuse? Of course your teens don't give in when these methods are used. Nor do the jobs get done, which is where it all started in the first place.

Use No Words

Another way to use the magic key to follow through is to use a look, a smile, a raised eyebrow, a pointed finger, or hands on the hips. These nonverbal signals can be more effective than any words at all. This kind of nonverbal communication is extremely effective when done with a friendly attitude and a twinkle in the eye to convey a sense of humor, as the following example illustrates.

Mary left the vacuum in the middle of the family-room floor. Her mother found Mary in her room, took her by the hand, led her to the family room, and pointed at the vacuum.

Mary said with exasperation, "Oh, Mom!" She then put the vacuum away and flounced back to her room.

Have confidence that helping your kids keep their commitments, even when it's not a priority for them, is the type of parenting that teaches them good habits to serve them throughout their lives.

Follow Up on Follow-Through

Follow-through won't be completely effective if you don't follow up afterward. Continuing with the earlier example of Andrew and his dad, Martin said to Andrew later that night, "Thanks for keeping your agreement to mow the lawn even though it was inconvenient for you at the time."

Andrew said, "I don't see why you couldn't wait for me to finish washing my car."

Martin said, "I can see how that might seem unreasonable to you. But our agreements are very important to me. I really appreciate you keeping the agreement even when you were angry."

In this encounter, Martin did an excellent job of focusing on and reinforcing the positive aspects of the encounter.

Decide What You Will or Won't Do

YOU MAY DECIDE that you will be available to help with homework on Tuesdays from 6:00 to 7:00 P.M. To follow through, you need to be sitting at the homework area whether or not your teen shows up. When your teen then begs for help on Thursday for a Friday morning test, say, "I have faith in you to handle this. However, I'm always available on Tuesdays." Avoid the lecture about the problems of waiting until the last minute.

If you decide that you are available for chauffeuring three days a week, follow through by refusing to be available at a moment's notice on other days. This does not mean you can't be flexible, but only with respectful advance notice.

Appropriateness, Dignity, and Respect

THERE ARE THREE key concepts essential to the effectiveness of follow-through: appropriateness, dignity, and respect.

It will be easier to follow through on what you say if it is appropriate—not only to the developmental stage of your children but also to the needs of the situation. Trying to maintain control over teenagers is not appropriate. Arriving at agreements through a problem-solving process that involves your teenagers is appropriate. Meaningless threats of humiliation and punishment are not appropriate. There is no need for humiliation and punishment when you follow through with dignity and respect.

Maintaining dignity and respect means understanding that normal teenagers will resist your priorities. But it also means avoiding manipulation. Once a consequence, solution, or plan has been mutually agreed upon, you do your teenagers a disservice by not following through with dignity and respect. You also need to retain dignity and respect for yourself as a parent, which means carrying out your responsibility to teach your teenagers certain life skills, whether or not they want to learn them. It also means respecting your teens' right not to be excited about the things you are trying to teach them and understand that, because of the individuation process, it is appropriate for them to resist. Finally, it means focusing on what needs to be done rather than on personalities. For instance, say, "I understand that you don't want to do it now, but our agreement was that you would do it now," rather than, "What do you mean you don't want to do it now? You're being inconsiderate and irresponsible by not keeping our agreement. What kind of a person are you?"

> Once a consequence, solution, or plan has been mutually agreed upon, you do your teenagers a disservice by not following through with dignity and respect.

Not Following Through

IT IS DISRESPECTFUL to your kids and yourself when you say you are going to do something and then you don't follow through. By failing to follow through, you send your children the wrong message.

LESSONS TEENS LEARN WHEN YOU DON'T FOLLOW THROUGH

1. They don't have to keep agreements. If you don't, why should they?

2. Your word doesn't mean anything. You're just blowing smoke. They may follow your example.

3. Manipulation works to avoid responsibility.

4. They can get away with all kinds of behavior because you don't allow them to be accountable by following through.

5. Love means getting people to "give in."

Avoid Manipulation

DOTTIE HAD FALLEN into a pattern of manipulation with her daughter Dani. Neither mother nor daughter knew how to deal with the other without trying to control the other's behavior.

Typically, Dottie would make threats and pronouncements but would not follow through. Dani understood this pattern well and knew she could talk her mother into or out of almost anything.

When Dani turned eighteen and wanted a car, Dottie decided to follow the procedure for follow-through. She set up a time to discuss car shopping and purchasing with her daughter. Because Dottie was concerned about succumbing to her daughter's manipulation, she did some advanced preparation.

Prepare in Advance

Dottie knew it would be difficult to be clear about her own limits once her daughter got involved, so she decided to make a list before sitting down to talk with Dani.

1. I don't want us to take advantage of each other.

2. I want to give when it feels good to do so. But when it doesn't feel good to give, I don't want to feel guilty.

3. I want to give from desire, not from demands and manipulation.

4. When I give, it needs to be without strings.

5. I want both of us to feel free to pursue her own interests as long as it doesn't hurt anyone else.

6. Without trying to fix things or change Dani's mind, I want to allow Dani to experience whatever feelings she may have in response to my behavior.

7. I want to feel free to give opinions and information without feeling that Dani must agree.

8. I want a plan that includes what both Dani and I are willing to do, so that we each pull our own weight.

With her limits clearly defined, Dottie approached the conference with confidence. During the meeting, Dani told her mother she wanted Dottie to cosign the loan for a new car and assured her that she could make the payments. Before agreeing, Dottie asked Dani to create a budget. When the first budget didn't include insurance or car maintenance and repair, Dottie asked for another. Based on the new budget, Dottie said she thought Dani could afford a car—but it would mean that Dani would have to work at least thirty hours a week and most of her money would go toward the car. Dani agreed.

Dottie and Dani found a car in Dani's price range, and Dottie cosigned. For the first two months, Dani did fine. But then she began missing work regularly. Although she complained about her job, Dani didn't look for another one. Eventually, she quit and then missed a car payment.

In the past, Dottie would have lectured and criticized, and then made the payment, "Just this one time." This time, Dottie said, "Dani, please give me the keys to your car. As long as you're making the payments, the car is yours. But when I have to make the payments to maintain my good credit, the car is mine. When you catch up on the payments, you can try again."

Dani threw a fit. She begged for another chance, told Dottie she hated her, tried shaming her with old stories about how unhappy she was when Dottie divorced her dad, and, finally, refused to give up the keys.

Dottie remained amazingly calm, saying, "I know how angry and upset you are. I'm not going to rip the keys out of your hands, but I'd appreciate your co-operation." Throwing the keys at her mother, Dani slammed out of the house.

Following Through Can Be Painful at First

WHEN YOU'RE NOT used to following through with your teenager, it can be very painful. One sign that you're using follow-through effectively is that you feel as bad as or worse than your teenager does. In the example above, Dottie felt like a wicked witch. But even though she wanted to cave in to make Dani happy, she knew in her heart that in the past caving in was what had helped to create the "monster" she was now parenting. Therefore, she held firm.

When Dani could see that manipulation wasn't going to work, she quickly found another job and caught up on the car payments. Dottie and Dani then made a new deal: Dani could have the keys as long as she agreed to give them to her mother anytime she missed a payment. After that, Dani seemed to have more respect for her mother and for herself. Increased self-esteem is one of the major benefits of follow-through.

Make Agreements

IN ANOTHER FAMILY, the mother of a seventeen-year-old boy shared the following:

> I remember the time Carl said he would be home at 1:00 A.M.—I said okay and went to bed at 10:00. For some magical reason, I woke up at 1:00 to use the bathroom. When I walked by Carl's room, I noticed his bed was empty. He wasn't home.
>
> Carl is the kind of kid who does what he says he will do, and I've always trusted him. So I started to worry that he'd been in a car accident.

I sat on the couch waiting for the police to call. When Carl walked in at 2:30 A.M., I was still sitting on the couch. He was shocked. "What are you doing up?"

I said, "I was waiting for the police. I thought you'd been in an accident."

Carl said, "You're crazy."

I retorted, "Why would I be crazy? Why would I have any reason not to believe you when you tell me something?"

"What am I supposed to do, call you at 1:00 A.M. if my plans change?"

"Sure."

"But that would wake you."

I said, "I don't care. It would be better than imagining you lying on a stretcher in an ambulance."

Carl responded, "You always worry too much. Why don't you just worry less?"

"Well, I wish I could, but I can't. If you told me you were coming in at 3:00, and I went to the bathroom at 1:00 and you weren't home yet, I wouldn't worry. But if you weren't there at 3:00, I would start worrying. That's the way I am."

It was important to me to show him how his behavior affects me. Then it was up to him to decide what to do about it. And he did. He said, "Since you're not going to stop worrying, why don't we have a range for my curfew? When I'm going out, I'll say I'll be home between 11:00 and 3:00." I agreed. I found it interesting that he started coming in at midnight after our discussion!

You may be quaking in your boots as you read this story about curfew. We aren't recommending a 3:00 A.M. curfew. We know that all kids are different and that some, like Carl, can handle the extra freedom without being irresponsible.

Carl and his mom made an informal verbal agreement that left Carl free to make his own decisions. When many parents reach this point, they feel that they have to get the agreement in writing as a contract with their teenager. But these parents wouldn't act that way if they were dealing with a friend, because it wouldn't be respectful or necessary. Anytime you do more or less than needs to be done in a situation, you set up a mischief shuffle.

An Agreement in Writing Is a Reminder, Not a Contract

If an agreement is put in writing, it should be done in the form of a record, not a contract. Some families make decisions at family meetings and record their agreements in a notebook. Others put a note on a calendar or on the refrigerator, until the new arrangement becomes part of the normal schedule. Some written agreements take the form of a job chart. The emphasis on putting the agreement in writing is to help people remember their commitments—it's not the commitment itself, because that's already been made verbally. Follow-through is the most effective way to help kids keep their commitments.

In the previous example, if Carl continued to come in later than he said he would, his mom's response could be to continue sharing her feelings. She could let Carl know how his behavior affects her. But if Carl persists, his mom may have to acknowledge that he says one thing and does another. At this point, Carl's mom can decide what *she* will do next. She may conclude that Carl feels insulted when she worries about him. If this turned out to be true, and if Carl didn't think his mother would change, he might decide to come in whenever he felt like it. At that point, she would have to deal with her problem some other way. She might decide to reevaluate her own behavior and learn to go to sleep

> If an agreement is put in writing, it should be done in the form of a record, not a contract.

whether or not Carl had returned home. Or she could say to Carl, "You aren't being responsible with your freedom, so let's go back to an exact, earlier curfew and try again. I can live with 11:30 or 12:00. You decide which of those is best for you."

What Works, What Doesn't

SOME OF THE more useless parenting tools include lecturing, overreacting, fixing, rescuing, guilt-mongering, shaming, and trying to make control look like it's for teens' own good. If you've tried any of these tools to get your teens to agree with you, you probably know that they don't work. And yet parents often persist, thinking that if they just use these methods long enough their kids will get the message. (Insanity was once described as doing the same thing over and over while expecting a different result!)

When you practice follow-through, you move in a positive and productive direction by communicating your feelings, sharing your values, listening to what your kids think is important to them, finding out what they want to do, and respecting their points of view. This means doing what needs to be done to achieve a goal, without expecting your kids to be as interested as you are in reaching that goal.

Follow-through encourages you to have faith in your kids. You can step back to give them room to decide what they will do for themselves. Follow-through allows you to teach skills, to do *with* and not *for,* to focus on solutions, and to be curious and listen.

Some Final Tips

IT'S EASIER TO follow through if you train yourself and your teens in advance. By spending time working *with* your teens on the necessary steps to achieve the agreed-upon goals, you can make follow-through much smoother. Don't negotiate a new agreement instead of following through on the original one. You need to start and finish with the same plan.

Many times teens don't follow through because parents don't give them a chance. Teens hate it when parents don't show faith in them. It's much better if parents ask their teens if they *have* done something they agreed to do rather than to assume the teens forgot.

Adults are not using their common sense when they expect teens to follow adult priorities. Follow-through is a respectful way to help teens live up to appropriate adult expectations and priorities.

Follow-through never involves threats. It allows you to keep your own power while letting your teens keep theirs. It feels good for everyone. Once you get in the habit of using follow-through, you can maintain a sense of humor when things don't go according to plan. Follow-through can be a wonderful way to enrich your relationship with your teens.

Follow-through helps parents to be proactive and thoughtful instead of reactive and inconsiderate. Once you understand that teens have their own priorities, even though they need to follow some of yours, you can see their resistance as cute, adorable, and normal instead of lazy, inconsiderate, and irresponsible. Follow-through can make parenting pleasurable, magical, and fun.

KIND AND FIRM PARENTING SKILLS TO REMEMBER

1. There is one surefire way to get your kids to keep their agreements, and it's called follow-through. It may be a lot of work for you in the beginning, but it will be worth every minute of the time you spend to train both you and your teen to use better habits.

2. Read the four steps, the four traps, and the four hints for successful follow-through again and again, because they are very different from how you would normally respond as a parent—and as a human.

3. You must be there at the first deadline to set up the follow-through. It won't work in the long run without you there in the beginning.

4. If you whine or complain that using follow-through is too much work, track how much time you spend reminding and nagging your teen instead.

Notice the effect that nagging has on you and on your teen. Keep a checklist of how often the task you are nagging about actually gets done. We call this a reality check.

5. Follow-through will help you use fewer words and your kids will hear you better.

6. Don't hesitate to prepare in advance and maybe even practice with a friend. You can always listen to the "Empowering Teenagers and Yourself in the Process" audiotapes for a live demonstration. It helps! (To order, call 1-800-456-7770.)

7. We do not recommend making contracts with your teens. If you need to write information down as a reminder for both of you, that is respectful and effective. Setting up a contract means you are treating your teenager like a client or an adversary. If you do sign a contract, don't be surprised by your teen's attitudes.

Practical Application Activity

1. Think of a situation in which you nagged your teen. (Dirty dishes in the bedrooms; leaving clothes, shoes, books all over the house; smelly animal cages, etc.)

2. Refer to the four steps, the four traps, and the four hints for effective follow-through and work with your teen to set up a situation to practice for a week.

3. Reread this chapter every time you feel the urge to nag. (The book will probably end up well worn.)

MY PLAN FOR THE WEEK

This week I will focus on

_____

_____

I will work on changing my attitude by thinking

_____

_____

_____

I will change my behavior by doing

_____

_____

_____

7

Does Your Teenager Hear Anything You Say?

Communication Skills

DO YOU AND your teenager really listen to each other? What happens to all those words you use? Why won't your teen use more words and talk to you? Would your teen talk to you more if he or she felt listened to, understood, and taken seriously? In this chapter, we show you how to communicate in a way that both you and your teen feel listened to and understood.

Even though listening is the primary ingredient of communication, it is the least developed skill. When parents ask, "Why won't my child listen to me?" we ask, "Do you model for your child what listening is all about? In other words, do you listen first?"

> When parents ask, "Why won't my child listen to me?" we ask, "Do you model for your child what listening is all about? In other words, do you listen first?"

So much has been written and said about listening that most people are aware of what it takes to listen well. However, most are not aware of why listening is so difficult to do. Simply put, listening is difficult because issues keep getting in the way. People usually take everything they hear personally; they want to defend their positions, explain, correct, retaliate, or tell a better story. Parents especially get extremely "ego-involved" with their kids—that is, they take things very personally, because they feel they may not be good enough parents. You might want to tape a copy of the following list on your bathroom mirror and read it every day until you overcome the ways you interrupt the listening process:

Barriers to Listening

1. Stepping in to fix or rescue so you can be a good parent, rather than listening as your teens try to figure things out for themselves

2. Trying to talk teens out of their feelings or perceptions so they'll have the "right" perceptions and feelings

3. Giving defensive explanations about your point of view

4. Interrupting to teach lessons on morality or values

5. Taking what teens say personally, and letting your own unresolved issues get in the way

6. Using what your teens say against them to punish, criticize, call names, and lecture.

By rearranging the letters in the word *listen,* you can find a primary key to good listening: *silent.* Be silent when listening, because you can't talk and listen at the same time. We know how hard it is to be silent while listening. It takes tremendous self-discipline. It means giving up the temptation to engage in any or all of the six barriers to listening, especially the first one. It's very hard to realize that your kids often don't need solutions—they simply need to be listened to, understood, and taken seriously. That's all!

A group of teens were invited to create a list of the top ten tips to help parents communicate better. They came up with more than 25 tips. Here are some of our favorites.

> By rearranging the letters in the word *listen,* you can find a primary key to good listening: *silent.* Be silent when listening, because you can't talk and listen at the same time.

TEENS' ADVICE TO PARENTS ON HOW TO IMPROVE COMMUNICATION

1. No lectures.

2. Make it short and sweet.

3. Talk everything out honestly.

4. Compromise.

5. Don't talk down to us.

6. Listen to us—don't talk over us.

7. Don't repeat yourself.

8. If we have the guts to tell you what we did wrong, don't be mad and don't overreact.

9. Don't pry or give us the third degree.

10. Skip the 20 questions.

11. Don't yell from a different room and expect us to come running.

12. Don't try to make us feel guilty by saying things like, "I did it because you couldn't find the time."

13. Don't make promises you can't keep.

14. Don't compare us with siblings or friends.

15. Don't talk to our friends about us.

Of course, there are times when it's appropriate to work on solutions with your teens. Later in this chapter we give suggestions on communicating for solutions. But first we cover some of the fine points about simply listening to your teens in order to understand them.

Skills to Help You Be Silent and Listen for Understanding

THE FOLLOWING SKILLS are effective only when you are sincerely interested in understanding the world of your teenagers and are willing to respect their reality.

1. The feeling behind what you do is more important than what you actually do. Being silent while you are reading the paper or thinking about something else doesn't count. Effective listening requires wide-open body language to indicate your interest.

2. Have respect for separate realities. Be open to the fact that there is more than one way of seeing things.

3. Show empathy. ("I can understand why you might feel that way or see it that way.")

4. Be curious enough to try understanding your teen's point of view.

Being curious means that if you do open your mouth, it's to ask questions that will invite more information from your teen. For example, "How did that make you feel? What about that was important to you? Could you give me an example of when I made you so angry? How often do I do that? Is there anything else that is bothering you? The last question ("Is there anything else that is bothering you?") is one that deserves more exploration. Many parents have shared with us that remembering to ask that particular question again and again has done more to help them get into their teen's world and understand core issues than anything else they have done.

"Anything Else?" Working on Your Attitude of Curiosity

AN IMPORTANT SKILL for demonstrating curiosity is to keep asking, "Is there anything else?" Too often, parents react to the first bit of information they get, although it usually isn't even close to the key issue. You discover the core issues and feelings when you avoid the temptation to respond to the surface information and instead keep asking this key question. There are many ways to ask: "Is there anything else about that that bothered you? Is there anything else you want to say about that? Is there any other reason you can think of? Is there any other information you could give me to help me understand?"

Use your creativity, but keep being curious enough to elicit more and more information. It may seem awkward and phony at first, but keep practicing. Once you get over feeling clumsy, it will become more spontaneous. You'll find yourself being truly curious and interested.

Adele shared the following story about her thirteen year old. While she and her daughter were visiting a friend, Adele volunteered her daughter to help the friend with some baby-sitting. However, she neglected to check with her daughter first, a point her daughter had raised on numerous occasions. Adele meant to be more sensitive to her daughter's needs, but sometimes she forgot. On the way home, she noticed that her daughter was sullen and moody, so she asked, "What's wrong?" Her daughter said angrily, "Nothing. You're just being your usual self. You volunteer my services without asking me."

Although Adele realized she had made a mistake, she could tell that her daughter needed some space before hearing any apologies. Therefore, Adele decided to wait and continue the conversation later. That evening she asked her daughter if she could sit on her bed for awhile. She said, "I don't care," so Adele sat down and began stroking her daughter's hair. Tears ran down her daughter's cheek as Adele said, "Sometimes life can be so difficult and sometimes one doesn't feel understood." After a few minutes she added, "I'm sorry that I was disrespectful of you by volunteering you for a job without asking you first. I made a mistake."

"It's not just that, Mom," she added.

"What then?" Adele asked.

"I felt too embarrassed to say no."

"Anything else?"

"I don't know how I can get my schoolwork done if I baby-sit after school."

"Anything else?"

"I don't like to baby-sit her kids because they are so difficult and never listen."

Adele nodded and said, "Thanks for letting me know your feelings. I'm willing to call and say I made a mistake if you like. Want to sleep on it?"

Her daughter said, "Okay, but maybe it will be all right. I'll let you know in the morning. Love you, Mom."

Adele demonstrated many important ideas about communication. Instead of making her daughter's moodiness a big issue by saying, "We need to talk about what happened," she waited until the situation had cooled down. Then she "hung out" by sitting on her daughter's bed. If Adele had demanded that they talk, her daughter would have taken this as a signal that a lecture or a punishment was on the way. Adele realized how much more effective it is to live what she believed than to preach what she believed. She wanted good communication with her daughter, so she had to work at becoming a better communicator first. In the long run, using this approach will mean that teens will be much more likely to "hear" their parents' actions than they are to "hear" the lectures. Although they may seem to rebel against your example for a short time, when you quietly and respectfully live what you believe, you'll be amazed at how many of your values your children will adopt when they grow up. Adele modeled waiting for the right time to talk, apologizing for her mistake, and listening to her daughter's feelings without judgments or trying to fix or change her daughter.

However, there are times when it's appropriate to communicate your feelings and desires directly, rather than by example. There are times when solving problems can only be accomplished by communicating verbally. To be an effective verbal communicator, you must call on different resources. The following are several options to consider:

RESOURCES FOR EFFECTIVE COMMUNICATION

1. Communicate from your heart and gut to develop a feeling words vocabulary.

2. Use joint problem solving to find solutions everyone can live with for a short time.

3. Learn the language of *powerful communication*.

4. Practice quick tips for communications.

Develop a Feeling Words Vocabulary

INSTEAD OF HIDING feelings, help your children identify and share their feelings. Since many adults don't know what feelings are, they can't help their teens, who are a bundle of feelings waiting to be spoken.

You need to learn to communicate from your heart and your gut using a feeling words vocabulary. Lectures, judgments, arguments, rationalizations, distractions, overreactions, and predictions of the future all come from your head. Sadness, loneliness, love, compassion, empathy, and understanding are feelings that come from your heart. Honesty, fear, anger, and courage are feelings that come from your gut. When it comes to communicating, not one of these is the all-time solution. There are times when judgment and analysis from your head will serve best. Other times call for listening to the love, compassion, or sadness of your heart. Still other times require you to be gut-level honest or to listen to your fears, anger, or courage. The solution to so many communication problems is to find the appropriate balance.

After Joyce's divorce, she realized that a big chasm had developed between herself and her daughter, Julia. When Joyce learned the skills of communicating from the head, heart, or gut, she was able to bridge that chasm. She shared the following excerpt from her journal:

> *About six months ago, Julia took me to a movie. Before the movie, we were talking, and I started to listen to what she was saying instead of arguing. I didn't realize I hadn't been listening until I started to listen. I could see how, in the past, I would go right to my head and would try to explain my point of view instead of listening to her from my heart.*
>
> *It took self-discipline to bite my tongue. When the conversation ended, I had this uneasy feeling that nothing had been solved. I hadn't done any of my usual behaviors, like giving her advice or telling her the "correct way" (my way) to see things. However, over the weeks I noticed our relationship got better, even though there was still some uneasiness. About a month after this first "listening" experience, I drove her home after a family dinner. She made it a point that she wanted me to drive her home. I could tell she wanted to say something to me, but she was nervous. So I decided to share*

with her from my heart. I said, "I feel so bad about the gap in our relation-
ship. We have this kind of superficial relationship. I love you, and I think
you love me, and when we spend time together it's very pleasant and cor-
dial, but it feels so superficial. I just wish there was something we could do
to close the gap." Julia said, "I'm not going to talk about this anymore. I've
been through a lot. I'm not getting into this stuff again."

I kept saying, "I think I'm a better listener now. I've learned a lot. I
used to think I knew how to listen, but I didn't. Please give me another try,
I want to know what you've gone through." So Julia started talking to me.
It was very painful to hear what she had to say. It was just breaking my
heart to really listen to her, because she told me that she felt that the person
who had always helped her deal with her pain had abandoned her when
she was in the most pain of her life. She wondered how I could really love
her and do that. She realized that many of the things she had believed were
just myths—that her mother was just a person but not the person Julia be-
lieved her to be.

Julia said, "In a way, I have to thank you because I'm a better person
for going through this, because I was just going along in life and having a
good time. All I thought about was where the next party was. I didn't really
take anything seriously. I figured life was just a game. When this happened,
I found out differently. Life is very serious, and I'm the one in control of
my life. Because of that, I made a lot of decisions about not abusing drugs,
about how I'm going to spend my time, about what's important to me, how
important school is to me. I don't think it's really bad, but it can never be
the same now because you're different than I thought you were. You were
my mother and now you're this person."

I was sitting there crying hard because I really heard Julia with my
heart. My heart was breaking, and I kept saying, "I'm just so sorry that you
had to go through this. I'm so sorry I couldn't listen to you. I heard every-
thing you said as a criticism—I couldn't hear what was behind it. I was
too defensive. I can imagine how invalidating that must have been. How
insulting that must have been to you! You know, I love you so much, and
it's so hard for me to see you go through pain. And to think that you
went through all this! I just wish I would've known. I wish I would've

understood. I wish I could have! You thought you saw me being happy, but I was going through incredible pain. You didn't see the pain; you saw something else. And someday, when you're ready, I'd like to tell you about what was going on for me then. I don't think this would be a very good time, but there's a lot you don't know and a lot you don't understand. I hope some day you'll want to know."

This was all happening in the car, in the driveway. The two of us were just sobbing, and I was holding her, and I said, "I just love you so much, and I feel so bad."

She said, "And I love you."

All of that big barrier got broken down between us. It was painful to listen from my heart, but it was worth it. I feel like I have my daughter back.

Communicate Gut Feelings

The heritage of our society is to discount or ignore feelings—especially those from the gut. You've been taught not to feel angry and not to be honest if it hurts someone else's feelings. (Isn't that an interesting paradox? It must be okay for other people to have feelings because you aren't supposed to hurt them, but you are supposed to suppress feelings of your own.) Although a great deal of lip service is given to developing as an individual, you are judged when you don't conform to the norm. The only way to conform is to discount the feelings that make you different.

If you don't learn to acknowledge your feelings, to listen to what they have to teach you, and to express them in ways that are respectful to yourself and others, your life will be superficial, without substance.[1] If you are able to do these things for yourself, you will then be able to teach them to your children.

Part of your job as a kind and firm parent is to help your kids acknowledge and understand their feelings, be comfortable with expressing feelings in a respectful manner, express feelings as information and not as absolutes, and help

---

1. See *Do-It-Yourself Therapy: How to Think, Feel, and Act Like a New Person in Just 8 Weeks* for more information on learning about feelings and how to express them.

them stand up for themselves. Children need to understand separate realities, to realize that people feel and think differently from one another. In addition, teenagers need to know that it's okay to have feelings, no matter what they are, and that they don't have to do anything about them. Having "bad" feelings does not make someone a bad person; everyone has these feelings. Actually, there aren't good or bad feelings, there are just feelings and emotions. No matter how intense those feeling are, the won't kill you, especially if you express them respectfully.

You teach your kids about communicating gut feelings when you hear their feelings and validate them and when you share own your feelings using the listening skills taught in this chapter. You need

> Part of your job as a kind and firm parent is to help your kids acknowledge and understand their feelings, be comfortable with expressing feelings in a respectful manner, express feelings as information and not as absolutes, and help them stand up for themselves.

to listen without thinking that you must "fix" anything, without getting defensive, and without explaining your position. You are much more respectful when you simply listen or employ your curiosity skills.

In addition to listening, one of the best ways to encourage kids to express their feelings is to model expressing your own feelings with complete honesty.

Honesty: A Tool for Developing a Feeling Vocabulary

Being honest with your teen about how you feel now and about how you felt and what you did as a teenager is extremely important. Often, parents are afraid to talk about what they did as kids because they think their kids will take it as encouragement to do the same things. But many teenagers have told us the opposite is true. Don't be afraid to be honest with your teen—it's an excellent way to encourage communication.

When her fourteen-year-old daughter, Erin, began going steady, Linda decided to be honest with her. She said to Erin, "I want to share some things that happened to me as a teenager . . . but I have to tell you, it's scary for me! I did some things that weren't good for me, and some things I knew my parents wouldn't like one bit—and I'm scared that if you know I did these things, you'll want to do them, too. But I'm not going to pay attention to my fears, because I think what I can tell you can be helpful."

Linda took a deep breath:

> Often, parents are afraid to talk about what they did as kids because they think their kids will take it as encouragement to do the same things. But many teenagers have told us the opposite is true.

I was sexually active from the time I was in the tenth grade. I was very lucky that I didn't get pregnant. I was having sex because I was looking for love . . . I didn't know that wasn't the way to find it. It was also a real moral issue for me, because I was taught that it was a sin to engage in sex before marriage. So I felt like a sinner, I felt guilty, and then I did it anyway—which made me feel even worse. I could never bring myself to ask anyone for information or ask about birth control. In fact, I kept promising myself I'd never do it again, but then I would. Then I'd feel guilty all over again.

I wonder what I would've done if I'd felt loved, . . . if I had information and even permission to use birth control, . . . if I knew I'd be accepted even if I did make those choices. I have a hunch I might've been much wiser in my decisions. I don't know if I would have abstained, but the chances are much greater that I would have in most cases—the times when I was more worried about being rejected than about what was right for me. I know I would have loved myself much more, and I wouldn't have had to look for love and approval in that way. That's why I want to tell you what I wish my parents could have told me.

I get scared that you'll get involved in sex before you've developed enough judgment to understand long-range results like pregnancy, your reputation, and disease. I wonder if you respect yourself enough to feel good about saying no if you want to, rather than feeling like you have to give in to someone else's demands. I wish I could protect you from being hurt by any mistakes you might make, but I know you have to make your own mistakes and learn whatever you learn from living your life the way you choose. Just know that I'll always be here to love you and accept you uncon-ditionally, and I'll be glad to give you information if you ever want it.

Linda used a lot of words—which is okay when you're sharing feelings from the heart and gut. She was amazed at how effective her sharing was. Erin told her all about the kids at school who everyone knew were "doing it." Erin told her mother that she didn't have any trouble saying no because she'd noticed how it wasn't long before everyone in school knew "everything;" she didn't want people to talk about her that way.

Linda would not have known what was going on for Erin if she hadn't decided to be honest with her. Aware that Erin might change her mind about sex as she grows older, Linda planned to keep the lines of communication open so Erin could feel free to use her mother as a resource anytime.

> It takes honesty and courage to get in touch with your own feelings, the source of those feelings, and what you want to do about them.

It takes honesty and courage to get in touch with your own feelings, the source of those feelings, and what you want to do about them. When com-municating honestly about feelings, it's easy to get sidetracked into explanations, rationalizations, at-tacks, defensiveness, and other reactions. Following the "I feel" formula—*I feel* _____ *because*_____ *and I wish* _____ —helps keep you centered on your feelings, the reasons for your feelings, and possible solutions. Notice the word *possible*. Asking for what you wish doesn't mean anyone else has the responsibil-ity to give it to you. Neither should you expect anyone else to agree with you or feel the same. Instead, the "I feel" formula is an effective procedure for honor-ing, respecting, and expressing yourself in a way that's respectful to others. (Use the Feeling Faces Chart on page 150 to help you identify your feelings.)

The "I Feel" Formula

The following are examples of the "I feel" formula. Note how the italicized words are used in the variations that follow. "I *feel* upset about the dishes not being done *because* I like looking at a clean kitchen and cooking in a clean kitchen—and I *wish* you'd do them before I start cooking."

FEELING FACES CHART

"I feel happy when you keep your agreement to do the dishes because the kitchen looks so nice. Now I can fix dinner in a good mood." As you can see, the last part of the formula was changed from "I wish" to "now I can." This doesn't mean other people are responsible for your good or bad mood. Some people can fix dinner in a messy kitchen and still stay in a good mood. It does mean that you've expressed how you feel.

"I feel hurt when you put me down, and I wish you wouldn't do that." In this case, the *because it hurts my feelings* was omitted since it's clearly understood. The formula is flexible; it provides guidelines, not rules. When appropriate, it's helpful to include the *because* and the *I wish* because they help us stay in touch with the whole picture and to give others as much information as possible.

"I feel happy for you for getting that A on your report card because I know how hard you worked for it." This comment ends with the focus where it belongs—on the effort rather than the person. To say, "I'm so proud of you for getting an A," leaves your kids feeling as though you won't be so proud of them if they don't get A's. Your children need to feel that you're proud of them no matter what.

"I feel upset about that F on your report card because I'm afraid you might be missing out on something that could benefit you. I wish you'd take another look at what a good education could mean to you." Rather than attacking character, comments like this invite your teens to look at how their behavior affects their lives.

"I feel really angry when you hit your brother because I dislike violence. I'd like you to consider other ways to express your feelings and other ways to get what you want." This comment models for your child that it's okay to feel angry but not okay to be disrespectful to others. It also allows room for follow-up on the issue of violence, which could be discussed at a family meeting or at another time when both parent and child are in good moods. At that time, a list could be made of possible nonviolent ways of dealing with anger and for getting what we want.

The "You Feel" Formula

In rare instances when your kids do open up to you and try to express their feelings (sometimes in disrespectful ways), you may react negatively (with a disrespectful parent response). If you tell your child he shouldn't feel that way or he should be more respectful, or if you counterattack him in any way, don't be surprised when he grows up with the idea that it's not okay to have feelings or that he should suppress them.

When you model the "I feel" formula, you help children learn how to honor and express their feelings in respectful ways. It helps to validate their feelings with the "you feel" formula—the word *you* differentiates this formula from the "I feel" formula. Sometimes it's easy to reflect what they've said because it's very clear. In these instances, it's important that you don't sound like a parrot. Your intent—to hear what your teen is saying—will come through if you validate the feelings behind the words instead of simply repeating the words.

DJ was watching television when his father came into the room and asked him to take out the garbage. DJ ignored Dad. Five minutes later, Dad came back into the room and said, "Turn off that TV right now and take out the garbage."

DJ said, "How come I have to do everything you want right now? How would you like it if I told you to turn off the TV and do something for me right now?"

Dad could see that he'd created resistance and defensiveness with his demand. Fortunately, he remembered the "you feel" formula and said, "You hate it when I tell you to do something right now and feel angry because I'm not being respectful of your time and interests. Do you wish I'd give you more warning or more choices about when it would be convenient for you?"

DJ said, "Yeah."

Dad said, "You're right. I was disrespectful. When would you be willing to empty the garbage?"

DJ said, "At the next commercial."

Dad said, "Good enough for me."

When Dad shared this example with his parent study group, he added, "Before, I would've escalated the problem by telling my son not to get smart with me instead of realizing I had been disrespectful to him."

A mother in the same group shared,

When my daughter used to tell me about her fights with her friends I would say, "Oh, honey, I'm sure it'll be okay tomorrow. You know you always have these fights, and they don't last long." She would stomp off to her bedroom and slam the door. Now, I ask something like, "You feel really bad when you have had a fight with your friend because you aren't sure you'll be able to make up, and then you won't have a best friend?" I see the relief in her face from feeling listened to and understood. Then she says, "Yes, but I'm sure we'll make up tomorrow." Instead of trying to fix problems or make them go away, it's actually much easier to reflect feelings with understanding. It's also comforting to know that she now feels validated rather than put down.

Reflecting Your Teens' Feelings Is Not Always Easy

SOMETIMES YOUR TEENS' feelings are not clear. This means listening with a "third ear" to what might be underneath an outburst and reflecting to them what you've heard. Your reflection may not be accurate, but if you present it in a friendly manner, with real intent to understand, your teens will help you out by correcting your perception.

Joint Problem Solving Works with Teens

WILLIE SAVED ALL his birthday and Christmas money from the time he was five, telling everyone that one day he would buy himself a really cool car. When Willie got his license, he told his folks he was going car shopping. His parents stopped in their tracks and said, "No way. You just got your license, and you're not ready to have a car of your own." "But I've been saving my whole life, and you never told me that before," Willie complained. "That's not fair, and you can't stop me. It's my money."

What a perfect opportunity for Willie and his folks to sit down and do some joint problem solving using the four steps for problem-solving.

FOUR STEPS FOR JOINT
PROBLEM SOLVING

1. Teen shares his or her issues and goals.

2. Parent shares his or her issues and goals.

3. If goals of teen and parent are far apart, brainstorm to find options.

4. Teen and parent pick an option they can both live with and try it out for a short time.

When Willie and his folks followed the process, Willie's issues were that he had waited forever and wanted his own car so he could experience the results of his years of effort. He wanted it to look a certain way, drive a certain way, and he planned to keep it perfect. He didn't want to share. His folks were worried that if he had his own car, he would think it was okay to go anywhere he wanted without checking in with them. They were also concerned that he'd let his school work slip because he was spending too much time in his car, on his car, and working to afford having a car. After much brainstorming, they decided that it was fine for Willie to buy the car as long as he agreed to continue to check in with them about where he was going and how often he'd be using the car. If his homework slipped, he agreed to give his folks the car keys until he caught up.

A fourteen year old wrote the following for a school paper entitled "Parents and Rules." You can tell that his parents have definitely embraced the ideas of joint problem solving.

When I think of my parents, I think of them as not being too strict. I think of them as being more of a type of a friend to me. They let me do a lot of things I want to do but sometimes take control and make what they call "the right decisions." On a scale from "strict" to "doesn't care," I would rate my parents at the halfway mark.

The reason that I would rate them at the halfway mark is because I have a good relationship with them. When we make up rules that I have to

follow, we can sit down and talk about them. Most of the time we decide
to make a compromise, which is the halfway mark. Some compromises that
we have made in the past are things like a curfew, wearing my bike helmet,
not doing drugs, calling and leaving messages so they can know where I
am, and doing certain things around the house to help out. Although some
of the things that I've listed are rules that I have to follow, like not doing
drugs, they are rules that are okay with me.

After all of the things I have listed, I found that having only a few
rules, ones that you can cope with, isn't so bad. It allows me to do the things
that I want to do and also allows my parents to not have to worry about
me. That is what I think about my parents and rules.

Learning the Language of Powerful Communication

WE'VE REPEATED OFTEN in this book that teens are struggling with ways to feel powerful. Being powerful is a good quality, as long as it is accompanied with respect and responsibility. As you learn how to communicate using the language of powerful communication, you'll be able to help your teen feel powerful without ending up in power struggles. Because parents have asked us, "But what do I say? Give me the words," we provide the following phrases to help you communicate to your teens that they are powerful. Saying this does not imply that teens have power over you; it simply means that they are powerful and can impact their world.

POWERFUL COMMUNICATIONS

Let's make a deal!

Let's negotiate.

Here's how we do it.

Would you be willing to _____?

Let's start here.

In our house, we _____

Tuesday is _____

Time for _____

When you have _____, then I'll _____

That's one way. I look at it differently. Want to hear what I think?

We can listen to each other without agreeing.

We'd like to do it this way until we have time to work out a plan we all like.

Let's try this out for a day, week, month, and then re-evaluate.

Let's start with a set curfew and change it as we need to.

You may drive our car, borrow my clothes, etc., as long as you _____; otherwise, I'll have to say "no" until I feel like trying again.

Compare these statements with your normal communication, which usually sounds more like, "Because I said so," or "When you have a home of your own, you can do what you want, and not until then," or "Do this and do that!" Quite a difference!

Quick Tips for Communication

THERE ARE MANY facets to communicating effectively. The following tips will serve as additional guidelines to help you keep respectful relationships with your teen.

1. Avoid the blame game
2. Stick to the needs of the situation, not the personalities
3. Keep it simple

4. Use only one word

5. Use ten words or fewer

6. Avoid words

7. Get permission before giving advice

8. Let your teens have the last word

9. Hang out

Avoid the Blame Game

One of the greatest barriers to effective communication is playing the blame game. If you're looking for blame, you will find it. And if you're looking for solutions, you will find them, too.

We saw a cartoon that beautifully illustrated the blame game. It depicted a father running after his child with a stick. The mother was calling, "Please give him another chance." The father shouted back, "But he might not ever do it again!" How often are you more interested in making your kids pay for what they have done through punishment, or at least through feelings of guilt, than you are in communicating for solutions?

A nice motto for any family (or any organization) is, "We are interested in solutions—not in blame." However, if you adopt this family motto, your kids will hold you accountable. Every time you get into your blame routine, one of your kids will say, "Are you looking for blame, or are you looking for solutions?" That's when you must have enough humility to say, "Whoops. Thanks for reminding me."

Stick to the Needs of the Situation, Not the Personalities

Rudolph Dreikurs taught over and over how important it is to "stick to the needs of the situation," which simply means doing what is appropriate to solve the problem at hand rather than predicting the future and making issues bigger than they are. If your teen hasn't done a chore, stick to the needs of the situation, which means to find a way to get the chores done. It is not helpful to make predictions that your teen will be an irresponsible bum for the rest of his life. For effective communication, focus on what needs to be done rather than on personal attacks.

Janice came home to find her daughter, Dionne, and four friends sitting on the couch watching television. The girls had left the kitchen in a mess after making brownies and popcorn. In the past, Janice had attacked her daughter's personality under similar situations. She'd say, "Dionne, I can't believe you'd be so irresponsible and leave such a mess! I want your friends to go home right now, since you obviously can't control what happens when they're here."

This time, she decided to stick to the issue rather than focusing on person-alities. She said, "Girls, it's a rule in our house that we clean up after ourselves. When do you plan to clean up, during commercials or as soon as the program is over?"

Dionne said, "Oh, Mom, we'll do it."

Mom said, "I know you will, honey. I'd just like to know when you plan to do it."

Dionne asked her friends, "Should we do it during commercials or after the program?" Her friends got into the spirit of the task, deciding they could all work fast during commercials to get the mess cleaned up.

Keep It Simple

We've talked a great deal about understanding and expressing feelings, as well as understanding your own and your teen's world. But watch out—it's very easy to go overboard and become engaged in "the paralysis of analysis." Again, it comes back to appropriateness and balance. There are times when the com-munication process is intricate because truths are buried. But there are other times when the situation is straightforward and needs to be taken at face value.

When we look at the language that teens have developed for expressing themselves via pagers and so forth, we are amazed and impressed at how well they keep communication simple. Here are a few of the commonly accepted codes (taken from a newspaper article by Loren Doppenberg of the *Santa Rosa Press Democrat*).

Pager Code Language

Code	Definition	Derivation
10	Perfect	Score of a perfect 10
13	Having bad day	Unlucky number
30	This is getting old	30 is over-the-hill
66	Let's hit the road	Route 66
121	Need to talk	One-to-one
226	I'm sick	Too, too sick
811	A semi-emergency	Less urgent than 911
1021	Not a chance	Odds are 10-to-1
1040	You owe me	IRS form 1040

Use Only One Word

Although chapter 6 covers the one-word method of follow-through, it's worth repeating in the context of communication.

When your teenager has left his towel on the bathroom floor, this is not the time to "get into his head" to try to figure out what feelings might have been behind his action. His feelings are obvious. He's a teenager—he doesn't care if towels get left on the bathroom floor! You're the one who cares. What you need to decide is whether you want him to pick up the towel or to feel bad, guilty, inconsiderate, and a failure.

If you want your teen to pick up the towel (with the hope that someday he might learn this life skill), the sum total of your communication should consist of one word, "Towel." If by some chance he doesn't get it, you can add one more word, "Bathroom." Because towels on bathroom floors are low on his priority list, it's within the realm of possibility that he still won't get it. At this point, you might use two words, but only if you run them together, "Bathroomfloor."

We hope you get the point that using only one word is more to help *you* learn self-discipline and respect than to help your teenager learn self-discipline and respect. Its ironic how often parents try to teach teenagers to be self-disciplined and respectful by using disrespectful methods that lack self-discipline. The one-word method gets results. Are you looking for blame or are you looking for solutions? One word can be very effective communication and follow-through.

Use Ten Words or Fewer

Another variation of the *less-is-more* school of communication is learning to use ten words or fewer. Again, this is an exercise for you in self-discipline and respect.

Sharon is the mother of two children. Every time she opened her mouth to speak, her son and daughter would walk away, roll their eyes, start reading the paper, or give her a blank stare while they thought about something else. Because they couldn't stand listening to her go on and on about what she thought and felt, her family had trained themselves to tune her out. Her daughter, Kerry, was the most blatantly disgusted with Sharon's verbosity, but her son, Terry, and her husband weren't much more patient with her.

When Sharon heard about using ten words or fewer, she knew she was a good candidate. She wanted to break the tune-out pattern so that her family would listen to her and take her seriously. First she decided to email her family members using her newly found skill.

To Kerry she emailed, "Bring garbage can up from the bottom of the driveway." To Terry she wrote, "Wear headgear, and floss today." (She wasn't ready to give up nagging, just nagging with so many words.) And finally she sent the following email to her husband, "Kids going to movies. Let's do dinner. Love you."

That evening as the kids were getting ready to go to the movies, Kerry asked his mom if she was feeling okay.

Sharon replied, "Yes" (one word).

"What do you want?" asked Kerry, feeling confused and uncomfortable.

Sharon answered, "To let you know I'm practicing saying less" (eight words).

"About what, Mom?"

"About everything, Kerry, and I'd like your help" (eight words).

Now Kerry felt more at ease—she got ready for her mom to give her the *no one ever helps me* lecture. But after tuning out for a few minutes, Kerry realized her mom wasn't talking. Shocked, Kerry said, "Mom, what are you talking about? What kind of help do you want?"

"If I go on and on, tell me to stop" (ten words).

Kerry said, "Sure, Mom, whatever you say."

As Sharon continues to work on the skill of using ten words or fewer, she'll learn to organize her thoughts clearly before she starts talking. She'll also get more attention from her family, as she has already discovered. Most importantly, she'll experience the real joy of conversation with the give and take that comes when people are truly engaged in effective communication.

Avoid Words

We've all heard the saying that a picture is worth a thousand words. The same is true of a look. Therefore, it is worth repeating that you can communicate very effectively by facial expression or body language without words, as discussed in chapter 6.

Upon coming home from school, Steve usually left his backpack, jacket, and other "droppings" all over the family room. He made a deal with his mom that he would pick them up after he had a chance to "chill out" for a few minutes but before he left the house to hang out with his friends. The next day his friends came by and wanted him to go to the lake. Steve said to his mother, "Can I go to the lake? I promise I'll pick up my stuff as soon as I get back." His mother put her hands on her hips and looked at him with a disbelieving smile on her face.

Steve said, "Come on, Mom. I promise."

Mom just continued to look at him, adding raised eyebrows to the smile.

Steve gave in. He said to his friends, "Come help me pick up my stuff. Then I can go."

For nonverbal communication to be effective, parents must have confidence and the ability to focus on the needs of the situation. Don't take the bait that your teens will throw at you in the form of disgust or coaxing. Keep long-range parenting in mind and your own issues out of the way. This takes maturity and self-discipline—characteristics we hope our teens will one day learn. So, what better way to teach than to model?

Get Permission Before Giving Advice

Most people who share their feelings are not looking for advice; they simply want someone to listen and to understand. On the other hand, most people who are in the listening position believe it's their job to give advice. Unless they ask for it, teenagers don't want your advice. Whenever you're tempted to give advice, first ask, "Would you like my advice?" Teens will usually respond "no," but occasionally they might say yes, or at least, "Oh, okay, if you insist!"

Let Your Teens Have the Last Word

We've heard of some ugly confrontations between parents and teens that have ended up with holes in walls, kicked-in doors, and even blows to those involved. Although it may feel like a monumental task, it is often best to let teenagers have the last word.

When you fight with your teen to determine who is right and who is wrong, are you making any headway? Are you really getting the respect you want (or showing any, for that matter) when you insist on having the last word? You will gain the upper hand when you restrain yourself. Just watch the shocked expression on your teen's face. If you are starting to argue, more angry words will only make matters worse. Instead of arguing, try a note, an email, a cooling-off period, or a trip to the family meeting agenda, which should be hanging in plain sight in your home.

Hang Out

Your teens can't talk to you if you aren't around. Just because your kids are older doesn't mean that they don't still need you. In some ways, teenagers act a lot like they did when they were two years old, needing you the minute you are busy doing something else nearby. So go for it! Read a book at the table as your teenager does her homework. Volunteer to carpool or pick her up from a friend's house. Work on a hobby or read the paper while she works at the computer. Ask if you can come into her room to listen to music with her. Invite her out for pizza with some of her friends. We'll bet you'll end up in conversation if you simply make yourself available, without any other agenda.

We have discussed several methods of communication between parents and teens. Some seem complicated because you need to dig beneath the surface to find the hidden truth. Others are simple, such as using one word, up to ten words, or no words at all. The point is to listen, to work out problems together, to understand your teen's point of view, to validate, and to practice emotional honesty yourself.

Another of our favorite communication tools is the family meeting. Because it is so important and involves so many skills, we have devoted chapter 8 to this important process. Don't skip the chapter thinking family meetings are too difficult or that it's too late to start them. You'll be amazed at how holding family meetings raises the well being of your family.

KIND AND FIRM PARENTING TOOLS TO REMEMBER

1. Look at the barriers to communication and find the ones you use most. Work at catching and stopping yourself from using them, even it it's midstream.

2. Review what teens have to say about how to improve communications and use as many methods as you can with your teen.

3. Ask "Anything else?" until your teen stops talking to really open your eyes to your teens separate reality.

4. Feelings aren't good or bad and you won't die from them, so work on developing a feeling words vocabulary to help you and yours express your feelings respectfully.

5. Although you may have grown up trying to be tactful and worrying about hurting others' feelings, you can probably communicate with much more honesty and still not offend anyone. In fact, you might even feel closer to others.

6. Of all the communication help in this chapter, the "I feel" and "You feel" formulas help the most when you learn how to use them with real feeling words.

7. Teens communicate better when you really listen to them and when you include them in discussions about issues that affect them.

8. The language of powerful communication can help you avoid power struggles, so put the list where you can easily access it.

9. Using fewer words, hanging out, and asking permission go a long way to make the communication you do have with your teen more effective.

Practical Application Activity

THE "I FEEL" PROCESS

1. Reread the pages in this chapter on the "I feel" and "You feel" processes.

2. Refer to the Feeling Faces chart.

3. Think of a situation in which, no matter how many times you tried to communicate something to your teen, you couldn't get anywhere. Look at the chart (on page 150) and find the feeling face and feeling word that best fits how you felt in that circumstance.

4. Write a sentence using the "I feel ____ because ____ and I wish ____" formula, making sure you use the feeling word from the chart after the word "feel." Read your sentence to your teen and see what kind of result you get.

MY PLAN FOR THE WEEK

This week I will focus on

_____

_____

I will work on changing my attitude by thinking

_____

_____

_____

I will change my behavior by doing

_____

_____

_____

8

Do Family Meetings Work with Teens?

F AMILY MEETINGS PROVIDE a time for everyone to have a chance to feel a sense of belonging and to experience making a contribution. At a well-run family meeting, you can help your teens build character as you all explore feelings, discover separate realities, and work together to find solutions to family problems. Your teens will improve communication and problem-solving skills while creating a family tradition based on giving and receiving compliments. Family meetings can be as important to families as regular staff meetings are to any well-run business. They can help a family find understanding and closeness.

A few basic tips ensure that your meetings are what you would like them to be. Hold regularly scheduled meetings, rotate the job of chairperson and recorder, use an agenda to which anyone may add items during the week, and seek consensus or temporary interim decisions. Include compliments and appreciations at the start of each meeting to stress the idea that working together means identifying the positive aspects of family life and not simply focusing on problems.[1]

Family meetings are a great way to communicate with teens because there is a cooling-off period before you discuss most issues. Many people say that teens don't like family meetings, but our experience is that teens don't like being lectured to, criticized, or bossed. If that is what happens at your family meetings, your teens won't want to attend. Remember, teens often come with an "attitude," so don't be put off by their style if they appear to be less than enthusiastic. We have both experienced what appear to be uninterested teens at meetings who are later heard on the phone telling one of their friends that they should have family meetings. As you focus on looking for solutions instead of placing blame, you are more likely to succeed in communicating at a family meeting.

Use Family Meetings to Open Communication

AT FAMILY MEETINGS, some issues may not get solved; they may simply be aired. That's okay. Your teens may often disagree with you in a conversation and then turn around and do exactly the thing they said they wouldn't do that you wanted. Because teens, and even spouses, often have completely different realities, it is important to have a time when everyone in the family can speak and be listened to with respect. Remember that listening doesn't mean agreeing; it simply means learning more about each family member's thoughts.

In the O'Brien family, Dad felt that everyone should sit down together for their meals. He came from a family where everyone ate three meals together.

---

1. For in-depth material about family meetings and how you can use them to transform the atmosphere in your home, see *Chores Without Wars* by Lynn Lott and Riki Intner or *Positive Discipline A–Z* by Jane Nelsen, Lynn Lott, and H. Stephen Glenn.

He felt that this was how it should be—that this was how a family shows love—and that he felt loved when people sat down and ate with him.

In Mom's family growing up, her father was working in other towns most of the time. Her own mother gave up trying to deal with fussy appetites and allowed the kids to fix their own food, except on Sundays when they would have a roast or chicken dinner. Therefore, Mom felt that mealtimes didn't matter, except for special occasions. To her, mealtimes meant the freedom to eat what you wanted, when you wanted, and how you wanted. Her definition of a family was one in which everyone had the freedom to come and go as they pleased. However, she also had a vague feeling that this was not how it "should" be done. Because her experiences didn't fit her image of the ideal family, she was subconsciously confused about liking it the way it was while feeling it should be different.

> Because teens, and even spouses, often have completely different realities, it is important to have a time when everyone in the family can speak and be listened to with respect.

The two teenagers in this family, David and Cindy, were more interested in doing their own thing than sitting together for family meals. Dad, feeling like the odd man out, decided he wanted to discuss his concern about mealtimes at a family meeting. The O'Briens, new to holding family meetings, asked their counselor to act as a moderator.

DAD: I feel really disappointed that I can't get more cooperation for something as simple as getting the family to have at least two meals together a week. (Dad's tone of voice expressed judgments rather than feelings.)

DAVID (defensively): Ah, you get more than two meals a week.

CINDY: Yeah, Dad.

DAVID: Okay, you've got it two days a week!

COUNSELOR: How about listening without interrupting and trying to find out how and why people feel the way they feel? David, see if you can find out why this is important to your dad.

DAVID: I don't care why.

COUNSELOR: You don't have to care. This is just an assignment.

DAVID: I *know* why.

COUNSELOR: Let's see if you can give three reasons why.

DAVID: He wants to spend more time with his family.

DAD: Yes.

DAVID: Because he loves us.

DAD: Yes.

DAVID: Because he wants us to have a good meal.

DAD: Yes.

DAVID: Because he wants to talk to us.

CINDY: Because he wants us to learn manners!

DAD: No. I want you to sit with me because I want to know you love me.

CINDY: Oh, you know we love you.

DAD: How would I know that?

COUNSELOR: Find out why that makes your dad feel loved.

DAD: Because when I grew up my family did that three times a day. That's why I got the perception that people who love each other do that.

COUNSELOR: Did you picture that's how it would be with your wife and children?

DAD: Not consciously, but yes.

COUNSELOR: So that gives you a feeling of love?

DAD: Yes.

COUNSELOR: David, what does mealtime mean to you?

DAVID: A time to get fed.

CINDY: I just hate it that when we're done eating, we have to just sit there!

MOM: It doesn't matter to me. My mother gave up on mealtimes. We all fixed what we wanted, except on Sundays.

COUNSELOR: Is there any way to work this out so everyone can get his or her needs met?

DAVID: I have a comment. I think we do eat together a lot.

MOM: So, your perception is that you eat with us more than we think you do?

DAVID: Yes.

COUNSELOR: What would be a normal mealtime in your house?

DAD: Just me.

DAVID: He's exaggerating.

CINDY: I get so hungry because I don't eat breakfast or lunch, so I come home and eat something, and he has a cow!

COUNSELOR: If you want your family to eat with you, one of the things you would have to give up is harping about what they eat. Have you guys ever had the system of taking turns picking out what you'll eat? When my kids were growing up, our family had a rule that you eat what you eat and you leave what you don't want to eat. Anyone could leave when they were ready to, but we at least started together.

MOM: I think that's one of the reasons we don't want to eat with Jim (Dad). He has so many rules about how it should be—what we should eat, how long we should sit there, and on and on.

DAD: I can see that I've done that. It just didn't occur to me that other people felt so differently about mealtime than I did. I'm willing to stop harping about what you eat, and I won't make you stay at the table when you are through. Under those circumstances, how many times would you be willing to sit down and eat with me?

DAVID: I wouldn't mind starting dinner most of the time together, at least four times a week, if you wouldn't put us down so much.

CINDY: That sounds good to me.

MOM: I'm certainly willing to be more considerate about what's important to you. I just didn't know it was that important. I'd also appreciate it if you wouldn't be so critical when we don't sit down together—because other things are more important on some days.

DAD: That sounds reasonable to me. So when will we have our next meal together?

MOM: How about tomorrow night?

DAVID: I'll be there.

CINDY: Me, too.

This family might have continued bickering for years if they hadn't learned to listen to each other's feelings and separate realities. With the counselor's help, they continued to have family meetings in which they heard each other's feelings and perceptions and then worked on solutions that were respectful to everyone. You can create this kind of openness and respect at your house by focusing on listening and curiosity.

Your family will run more smoothly when you hold weekly family meetings. During these meetings, in addition to sharing mutual appreciations and discussing issues of concern to individuals or the whole family, you can plan menus, calendars, shopping trips, outings, and other joint activities. If you are like most families, you will need to discuss guidelines for the use of televisions, computers, and phones. Family meetings are an excellent time to give out allowances, especially if that is something that easily is forgotten at your house.

GUIDELINES FOR EFFECTIVE FAMILY MEETINGS

1. Start with compliments and/or appreciations.

2. Prioritize items on the agenda. Ask if there are any items that can be eliminated because they have already been handled. Ask if any need top priority.

3. Set a time line for the meeting. Use a timer and a designated timekeeper. (Teens are more comfortable when they know when the meeting will end.)

4. Discuss each item and let everyone voice his or her opinion without comments or criticism from others.

5. If the problem calls for more than a discussion, which is more often than not, brainstorm for solutions.

6. Choose one solution that everyone can live with (consensus) and try it for a week.

7. Table difficult issues to discuss at the next regularly scheduled family meeting.

The more you adhere to these guidelines, the better your meetings will go. This doesn't mean that every meeting will be a huge success, but over time, you'll have increased cooperation and respect in your family. If you are having problems, remember that it takes time for everyone to practice and learn the skills necessary for effective family meetings. Have patience and keep practicing. When families aren't used to working this way, it takes time and patience to be efficient and effective—but it's worth the effort. You might also see if any of the following hints would improve your family meetings.

Hints for Improving Family Meetings

1. Hold family meetings at the same time each week, not only when there's a crisis.

2. Although family meetings with older kids can be quite rewarding, they can also be difficult to arrange because of busy schedules. One family solved the problem by setting the next meeting date at the end of each meeting.

3. Working together takes time and practice, but the goal is progress not perfection. All family members must have the opportunity to be present. Some family members may refuse to come, and younger children may get restless and leave in the middle.

4. Be sure that kids feel they're taken seriously and treated as important, contributing members of their family.

5. When someone shares at a family meeting, everyone else should listen respectfully, without arguing or correcting.

6. Have family members take turns running the meeting or making notes of the decisions.

7. When working on solutions for agenda items, consensus is a key ingredient for success. If not everyone agrees on a decision, dissenters will probably undermine any progress that could be made.

8. Talking about controversial subjects without trying to decide on a solution is often helpful. For extremely controversial issues, it may take several meetings to reach any kind of consensus.

9. It's okay if your family can't reach agreement. Live with the results of indecision, which usually means keeping things the way they've been or doing as the parents say until the issue can be worked out at a future meeting.

10. Lecturing or giving orders defeats the purpose of family meetings.

11. Focus on items that are less controversial, such as time for fun, allowances, and so on, until kids believe their input is wanted and respected.

When we counsel families, it's often obvious to us that they could solve many of their problems themselves through family meetings. But families usually don't spend time together. Instead, parents leave lists of orders for the kids—which the kids resist doing. And the kids can never find a good time to ask their parents for help, so they become demanding instead. The more responsible family members do more than their share of work, and then, feeling resentful, they nag and punish other family members for being lazy.

Although it may seem more efficient to issue orders and plan for your teens without their input, it's less effective than the long-term parenting that teaches your children life skills. Bryce and Barbara's story, below, provides an excellent example.

> Although it may seem more efficient to issue orders and plan for your teens without their input, it's less effective than the long-term parenting that teaches your children life skills.

Transcript of a Family Meeting

Bryce and Barbara had been married for five years. Like many stepfamilies, their lives were extremely busy because both parents worked, so they handled everything on the fly. On top of that, Bryce's daughter from his first marriage lived with them on weekends, holidays, and summers. Therefore, whatever schedule they established changed at least once a week. Their family counselor suggested holding family meetings as a way to reduce confusion and chaos. They began learning the skills for family meetings at their counselor's office and were making excellent progress. Following is a transcript from one of their meetings. Everyone was present: Barbara's two kids from her first marriage, seventeen-year-old Todd and fourteen-year-old Laurie, and Bryce's daughter, fourteen-year-old Ann.

BRYCE: I'd like to start our meeting with appreciations. I'd like to let Todd know I appreciate that he cleaned the garage yesterday. Ann, I want you to know I appreciate you leaving your boyfriend behind so you could spend the summer with us.

ANN: I'd like to thank Todd for offering to drive me to the mall today. I appreciate Mom for taking me miniature golfing.

TODD: I'd like to thank Mom for letting me sleep in the last few days.

BARBARA: I'd like to thank Dad for cooking dinner last night.

LAURIE: I'd like to pass.

(Imagine, just for a minute, how people in your family would feel giving and receiving appreciations. It is so seldom that people take the time to say something nice to one another. We are sure you and your family would enjoy meetings if only for the positive reinforcements.)

TODD: Since I volunteered to be in charge of the meeting today, I'd like to make up the agenda. Who has something they'd like to put on the list?

BARBARA: I'd like to work out the transportation for Ann and Laurie's tennis lessons. I'd also like help with the shopping and cooking. And I've been emptying the dishwasher twice a day, and I don't want to do that anymore.

BRYCE: I'd like to find a time this week that we could all go out to dinner together.

LAURIE: I don't want to share my room with Ann. I don't think it's fair.

ANN: Maybe I should have stayed home this summer.

TODD: Ann, is that something you want on the agenda?

ANN: No, but I don't think Laurie likes having me here.

TODD: We can talk about that when it comes up. Right now, I'm just trying to make the agenda.

ANN: I'd like to talk about a baby-sitting job Mrs. Hansen wants me to do this summer.

TODD: I want to talk about our trip to Los Angeles.

COUNSELOR: Todd, you've done a great job setting up the agenda. Since your time is limited, perhaps you can start at the top and take the list of unfinished items home for your next family meeting. It's okay not to finish everything today. Your family has a lot to talk about.

TODD: I'd like to start with Laurie's complaint, since that seems like the most important.

COUNSELOR: Why don't you check with the rest of the family to see if they agree?

(The family agreed and the meeting continued.)

LAURIE: I don't think it's fair just because I'm the only girl in the family that I have to share my room when Ann comes. I like Ann, but nobody even asks me if it's okay. Ann gets up earlier than I do, and she makes so much noise that I can't sleep. And I don't like listening to Ann's music all the time.

TODD: Does anyone else want to say anything about this?

BARBARA: I'm sorry, Laurie. I had no idea you felt this way. You're right, we just assume Ann will stay with you, and we never ask. I can't imagine where Ann would stay if she weren't welcome in your room.

BRYCE: Laurie, if you had more choice and could work out the wake up and the music with Ann, would it be okay for her to say with you?

ANN: I could use my earphones when I listen to my music. I try to be quiet in the morning. Maybe I could leave my clothes in the bathroom and get ready in there.

LAURIE: Now I feel like a real brat. (She starts to cry.)

BARBARA: Laurie, I'm glad we have a place where we can say how we really feel about things, and I'm glad you had the courage to tell us how upset you were. We weren't being considerate of you, and we didn't realize it. Now we do. I know we can work this out.

BRYCE: I've been thinking of moving my home office to the main office downtown. If I did that, it would give us another room. In the meantime, Ann could use the foldaway bed.

LAURIE: I *want* Ann to stay with me! I just wanted to be asked. And Ann, you can get ready in our room in the morning; you're not really that noisy. But I would like it if you'd use your earphones when you listen to the stereo.

ANN: Thanks, Laurie. I'd much rather share a room with you than be alone in Dad's office.

COUNSELOR: When do you think you will have a family meeting at home so you can finish the rest of your list? I'd also like to recommend that you keep a notepad handy somewhere at home so you can write things to discuss at family meetings as they come up. Your family shows us how much nicer it is to work together than to have to figure everything out alone. Thank you.

The rest of the session was spent trying to find a time everyone could be together for the next meeting—not an easy task in most busy families!

Use Family Meetings to Establish Cooperation

RELATIVELY SPEAKING, TEENAGERS will be more motivated to partici-pate in household chores if they have been involved in working on a plan. We say "relatively speaking" because, again, chores are the parents' priority, not the kids'. As a parent, your task is not to make your teens like doing chores, but to gain as much cooperation as possible, which benefits you and your kids in the long run.

Chore Cooperation Through Family Meetings

One way to improve the chore situation at your house is to use the following strategy. During a family meeting, the family makes a list of household chores that need to be done. Next to each item, the recorder notes the family consensus on how often that particular chore needs to be done and what the deadline should be for getting it done. Finally, family members pick which chores they would be willing to do that week. Some of the more unpopular chores, such as cleaning toilets, may have to be placed in a hat for some lucky person to draw. It's good to have one person monitor the chore list each day to see whether chores have been completed by the deadline. If a chore doesn't get done, the monitor finds the responsible person, lets him or her know about the missed deadline, and reinforces that it's time to do the chore. In many families, the youngest child likes this job and does it very well. Parents should avoid monitoring if they've been nagging the kids to get things done.

When families use this kind of chore routine, they find that deadlines work best if they are set for times when people are most likely to be around the house, such as first thing in the morning, after school or work, before dinner, or before bedtime. Follow-through (as discussed in chapter 6) is effective for holding people accountable for their agreements.

Some families find that cooperation about chores increases when everyone works together. Perhaps it's that old "Misery loves company," but setting aside an hour a week for housework when everyone is present to work together usually succeeds better than hoping things will get done at different times during the week. Of course, there are also the daily chores that can't wait, but even those go better when families have a chore time when everyone is doing something to help the family.

Some families are deeply involved in power struggles around chores. When this is the case, it may take smaller steps at a family meeting to progress toward cooperation, such as asking each

> Some families find that cooperation about chores increases when everyone works together. Perhaps it's that old "Misery loves company," but setting aside an hour a week for housework when everyone is present to work together usually succeeds better than hoping things will get done at different times during the week.

family member what *one* chore he or she would be willing to do daily until the next family meeting. The idea is to try something for a week and at the next meeting discuss and evaluate what everyone learned. We know this is a slow process, but building family involvement when discord has been the norm often starts slowly and then snowballs into something wonderful.

Dealing with the Boob Tube and Other Distractions

MANY FAMILIES SPEND more time watching television or sitting in front of a computer screen alone than they do with each other. These activities can become very addictive, and they can provide safety from dealing with family issues—like talking with each other. A surefire way to prove just how addicted your family is to TV is to announce that there will be no TV for a week. Look for the panicked look on family members' faces as they consider the thought of filling time without numbing out in front of a TV or computer screen.

Family meetings provide excellent time for tackling the problem of too much television. A good way to start is to use the following steps for putting the problem on the family meeting agenda:

1. During the family meeting, invite a discussion about how you each view the purpose of televisions.
2. Ask family members to discuss their fears about turning off the television. (Family members may deny that they have any fears about this,

so ask them to brainstorm what they would do if the power went out for a week.)

3. Share your concern that the TV (or computer) is becoming more important than family time and other worthwhile endeavors.

4. Brainstorm ideas about a reasonable amount of TV time. (This may take several sessions.) If you can't handle having no televisions, we strongly recommend having only one TV in the house rather than one in every room.

5. Once an amount of time has been agreed upon, teach your children to schedule their TV watching thoughtfully. Have a *TV Guide* at the family meeting every week, and let family members choose the programs that are important to them. This should come out to about one hour per evening per person. For example, in one household, Dad chose to watch the news from 6:00 P.M. to 7:00 P.M. There was one half-hour program that both kids wanted to watch together, and they each had one they wanted to watch separately. They each decided to do homework while the other was watching the program that didn't interest them. Mom and Dad agreed to watch the program that the two kids were both interested in (partly for some passive family time, and partly so they would be in tune with their kids' interests). Even though Mom and Dad were reading or doing other tasks during the alternate programs, they could still be aware of what was going on. They could later use some of the TV material for discussion or curiosity questions about what their teens thought about what they were watching.

6. Schedule some special family time (even if it is only five or ten minutes) for sharing special interests or events of the day. You might be surprised at how much your kids will share if you joke with them about "enduring this" for just ten minutes.

We live in a very "speeded up" society. It is easy to get sidetracked from what is most important to you—your family. Making the effort and taking the time to hold regular family meetings can help maintain a balance of priorities and all the other little things that need to be done. In fact, family meetings can get the whole family involved in helping with all those other things.

> We live in a very "speeded up" society. It is easy to get sidetracked from what is most important to you—your family.

A Word of Encouragement: Don't Expect Perfection

ONE FINAL TIP regarding family meetings: Don't expect perfection. It takes time for family members to believe that their thoughts and ideas are important to others. It takes time for family members to learn the skills for successful family meetings. Adopt the perception that mistakes are wonderful opportunities to learn and keep learning. Many families find that it is more fun to read their old family meeting journals (lists of compliments, problems, and solutions) than it is to look at family photo albums.

KIND AND FIRM PARENTING TOOLS TO REMEMBER

1. Instead of dealing with issues in the heat of the moment, use family meetings to work out issues after cooling off. Putting an item on the agenda allows for cooling off time before the family meeting occurs.

2. Family meetings are worth the effort because of the high degree of belonging and significance your teens will feel as a result of participating.

3. Family meetings are good places for discussion without worrying about coming up with a solution.

4. Family meetings work best when held regularly and not in the middle of a crisis or at the whim of a parent.

5. Unless you can reach a consensus about an issue, don't initiate any new family procedures. Stick with what you currently are doing or, as a parent, decide how it will be temporarily. Then, keep the discussion open until all family members come up with something they can all live with.

6. Use family meetings to discuss any and all topics, whether mundane or extraordinary.

Practical Application Activity

At first, family members may feel uncomfortable with complimenting or think it is silly. If you have faith in the process and give your family members opportunities to practice at the start of each week's family meeting, skills will grow, and so will the good feelings in your family. To get your family started, use this activity at a family meeting.

1. Ask family members to think of a time when someone said something that made them feel good about themselves. Take turns sharing the examples.

2. Ask family members to think of something for which they would like to receive a compliment. Remind everyone that sometimes it helps to ask for what you want so that you get noticed for what is really important to you.

3. Ask family members to say what they would like to be complimented on and then invite the others to give the compliment. For example, your teen might want a compliment on how he or she remembered to return the car with gas in the tank (even though it might be only a dollar's worth). Dad says, "Thank you for being thoughtful about returning the car with gas in the tank. It's nice to be able to get to work in the morning without having to stop at the gas station." Notice that Dad doesn't say anything about how little fuel there is in the tank.

4. Remind family members that when receiving a compliment, it is helpful to say, "Thanks," so the person giving the compliment knows it was received.

5. At another family meeting, you could suggest that family members take turns giving appreciations by starting with, "Thank you for . . ." or "I appreciate . . ." or "You make my life richer or easier because . . ."

MY PLAN FOR THE WEEK

This week I will focus on

_____

_____

I will work on changing my attitude by thinking

_____

_____

_____

I will change my behavior by doing

_____

_____

_____

9

How Do You Spend Time That Counts?

Dᴜʀɪɴɢ ᴛʜᴇ ᴛᴇᴇɴ years, when your children spend less and less time with you, it's more important than ever to connect in ways that really count. Unfortunately, there are several conditions that make quality time especially difficult to achieve: busy schedules, teenagers' preference to be with their friends, and time spent lecturing, judging, and punishing.

Brian decided to try spending quality time with his son, Ted. Brian's attempts to control Ted's use of drug and alcohol had damaged their relationships. He had grounded Ted, taken his car away, and lectured ad infinitum ("How could you do such a thing? You'll ruin your life forever. What have we done wrong?"), but all to no avail. Ted got more defiant and more rebellious, and the father-son relationship deteriorated badly. Brian was thoroughly discouraged, but decided to take a class called "Empowering Teens and Yourself in the Process" before giving up completely. The very first night of the class he heard something that would later change his life, as well as his son's. The facilitator said, "Sometimes you get the best results by forgetting about behavior and focusing on the relationship." Brian thought that sounded pretty simplistic, but he also realized that trying to improve his relationship with his son certainly couldn't do any harm—even if it didn't do any good.

The next day, Brian showed up at Ted's school during his lunch period and got permission to take his son to lunch. Brian had decided that his whole purpose would be to enjoy Ted's company—no matter what. When Ted saw his dad, he asked belligerently, "What are you doing here?" Brian replied, "I just wanted to have lunch with you." During lunch, Brian focused on his purpose, avoiding third-degree questions. He didn't even ask Ted how his day was. Ted was completely surprised and very suspicious all during lunch, waiting to be criticized or lectured. The entire lunch was spent in silence. Afterward, Brian took Ted back to school and said, "Thanks for having lunch with me. I really enjoyed being with you."

Brian continued showing up at Ted's school for lunch every Wednesday. It took three weeks for Ted's suspicions to disappear. He then started telling his father small things about his day, and his father did the same. Ted even began asking questions about work and college. Brian was careful to answer Ted's questions without lecturing.

Meanwhile, Brian had stopped trying to control Ted through punishment and withdrawal of privileges. Instead, he focused on Ted's assets, even though he had to dig to get past his fears about Ted's rebellion. He told Ted how glad he was to have him as his son and described to Ted how thrilled he had been the day he was born. Brian found it easy to tell stories about the cute things Ted had done as a child. Ted would shrug and give the impression that he thought these stories were "stupid." However, during this time, Brian noticed that Ted showed up for dinner more often and sometimes brought his friends over to watch television.

One day, three months into the lunch routine, Brian got stuck in a meeting that lasted through the lunch period. That night, Ted said, "What happened to you today, Dad?"

Brian apologized, "I'm sorry. I didn't know you were expecting me. We never said it would be a regular thing. But I'd love to make it a regular routine; how about you?"

Nonchalantly, Ted said, "Sure."

Brian said, "I'll be sure to leave a message if I ever get tied up again."

Brian felt pleased and gratified about the effectiveness of spending quality time with his son. He didn't know if Ted stopped experimenting with drugs and alcohol, but he knew his control efforts hadn't had a positive effect. Now, at least, the damaged relationship was being repaired, and Brian was grateful that the importance of this had gotten through his own thick skull. He felt satisfied that he was providing good memories for his son and letting him know from experience that his father loved him unconditionally. Ted's behavior improved considerably. He stopped being disrespectful. In fact, he started being considerate about letting his parents know when he would be home. Brian felt he was creating an atmosphere in which his son could think more about how his behavior affected his life rather than spending so much energy on "getting even" with his dad for the lectures and criticism.

What About All the Lessons I Have to Teach My Teenager?

SPENDING QUALITY TIME with your teenager may sound like wonderful advice under normal circumstances, but what if your teenager is involved in drugs, has stolen your car, has lied to you, or has burned your house down? Think of all the things that you're tempted to do, such as ground your teen forever or perhaps imprisoning him or her. Will your methods solve anything? Or will they only increase your stress while widening the gap between you and your teenager? Remember all the mistakes you made as a teenager. If you didn't make any, think of the price you paid by becoming an approval junkie. When you were a teen, how would you have responded to the methods you now use with your teen? How would you have responded if your parents had shown an interest in just being with you?

You might be surprised at how many conflicts are resolved when you focus on spending quality time instead of spending time on the problem. (See chapter 14 for more information about what to do about behavior that scares you.)

Hang Out and Just Be Available

WE WERE IMPRESSED with Brian's commitment to spending time that counts with his son. He demonstrated true dedication by being willing to take time off from work to make his son a priority.

We've found it can be equally effective just to "hang out," to be available at certain times when you know your kids will be around. The pitfall is expecting

Hanging out means being available to listen if your teens want to talk—and if they don't. It means being a "closet" listener (not making it obvious that you're listening). It means listening to who they are rather than focusing on their words.

that your teens will overtly notice or care or that they will talk to you. Although it may seem that they don't notice or care, if you're really available, your teen will feel it. The energy you create when you're truly available is different from that when you're "there" but preoccupied with other concerns or too busy to be bothered.

Teenagers can tell when you expect something from them—and with teens, expectations can create resistance. We've heard many parents complain, "Well, I'm available, but my teenager still won't talk to me." Hanging out means being available to listen if your teens want to talk—and if they don't. It means being a "closet" listener (not making it obvious that you're listening). It means listening to who they are rather than focusing on their words. Five helpful tips will increase your chances of making the time you spend hanging out with your teenager count as quality time.

TIPS FOR SPENDING TIME THAT COUNTS

For at least five minutes a day, spend time with your teenager while keeping:

1. your mouth shut (listening)

2. your sense of humor intact (perspective)

3. your ears open (curiosity)

4. your heart emanating warmth and gratitude (love)

5. a desire to understand your teen's world (focusing)

Keep Your Mouth Shut

For just five minutes a day, take Archie Bunker's advice and "stifle yourself." There are very good reasons for keeping your mouth shut. When your mouth is open, what are you usually saying? Can you resist the temptation to lecture, moralize, show disappointment, play psychologist, or try to teach lessons?

Imagine the effect on your teenager of receiving five minutes a day with you without hearing your lectures, your judgments, or your disappointments. We know you think it's your job to make sure your teenagers avoid all mistakes that could ruin their lives. We know you're especially concerned about big mistakes, such as lying, stealing, cheating, sex, and drugs. We know you think it's your job to help them overcome little mistakes, such as irresponsibility, inconsiderateness, self-centeredness, and lack of motivation. But remember that indirect methods sometimes have a greater affect than direct, and often misguided, methods.

> Imagine the effect on your teenager of receiving five minutes a day with you without hearing your lectures, your judgments, or your disappointments.

In *Raising Self-Reliant Children in a Self-Indulgent World* (1988), H. Stephen Glenn and Jane Nelsen list five barriers to good relationships: assuming, rescuing or explaining, directing, expecting, and adultisms (e.g., "How come you never . . . ? Why can't you ever . . . ? How many times do I have to tell you? When will you ever learn?"). Glenn and Nelsen claim that a relationship can improve 100 percent simply by eliminating these barriers. Where else can you get a 100 percent return by purposely doing nothing?

A thirteen-year-old teen, whose mother rarely indulges in the five barriers to good relationships and mostly uses the principles of kind and firm parenting, wrote the following for his school project on the reasons why he likes his mom so much. We hope it can be an inspiration for you.

My mom is the best because she is cool, nice, friendly, loving, supportive, in touch with what's happening in my life, takes me places, buys me things that I need in life, tries to help me out even if I don't need the help, always makes sure that I am safe, if I'm on a trip she will call me every day, she is giving, she keeps me in touch with all of my relatives, she can always crack a lame joke, she will never admit to her coffee addiction, she has many shoes but won't admit to it, and she is very healthy. These are some reasons of why I like my mom. She is the best person in the world.

Keep Your Sense of Humor Intact

How does behavior affect you when you don't have a sense of humor? You lose perspective and objectivity. In this state of mind, it's easy to believe your teenager is a finished product. You imagine the worst things that could happen. But a sense of humor can help you realize that all your fears and insecurities are yours.

One way to put the teen years into perspective is to get together with a bunch of adults and tell each other stories about what you did as teenagers that you hoped your parents would never find out about. If you "lighten up," we predict your teenagers will be more willing to hang out with you a little more often.

Sometimes it is difficult to keep your sense of humor, even if you want to. You may have experienced moments similar to the following, when you really wanted to wring your kids' necks while you were *having fun together*.

Mark, age fourteen, is a first-born child who, by age eight, could not stand to lose at games. His father, Alan, contributed to Mark's bad attitude by always letting him win at chess because he hated it when Mark got upset and cried. Alan knew it was important to spend special time with Mark, but the time they spent together was not fun. One day Alan decided to change his attitude. He played his very best against Mark. Naturally he won, and naturally, Mark pitched a royal fit.

As Mark pouted and cried, Alan said, "Okay, kiddo, you're in big trouble now. I forgot to tell you that this game was for the Grand Championship of the Universe, and you now owe me one million dollars because you lost."

Mark looked at his father, trying to continue his pouting, but Alan's joke was so dumb that Mark couldn't resist sending a barb his way. "Dad," Mark said, "I hope you don't think that was funny, because it wasn't."

Alan grabbed his son in a big bear hug, playfully threw him to the ground, and said, "Take it back, take it back, or I'll have to do my Jesse Ventura imitation."

Mark started to laugh and said, "Dad, you are *too* weird."

Even though Mark called his dad weird, he learned a lot from Alan's sense of humor. Not only did he start losing with more grace, but also his own sense of humor improved.

A few weeks later they were playing catch in the backyard. Alan threw a bad ball that Mark couldn't catch. After running after the ball, Mark said, "Nice throw, Dad. Lousy catch, Mark."

Randy provides another example. He wanted to try snowboarding. But when he and his mom, Karyn, got to the ski area, all he could do was make negative comments about how stupid everything was, how far it was from the parking lot to the ski hill, how lessons were for idiots, how he had *never* said that *he* wanted to go snowboarding, and how his mom was *always making him* do things he hated. Karyn was ready to get in the car and drive the three hours back home, when she suddenly remembered her first ski experience and how fearful she was of failing. Not only did this help her get her perspective back, but it also made her chuckle and remember her sense of humor.

"Randy," she said, "let's make a deal. I'm going to take a few runs and get the kinks out of my legs. Why don't you hang out in the cafeteria and have a hot chocolate? I'll come check with you in an hour or so and see if you'd like to give snowboarding a try."

"Don't bother," Randy said, "this is a *stupid* place, a *stupid* sport, and I'm *not* going."

"Good idea," Karyn said, "because knowing you, you'd probably *never* be able to stand up and would spend the *entire* day on your butt and have a *totally* miserable time. See you later. Love you, honey." And off she went.

Of course, when she came back an hour later, Randy had been watching out the window, wandering around looking at everyone else who was falling all over the place, and realizing that he could do at least as well as the people he saw from the lodge window. With as much negativity as he could muster, he said, "Well, if I *have* to, I guess I'll take a lesson."

"That's the spirit," Karyn said. "Of course you *have* to, because *I* said, and I know you *always* do everything I say. Come on, let's get you signed up for the class." Without another word, she put her arm around Randy, and they marched off together.

Karyn saved the day because she was listening to Randy's "coded" message instead of his words.

Keep Your Ears Open

When your ears are not open, you miss knowing who your teenagers really are. You have to be a good listener to get into their world and learn about their reality. When you really listen, you hear what is going on underneath their words—you may even decipher the code.

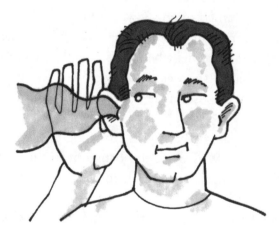

Your ears and mouth cannot be open simultaneously. With your mouth shut, you'll be surprised at how much you can hear, although sometimes what you get is nonverbal, at the feeling level. Young people who are used to lectures, judgments, expectations, and disapproval have done a lot of closing down. They've created defensive or offensive strategies for self-protection and self-preservation and may not open up right away.

Keep your ears open without expectations of what or how you will hear. One mother said, "I kept my mouth shut and my ears open for a month, and my teenager still wouldn't talk to me." This mother's son could probably sense that her silence was full of expectations. Instead of trying so hard, simply hang out until your teens get the idea that it might be safe to share something—even nonverbally. When you're willing to hang out, you may find your teenagers more willing to hang out around you. Don't underestimate the value of sim-

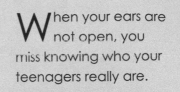

When your ears are not open, you miss knowing who your teenagers really are.

ply being around so they can absorb good feelings even when words are not used. Since some teenagers never open up and tell all, drop all agendas and just be with them—with your mouth shut and your ears open.

Keep Your Heart Emanating Warmth and Gratitude

What do you emanate when you don't emanate warmth and gratitude? Self-righteousness and conditional love are two possibilities. But with your mouth shut, your sense of humor intact, and your ears open, your heart will naturally emanate loving warmth and gratitude. In this state of mind, compassion, wisdom, and gratitude are all you have left! When you see your teenagers from this state of mind, they will look different to you. You'll also find this state of mind very inviting and nurturing. It creates energy that can be felt by anyone

around you. You'll see possibilities and solutions with your teens rather than mistakes and problems. There is a catch, however: You won't see anything until you expect nothing. Possibilities may not appear until you have gratitude for what you already have.

Grandpa Louie, who was very good at expressing encouragement and at seeing past the surface behavior to the good in others, was visiting his daughter and her stepson, Rico. Rico stayed out late, left his room in chaos, ran out of gas, got bad grades, and was usually in trouble for one thing or another. Every time Grandpa saw Rico, he said, "Rico, you're all right!" Rico looked at him quizzically, waiting for the catch, as the corners of his mouth turned up. Grandpa Louie must have told Rico he was "all right" at least a hundred times, until Rico looked at him and said, "Grandpa, I know what you're going to say . . . I'm all right. Right?" Grandpa just looked up and grinned. This special time that Grandpa spent with Rico was unscheduled and took only seconds at a time. However, the boost to Rico's self-confidence was immeasurable in an environment where he was hearing so many negative comments.

> You won't see anything until you expect nothing. Possibilities may not appear until you have gratitude for what you already have.

Hugs are another way to take only seconds for time that counts. With teens, be sure you don't hug them in front of anyone else. You may even have to use your sense of humor and say, "I know you can't stand hugs from me right now, but I might die without one. Could you please spare your dignity for three seconds to save my life?"

Here's a cheery thought that came to us by email. It's called The Universal Hug. You might want to try it out today.

No moving parts, no batteries
No monthly payments and no fees
Inflation proof
It can't be stolen, won't pollute
One size fits all
Do not dilute

It uses little energy, but yields results enormously
Relieves your tension and your stress
Invigorates your happiness
Combats depression
Makes you beam, and elevates your self-esteem
Your circulation it corrects without unpleasant side effects
It is, I think, the perfect drug
May I prescribe, my friend . . .
The hug (and of course, fully returnable!)

Keep a Desire to Understand Your Teen's World

What is the opposite of trying to understand your teen's world? Trying to mold him or her into living up to expectations; trying to make a petunia into a rose.

A desire to understand the world of your teenager comes naturally from a loving state of mind. Right and wrong become moot issues. Understanding and respecting separate realities becomes fascinating. Notice how the parent in the following story really understood and tuned into the world of her twelve year old, as related by him in a school assignment called, "My Most Treasured Memory."

> What is the opposite of trying to understand your teen's world? Trying to mold him or her into living up to expectations; trying to make a petunia into a rose.

My most treasured memory happened to me this spring when we went to visit my grandma and my half grandpa. It was during Easter and my family and I had just arrived in Arizona. We had left home while it was snowing, so it was like having an extra summer. There were two pools in the neighborhood. There was also a golf course down the block. My mom decided we were going to the Olympic-sized pool. That's when she told me that I could drive the golf cart. I asked, "All by myself?" and she replied, "Yes, with me in the passenger seat." I was so thrilled. It was one of the happiest moments in my life.

Time That Counts

HAVE YOU INSISTED that your teen spend more time at home and then complained because he or she would rather be with friends? When you understand your teen, you will know that this is normal behavior, both for you and your teen. Ask yourself, "What is there at home for my teen to enjoy?" Even though most teens prefer their friends, you can find ways to increase the chances that they will enjoy spending some time with you.

Participants at an *Empowering Teens and Yourself in the Process* workshop brainstormed the following list of ideas for spending time that counts with teenagers. They based this list on an understanding of teens.

We suggest referring to this list often. It may inspire you to spend time that counts with your teenagers in ways you haven't thought of or that get lost in the shuffle of busy lives. End every family meeting by planning at least one family activity from this list or from a list that comes out of your own family brainstorming (see chapter 8).

IDEAS FOR SPENDING TIME THAT COUNTS

Listen without judging

Validate their feelings

Stop nagging

Take extended trips

Go on day trips

Take walks together

Do activities planned by them

Tell stories about your own childhood

Watch their television programs

Look at photo albums of when they were little

Hang out with them

Work less, play more, be available

Go to concerts or ball games

Go to a flea market

Work on creative projects (arts and crafts)

Ask for their opinions

Cook together

Make home a comfortable place for their friends

Keep a sense of humor

Remember that differences are okay

Avoid overreaction

Work on mutual respect

Invite them to see you at your job

Do activities of their choice with them

Support their activities and interests

Share about yourself if they're interested

Include them in your discussions

Work on joint problem solving

Schedule regular family meetings

Ask for their help

Give choices

Practice role reversal and role-playing

Allow them to make their own mistakes

Show interest in their world

Backpack together

Take care of yourself and your own issues

Go to a retreat together

Learn what's normal; don't take it personally

Treat them to activities they enjoy but can't afford

Take time off from work to be with teen

Eat together or go out to a restaurant

Play games together

Spend special time alone with each child

Plan an event together

Plan vacations ("What do you want to do?")

Have faith

Have trust

Laugh a lot

Short periods (even minutes) of quality time a day, a week, or even a month can do wonders to improve your relationships with your teens. Focusing on spending quality time with your teens will help you remember to get into their world, see them with perspective, and bring back the joy of being their parent.

During therapy, we often recommend that parents spend quality time with their kids, but it doesn't always happen. And when it doesn't, surprisingly, the young people often tattle that their parents haven't done their homework. One excited preteen announced in a session, "Mom finally did that thing you were saying—that 'special time.' It was *so* much fun."

Short periods (even 5 minutes) of quality time a day, a week, or even a month can do wonders to improve your relationships with your teens.

"What did you do?" her therapist asked, thinking that they went out to dinner or to the movies as they had discussed week after week.

"We lit about a hundred candles, put the stereo on really loud, and danced around in the living room. We're going to do it again sometime, aren't we, Mom? It was the best!"

What parent wouldn't want to create some quality time with their teen when they get results like that!

Time That Counts with Each Child, Individually and Together

As you can see from the candle story above, children feel special when you care enough to spend one-on-one time with them. Although you know it is important to spend time with each of them individually as well as during family time, it's not always easy to do because of sibling rivalry. Remember that children are always making decisions based on their perceptions of their experiences, and sometimes they believe that they aren't loved if they aren't part of everything. A child may feel threatened by your desire to spend one-on-one time with another child and create a scene or diversion so you will include him or give him time instead of his sibling. In addition to being difficult to deal with in the moment, these diversionary behaviors can also have negative effects that could greatly influence their futures.

Through help and understanding, you can offer encouragement that stops unhealthy patterns from developing in the first place. In the following story, the mother could have helped her daughter to refocus and to feel loved, important, and empowered. However, the mother did not know about sibling rivalry and its effects on teens.

When Arnell was twelve years old, her Uncle Jack wanted to fly Arnell's fifteen-year-old sister and mother to visit him. He did not invite Arnell because he thought she was too young. Arnell whined and cried until her mother said she could go. Even though she got to go, she still thought that her uncle liked her sister more. In her eyes, that meant that she was not worth liking. There was also a part of her that wasn't proud of her spoiled brat behavior, so she could see why he wouldn't like her.

As Arnell grew up, she tried to prove that she was a worthwhile person, but no matter how much she accomplished, she never quite felt good enough. She decided to see a therapist to work on a problem she was having with a best friend. She and her friend were in business together and were having experiences that threatened the survival of their business and their relationship. The therapist asked Arnell to share an early memory. When the memory about the trip to her uncle's came up, the therapist asked, "Do you think this memory relates to the problem you are having with your friend?"

Arnell thought a minute and then got a sheepish look on her face. "I just realized that I thought my sister and uncle were the ones with all the power, but I'm the one who was very powerful. I got my way. They didn't."

The therapist asked, "What advice would you give that twelve-year-old girl, based on your new understanding?"

Arnell said, "I would tell her that she has nothing to prove and that when she understands this, she can accept that she is a very powerful little girl. She can use her power in very constructive ways. She can be considerate of others and let her sister have some special time with her uncle. Then she could ask him to get out his calendar to find a time when she could visit."

"How could this advice help with your friend?"

"I'm also very powerful in our business. However, sometimes I'm trying so hard to prove my own worth that I get very insensitive to the needs of my friend and end up getting my way without considering hers. When she tries to call me on what is happening, I am very defensive. Instead of just listening to the reality of what is happening, I refuse to take any responsibility. I see it all as blame or an attack on my worth. I could avoid a lot of mischief if I would just accept how wonderful I am and quit trying to prove it. Then I would have plenty of energy left to be sensitive and nondefensive with my friend. We could just focus on solutions to problems."

If Arnell's mother had seen what was going on when Arnell started to whine and plead to visit Uncle Jack, she could have validated Arnell's feelings instead of giving in to them. She could have said, "I'll bet you are feeling very jealous of your sister right now. I can understand how you would feel that way.

I'll bet your uncle would be happy to have you come spend time with him. Would you like to call him and arrange for a date, or would you like me to help you?"

You may want to use the advice we would have given Arnell's mother to help you refocus your children when they inappropriately try to manipulate you into spending time with them. By reading between the lines, you can help them understand their worth, even when they don't always get what they want. However, the only way you can read between the lines is to stay connected.

Stay Connected During the Teen Years

THE FOLLOWING IS an excerpt from the July 22, 1999, *San Francisco Chronicle* article, "Angry Teens and Fed-Up Parents Grope for Way Out of Conflicts:"

> *Research consistently shows that the steady presence of even one caring adult can alter a teenager's life for the better. But a Temple University study of 20,000 high school students found that about 30 percent of parents were significantly uninvolved in their kids' lives.*

We encourage you to do your part to change those statistics and reap the benefits for both you and your teens by spending time that counts!

KIND AND FIRM PARENTING TOOLS TO REMEMBER

1. When it's the hardest to spend time with your teen, it's very important that the time you do spend is quality, lecture-free time.

2. Don't expect your teens to be open with you if you don't have a good relationship first. A good relationship takes time for getting to know who your teens are instead of telling them how you want them to be.

3. Just hanging out, which means being around, available, and without an agenda, seems the best way to start spending time with your teen.

4. Keep the Time That Counts list handy so you and your teen can find ways to enjoy being together on a regular basis.

Practical Application Activity

FUN THINGS TO DO

If you did nothing more than remember to have fun with your teenagers on a regular basis, you would be surprised how much your relationships would improve—and how much more you would enjoy life in general. Unfortunately, you can get caught up in busy schedules and in dealing with problems. The purpose of this activity is to serve as a reminder of the importance of having fun and to provide inspiration and motivation to do it.

1. Look back at the list called "Ideas for Spending Time that Counts." Check off some of the activities that appeal to you. Now give the list to your teens and ask them to check off, in a different color, activities that appeal to them. Then ask others in the family to do the same.

2. Schedule a "Fun Things to Do" meeting, and bring the list. Circle the items that more than one person has marked.

3. Brainstorm more fun things that all family members have in common. Add those items to the list.

4. Each member of the family then presents one thing that he or she would like to do for fun as a family. If the rest of the family agrees to participate, schedule the event on a calendar on a date that suits everyone. There should be a date planned for each member of the family's favorite activity. Then have fun together.

MY PLAN FOR THE WEEK

This week I will focus on

_____

_____

I will work on changing my attitude by thinking

_____

_____

_____

I will change my behavior by doing

_____

_____

_____

10

How Do You Help Your Teen Handle Life's Difficulties When You Aren't Nearby?

I N O N E O F her books, mystery writer Martha C. Lawrence shares a passage that reflects our hope for what you will choose as a long-term goal for your teens.

> *I solemnly promise that, to the best of my ability, I will help this child to grow up with love for the right and the courage to do the right; with the ideals of integrity and large-mindedness; with love for others of whatever race, nation, or creed; and with faith that the power within her is stronger than any power without her.*[1]

This chapter teaches the tools and steps for long-term parenting to help your teens know that they are loved just as they are, unconditionally. The chapter provides a foundation on which teens can build their inner resources. By using long-term parenting, you empower, rather than enable, your teens.

---

1. Found on p. 184, in *The Cold Heart of Capricorn,* by Martha C. Lawrence, St. Martin's Press, 1998.

Empowering vs. Enabling

IN THIS BOOK, the word *enable* refers to behavior that puts the parent between the child and life experiences and that minimizes the consequences of the child's choices by rescuing the teen. Enabling behavior encourages an unhealthy dependence in your teens and prevents them from learning to do things for themselves.

Typical Enabling Behaviors

Waking teens in the morning, doing their laundry, fixing their lunches, picking out their clothes

Loaning money and/or giving extra money after teens have spent their allowance or used specially earmarked funds, such as a clothing allowance, on something else

Typing papers, researching, delivering forgotten homework or lunches to school, lying to teachers when teens cut classes or skip school

Feeling sorry for teens when they have a lot of homework or activities, excusing them from helping the family with household chores

Pretending everything is fine, when it clearly isn't, to avoid confrontation

Empowerment, on the other hand, helps children grow to be responsible young adults instead of dependent, rebellious people. In this book, the word *empower* refers to turning over control to young people as soon as possible so they have power over their own lives and having faith in them to learn and recover from their mistakes.

Typical Empowering Behaviors

Listen and give emotional support and validation without fixing or discounting

Teach life skills (which can be very difficult to do if you don't have those skills yourself)

Work on agreements through family meetings or the joint problem-solving process

Let go (without abandoning)

Decide, with dignity and respect, what you will do

Share what you think, how you feel, and what you want without lecturing, moralizing, insisting on agreement, or demanding satisfaction (see chapter 7)

Use dignity and respect while sticking to issues

Sometimes parents think these suggestions feel like "doing nothing" because they don't include punishment or control. However, when parents follow these suggestions, they are doing a great deal to ensure long-term results when they follow these suggestions.

As you look at the two previous lists, you may become vividly aware of how skilled you are in enabling responses and how unskilled you are in empowering responses. Because we believe that enabling responses are second nature to most parents and because we have given many examples of these responses throughout the first nine chapters, this chapter concentrates on the empowerment skills.

Empowerment: The Foundation of Long-Term Parenting

> Empowerment is the process of developing courage, responsibility, cooperation, self-love, and social consciousness.

EMPOWERMENT IS THE process of developing courage, responsibility, cooperation, self-love, and social consciousness. By helping your teens develop and internalize these skills and attitudes, you can lead them to a healthy, happy, productive life, whether or not you are there. Empowerment invites teens to think for themselves, to think about their behavior, to make their own decisions, to live with their mistakes, and to have good memories of unconditional love.

Courage is the ability to cope when the going gets tough, which is obviously very important for teenagers' tough times. Teens experience extremes in

emotion, changes of loyalty from parents to friends, and a whole new world of temptations. Some teens go to the extreme of suicide because they lack the courage to deal with tough problems. These teens haven't learned to have faith in themselves, knowing that there is always another day and that they can make it.

How Do You Help Establish Courage in Your Teens?

Have faith in them and in yourself

Let them know that mistakes are opportunities to learn

Give them opportunities to try again, rather than punishing or rescuing them

Work on agreements, solutions, and plans to overcome problems

Show them that what happens now is only for now and that tomorrow is another day

Most people think a responsible teen is a perfect teen. This is not true. *Responsibility* is the ability to face mistakes and to use them as opportunities for growth. Responsibility is the knowledge that you are accountable for your behavior and that your actions and choices affect your life.

How Do You Help Establish Responsibility in Your Teens?

Be consciously irresponsible (don't do things for them and don't nag them)

Don't punish them for mistakes

Help them explore the consequences of their choices through friendly discussions and curiosity questions

Teach problem-solving skills for correcting mistakes

Don't pamper them to help them avoid pain

Give them supportive opportunities for accountability

Maintain your sense of humor and help your teens stop taking themselves and others so seriously

If you ask most teens what they think parents mean by *cooperation,* they will tell you, "Do what parents want." If you further explore teens' thoughts on this, they will tell you how they often agree to "cooperate" simply to avoid arguments and hassles. They say that they will then do what they want so they don't feel they have given up "who they are."

Cooperation is the ability to get along with other people, to make a contribution, to be part of the scene instead of the focus of it, and to practice give and take. Notice that the definition does not include the ability for teens to follow your orders! When teens are respectfully involved in the problem-solving process, and in choosing the solutions, they are more likely to cooperate.

How Do You Help Establish Cooperation in Your Teens?

Hold family meetings

Hold problem-solving sessions

Work out agreements together with true dialogue

Be nonjudgmental (using we, not you or I, when solving problems)

Be curious about your teen's friends instead of dictating who your teens' friends should be

Have a conversation with your teen about their choices of friends and activities instead of controlling and judging what is acceptable

Be reasonable about phone time, email, and other channels for socialization

Self-love is the ability to know your thoughts and feelings and accept them without judgment. It is also the capacity to respect and value differences in yourself and in others instead of seeing differences competitively or judgmentally. Self-love embodies the desire and skills to care for yourself, including how you treat your body. (You may hear self-love referred to as self-esteem. We prefer *self-love, self-respect,* and *self-confidence.*)

How Do You Help Your Teens Establish Self-Love?

Give them unconditional love

Respect their thoughts and feelings without having to agree with them

Take care of yourself in respectful ways and support your teens in taking care of themselves in respectful ways

Back off and don't make a power struggle out of your teens eating junk food, staying up too late, or abusing their bodies in countless other ways. The teenage years are not forever!

Love them when they dress like their peers, color their hair, or otherwise follow the latest fashions that seem obnoxious to you

Provide reality checks about the average weight of most people, how advertisers distort images, and how much influence the media has on society's image of what constitutes beauty

Remind them of who they are to you, show them their baby pictures, and tell them a million times that you think they are great—even if they say, "You're just saying that because you're my parent."

Social consciousness requires a deep respect for self and others. It is the desire to want to contribute to your world because you know you belong and you can be significant in positive ways. By doing what you enjoy in life while helping, or at least not hurting, others, you find happiness and feel good about making a contribution. You reject a victim mentality in favor of knowing that your future is shaped by what you do in the present.

How Do You Help Your Teens Establish Social Consciousness?

Discuss the news, current events, movies, television shows, and literature

Show them other places where people live differently from how you live

Encourage correspondence with people from other countries, cultures, and circumstances

Set up volunteer opportunities for both of you

Expect your teens to help out grandparents or other relatives whose needs and experiences are different from theirs

Help them explore, through curiosity questions, what they might not think about without your help, such as how other people feel when they aren't treated respectfully

Acknowledge their altruism and loyalty, even if you don't agree with the cause

It's important to note that many of these qualities can occur in negative ways as well. Gang members can have courage, be responsible, get along with others, like themselves, and contribute to a group. Our emphasis is to help your teens build character by developing qualities and characteristics in constructive, respectful ways that add something positive to the world. If what you're doing is not working to meet these long-term goals, then it's time to try something different.

Teaching these skills will be more difficult if you have always held a tight rein on your teens rather than encouraging independence. However, it's never too late to take steps in the right direction. Taking one step at a time is a great way to start on long-term parenting. Over time, your teens will notice and respond to your changes. Because you may have bounced from one new parenting manual to another, it will take some consistent effort on your part to convince your teens that you really intend to parent differently. They've learned to pay more attention to your behavior than to your words and may have developed a lot of bad habits in reaction to your old parenting styles.

> Our emphasis is to help your teens build character by developing qualities and characteristics in constructive, respectful ways that add something positive to the world.

But Am I Really Doing Anything?

ALL OF THE previous suggestions (and several that follow) are specific empowering behaviors that you can use when dealing with most problems with your teenagers. As pointed out earlier, it may be difficult to realize that you are really doing something when you use these suggestions. This is because they are so different from the conventional approaches. Therefore, we suggest that you participate in the following experiment first. The best way to do this experiment is with another person, but if that isn't possible or you don't want to, read the script and imagine yourself in the teen's shoes. If you do this with another person, and we recommend doing it with your teenager, you read Sonja's lines and the other person reads the parent's lines. As you read the script, notice how you are feeling when you pretend to be Sonja and pay special attention to what you are deciding.

To set the scene, picture the following: Sonja refuses to do her homework and the teachers have been sending notes home saying that her grades are dropping because of this. A typical enabling conversation sounds like this:

PARENT: Sonja, you have to turn in your homework or you'll get bad grades.

SONJA: I do turn in my homework.

PARENT: No you don't, and don't lie to me. Your teachers have sent me notes about the problem and your grades are dropping.

SONJA: Well, the classes are stupid, and I don't like the teachers.

PARENT: Oh, and you're so smart? Consider yourself grounded, young lady! You will not go anywhere, talk on the phone, watch TV, go on the Internet, or use the car until your homework is done. I'll be checking it each day to make sure and I'll have your teachers send home weekly progress reports.

SONJA: Fine, I'll do my homework, but you're not fair.

When most people play out Sonja's part in the script they end up feeling angry and controlled. They decide that they'll say or do whatever they can to get their parents off their backs, but they won't turn in their homework. Or they'll pretend to go along until their parent tires of monitoring, which should only take a few days. Or although they may do the homework and turn it in, they won't have given it their best, which allows them to hang on to a thread of personal power. We have never heard anyone decide, "Wow, my parent really cares about me and is helping me learn the importance of persistence, responsibility, and commitment."

Now read the following list. Continue to pretend that you are Sonja. But instead of being enabling, your parent responds with one of the following suggestions. Notice if your thoughts or feelings change in any way.

1. Show Faith: "I have faith in you. I trust you to figure out what you need. I know that when it is important to you, you'll know what to do."

2. Respect Privacy: "I respect your privacy, and want you to know I'm available if you want to discuss with me what is really going on."

3. Express Your Limits: "I'm not willing to go to school to bail you out. When your teacher calls, I'll hand the phone to you or tell her she'll need to discuss it with you." (A respectful attitude and tone of voice is essential.)

4. Listen Without Fixing or Judging: "I would like to listen to what this means to you."

5. Control Your Own Behavior: "I'm willing to take you to the library when we get an agreement in advance for a convenient time, but I'm not willing to get involved at the last minute. If you need my help with your homework, please let me know in advance."

6. Let Go of Their Issues: "I hope you'll go to college, but I'm not sure it's important to you."

7. Work Out a Plan *Together:* "Could we sit down to work on a plan regarding homework that we both can live with?"

8. Love and Encourage: "I'm concerned about your failure to turn in homework, but I love you just the way you are and respect your right to choose what is best for you."

9. Ask for Help: "I need your help. Can you explain to me why it is not important to you to do your homework?"

10. Share Your Feelings: Share your truth by using the "I feel ___ because ___ and I wish ___" process without expecting anyone else to feel the same or to grant your wish. This is a great model for children to acknowledge their feelings and wishes without expectations. "I feel upset when you don't do your homework because I value education so much and think it could be very beneficial to you in your life, and I really wish you would do it."

11. Use Joint Problem Solving (Similar to No. 7, with some additional steps): "What is your picture of what is going on regarding your homework? Would you be willing to hear my concerns? Could we brainstorm together on some possible solutions?"

12. Communicate Respectfully: "I'm feeling too upset to talk about this right now. Let's put it on the agenda for the family meeting so we can talk about it when I'm not so emotional."

13. Give Information, Not Orders: "I notice you spend a lot of time watching television and talking on the phone during the time you have set aside for homework. I notice you often leave your homework until the last minute and then feel discouraged about getting it done. I'd prefer that you do your work first."

At first, these empowering statements and actions may not seem as powerful as they really are if you are used to the short-term benefits of controlling, rescuing or abandoning. But if you really let yourself role-play the situation and honestly check to see how you feel as Sonja, you'll probably find that many of the options invite discussion or an increase in personal responsibility instead of resistance and sneaking. You might want to use the list to role-play a problem, other than homework, that you are experiencing with your teen to understand that these suggestions are effective for many situations.

These statements and actions do turn over control to your teens so they have power in their own lives. One of the difficulties for you may be that this power often leads to mistakes and failure. When you understand that learning from mistakes and failure is an important part of a successful life process, you will also understand the importance of using these empowering statements and actions.

Tips for Empowering Teens and Focusing on Long-Term Parenting

THE FOLLOWING LIST provides more tips for long-term parenting. Many of these tips have been discussed in more detail in previous chapters, but keeping this list handy serves as a friendly reminder. (We repeat some concepts again and again because we know they are stumbling blocks for many parents.) Implementing any of these suggestions will help your teens grow into responsible adults and will also invite a better relationship between you and your teen.

1. Use your parental authority wisely; save your "no's" for the really important things. With preadolescents, a "no" once a week is plenty. By the time your kids are fourteen, once a month should do; and by the time they are seventeen, once a year should be enough (see chapter 7).

2. Encourage, or at least don't block, safe rebellion, which allows teens to experiment without hurting anyone. Examples of safe rebellion include such things as music, hair, cosmetics, fashions, room decorations, use of time, friends, and so on. Stay in the now and remember that what your teens do today is not what they'll do forever and is not a mark of their character—it's just part of their growing process.

3. Because teens have a great need for privacy, give them some space to withdraw into their own private world. Ignore their moods and don't get into their doldrums. Love them even when they're in a bad mood, because the mood will probably get better soon. (See chapter 14 for a discussion of moods that might be an indication of more serious problems.)

4. Support your teens' roles, fantasies, ideas, and interests, even if you feel they aren't worthy of your teens' time. Your teens need you to be their cheerleader and advocate. If they decide to try something and it fails, they'll learn more from that failure than if you discourage them from trying at all. Remember, you provided your toddlers with opportunities to explore, and you need to do the same for your teens. These opportunities may include the use of cars, telephones, and computers; attendance at concerts and lessons; and so on. This is not to say you should pay for everything, but you could help your teenagers budget to get the things they really want. Also, it does not mean that you should not educate yourself about possible dangers and have friendly discussions with your teen about what you learn.

5. Say things with a smile. Although this isn't always easy, your teens hear you better when you keep your sense of humor instead of getting uptight. Saying "I notice" can be much gentler than "You never." Have faith in your teens to figure things out, to learn, and to grow. This faith will help you maintain your sense of humor.

6. Let your teens know you love them. This is easy. Simply tell them. Write them notes. Tell someone else when they can overhear you. Trust teenagers to be teenagers, and you'll find them easier to love. It's hard to feel loving when your expectations are crushed, but if you count on your teens to act like teens, you won't feel disappointed very often.

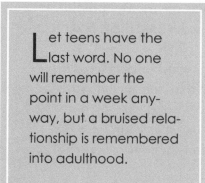

Let teens have the last word. No one will remember the point in a week anyway, but a bruised relationship is remembered into adulthood.

7. Avoid lectures and ask permission to give information. It's too late to force them to learn lessons through lectures, so give it up. It's not too late to teach, but only when your help is requested. You can ask your teens if they'd like to hear what you think or if they want or need your help. If they say "no," then back off. Because teenagers think they know everything, don't argue. Let teens have the last word. No one will remember the point in a week anyway, but a bruised relationship is remembered into adulthood. If you give information, give it without strings or demands that it be followed.

8. Count on teenagers to be obnoxious. Instead of letting it bother you, step back and try to see it as cute. When they push you too far, set your own

limits and follow through or give them a choice you can live with. It's easier to do this than to try to change a teen. Don't ever embarrass or correct your teens in front of their friends, and *never* compare them to their friends or siblings.

9. Learn to listen without giving advice or trying to fix things. Just listen. Teens feel better when they feel heard. If you have something to say to teens, speak from your feelings and your ideas rather than lecturing them or trying to tell them how to think. Watch out for making judgments and placing blame. Use the word *we* when working things out. Finger-pointing with teens leads either to loss of faith in themselves or to revenge against you.

10. Validate your teen's biological clock. Eliminate the shame and guilt teens may have for doing what is normal at their stage of development. It's a great relief to your teens when you let them know it's okay to feel and think exactly the way they do.

Three Families Switch to Long-Term Parenting

WHEN YOU LEARN how to empower your teens, you can reverse some very discouraging situations. In the stories that follow, three different families implemented long-term parenting to help their children think for themselves, make their own decisions, and have good memories of unconditional love.

Patsy's Mom Exchanges Lecturing for Listening

Negative rumors about Patsy were being spread around school. She was so unhappy about this that she wrote poems about suicide. Around her friends, she pretended she didn't care—she acted flip and made a lot of jokes, but inside she was torn up.

When Patsy told her father that she wanted to change schools, he lectured her about how you can't run away from trouble (Edward, her father, was afraid that Patsy was trying to take the easy way out). These lectures made Patsy even more upset; she wondered why her father couldn't simply support her.

When asked what it was about her father's lectures that bothered her, she said, "What if he's right? If he *is,* then I'm wrong. If I'm wrong, what have I got left? I don't know if I can trust myself."

Patsy's father decided to use some of the tips for long-term parenting. He said to his daughter, "Honey, I have faith in you to do the things that are right for you. If you need my help, let me know, and I'll be there. If you still feel this way in a couple of weeks, we'll call the school together and figure out a plan that works for you."

By suggesting that Patsy see how she felt in a few weeks, Edward showed that he trusted Patsy to be a teenager, who can feel one way so strongly one minute and the next feel totally different. He was also implying, "I have faith in you even when you're doing things I don't necessarily approve of or would do in the same way." This attitude gave Patsy a chance to find out what she wanted, who she was, and how she wanted to live her life. With this support, Patsy could learn from her mistakes instead of trying to please her father or rebelling against him. In making her own decisions and her own mistakes, she could learn and perhaps even change her mind.

When Edward decided to listen to Patsy instead of assuming he knew how she should think, he found that Patsy lived in a completely different world from his own. Patsy was not worried about grades or about how she did in school; instead, Patsy worried about whether she could handle going to school at all because of the name calling and the way her peers treated her. She was concerned about one of her friends, who was afraid she might have been pregnant. In addition, guys were trying to get Patsy to go to bed with them; she was trying to figure out how to be popular; and she worried about what others thought of her. On top of all that, she was trying to please her parents. Patsy was simply thinking and feeling like the sixteen year old that she was, and not like the grown-up that Edward expected her to be.

Brandon's Dad Stops Interfering

Sixteen-year-old Brandon went in to see his counselor. He was feeling angry and depressed. His relationship with his father was at an all-time low. Brandon told his story, which is very typical for kids his age:

> I started off the first six weeks of school this year with fairly good grades for me. I got mostly B's and C's and a D in Spanish. My father had been staying off my back about school for the first time ever, because my grades were

better. But then my grades started going down. When my dad checked up on me and found I was getting a 1.9, he said I wasn't keeping our "agreement." This agreement was that I couldn't drive unless I had a 2.0 or better. When I make an agreement with Dad, he tells me what I have to agree to and I say yes. It doesn't feel like I have any choice.

My dad decided I had to go to summer school to raise my grades. He didn't talk to me about this—he just signed me up and told me I was going. I don't ask him to do any of this stuff for me, he just does it. I don't like it at all, but I figure I have to do as he says. So, when I raised my average to 2.0 in summer school, I told Dad I was ready to start driving again. But then he said summer school didn't count and that what I needed was consistency. At that point he went too far. I decided he was unreasonable and unfair and I wouldn't do anything he wanted.

Brandon decided that whatever his father said was the way it had to be and that he had no choice in the matter. Brandon said his father overreacted about everything, making simple things much harder than they needed to be. This was stressful for Brandon, who felt angry and without control over his life. He had learned to go along with his father on the surface, but he would get revenge later by doing poorly in school.

Brandon did not think about what was important to him or how he wanted to do in school. Instead, school became a big bargaining chip in the game of driving a car. When he felt he couldn't win the game, he no longer had any reason to do well in school.

Brandon also felt that he couldn't tell his parents the truth. One night he went to a party but told his folks he was staying at a friend's. His counselor asked, "Why didn't you tell your folks you were going to a party and staying out all night?" Brandon replied, "You just don't say that to your parents. They don't know that I go out and do that. I figure I'm having fun and they're not hurt by it—they don't have anything to do with it. It would be like me asking them where they're going every minute of the day and telling them they have to call in every hour. This is the way I have fun, and it's none of their business."

Brandon's counselor then asked, "Why do you go out and party when you know your parents wouldn't approve? Why not do activities that your parents would approve?" Brandon said, "They're older than me and have different interests than me. I like to be out, be with my friends, and meet people." The counselor asked, "Do you think you like to party and drink because you see your folks do it?" Brandon said that the last thing he would ever do is anything his folks did.

Brandon then shared how bad it got when his dad found out that he wasn't where he said he would be. When Brandon tried to explain to his dad what had happened, his father didn't believe him. Brandon then decided that he really didn't care anymore about anything his father said. According to Brandon, his father had always tried to get him to do things the way he would do them. His father told him that his friends were a bad influence. Brandon decided that he couldn't relate to his dad and that he would just have to put up with him until he could leave home for good.

Brandon's counselor asked, "If you could give advice to your folks about how you wish they would treat you and what would help you, what would you tell them?" Brandon said he wished they would leave him alone and let him make his own decisions. He said he couldn't control how his folks thought, but he wished they would understand that his decisions were different from theirs. He said, "I'm not them."

Brandon's counselor then asked, "What do you think would happen if your folks really did back out of your life and stopped checking up on you?" Brandon replied, "I'd be less stressed. I wouldn't have to worry about so many things. If I made a mistake, I'd have to live with it myself—I wouldn't have to listen to them tell me I did wrong or I was ruining my life. I could decide what things were mistakes to me. If Dad stayed out of my school, I wouldn't have to use school as a way to get back at him. I wouldn't have to worry about how I acted or what I said in class."

With the help of the counselor and reading the first edition of *Positive Discipline for Teenagers,* Brandon's dad realized that he wasn't using his parental authority wisely; that, in fact, his methods were backfiring. He told Brandon, "You know I'd like you to do well in school, but I realize I've been trying to control something that is your business. I've been worrying more about what others will think of me than about how all this affects you. I'm sorry. I intend to turn school over to you. If I forget, I hope you'll help me remember by telling me I have my nose back in your business."

Brandon's dad shared that it would probably never be okay with him for Brandon to party where alcohol was involved, but he wanted his son to know that he would always love him. Brandon's father shared his fears about the parties and said he would work on having faith in his son.

Brandon was relieved but suspicious. He knew his parents loved him, and he knew he loved them, but his feelings had been badly bruised. It would take consistency on the part of both parents to convince Brandon that they meant what they said.

Patrick's Parents Let Him Grow Up

Patrick's parents had trusted him with the family car to take his first long-distance trip. Even though Patrick felt ready, this was a big jump for his parents. The only thing they asked was that Patrick drive straight through and not take any side trips, which is about the same as telling a three-year-old not to eat the cookies on the coffee table!

Patrick intended to obey his parents, but, of course, something came up. He decided he just had to take a side trip to another city 150 miles out of the way. While he was there, he used his parents' credit cards. Figuring his folks always caught him if he did something they didn't like, Patrick saw no point in hiding any of this from them. But when he told his parents, they were very angry and felt betrayed. They did and said all the predictable things a parent would in this situation. They expressed their disappointment, grounded him as punishment, and, when he explained why he had done what he did, told him he didn't know his own feelings. Then, when Patrick got depressed, his worried parents called a counselor.

Patrick shared his story with the counselor, saying he was afraid there was something wrong with him. He figured he was a bad person and questioned his own thoughts, feelings, and motives. It hadn't occurred to him that his parents might be having a hard time letting him grow up. He didn't think that he might be misbehaving as the only way to do what he thought was right.

When Patrick's parents came to the counselor's office so that Patrick could share his feelings and thoughts with them in a safe place, they weren't prepared for what they heard. Patrick explained that he wanted to grow up, and he wished they would let him. He asked them to stop threatening him, because he didn't want to have that kind of relationship with them. He explained that he felt guilty and bad when he had to lie to them. Instead, he wanted to share his thoughts and feelings without being told they were stupid or wrong.

Patrick asked his mom and dad to support his ideas with enthusiasm. He told them he could learn more from trying things out and making mistakes than from being protected by them. He said, "I want to taste the world for myself, not through you." He recognized that his parents were scared, but he wanted them to have faith in him.

Although Patrick's parents were shocked, they were also proud. They had been unaware of many of the things he said. They wanted to be on his side and didn't realize how far off base they had been.

Stay in Denial or See It as It Is

DENIAL IS THE ability to go through life with a paper bag over your head and earplugs in your ears, watching a screen inside your brain that shows a movie of how you wish it would be (or how you are afraid it is), instead of how it is. It seems easier for many parents of teens to stay in denial about their teens than to see them as they are. It is difficult for parents to see teens as going through a stage in their development toward adulthood.

> Denial is the ability to go through life with a paper bag over your head and earplugs in your ears, watching a screen inside your brain that shows a movie of how you wish it would be (or how you are afraid it is), instead of how it is.

When you treat your teens like incompetents—monitoring them, supervising them, controlling them—you stop them from growing up. Often, you are more controlling of teenagers than you are of a three year old at a playground. You may give the three year old more room to learn how to use the playground equipment than you give a sixteen year old to learn how to use a car.

Many small children will not try playground equipment if they think they can't handle it. If your child does climb up the big slide before he or she is old enough to handle it safely, do you stand on the sidelines and give a lecture, or do you run to the bottom of the slide to give support? Usually, you encourage your child to try, in the process teaching your child a few skills. In this sense, teenagers are no different from toddlers. There are many things they won't do if they don't think they can handle them. They have as many fears as anyone else has. They need the same kind of help that you would give a toddler. Your teens need your encouragement, your support, and your help in building skills.

But What About Questionable Behavior?

ALTHOUGH QUESTIONABLE BEHAVIOR is covered more thoroughly in chapter 14, it is worth addressing at least one point here: If you are worried about your teen's behavior, sit down and talk with her. Let her know that this behavior scares you and that you would really appreciate it if she would educate you. Let her know that you want to know about this behavior from her perspective. What is she thinking, feeling, and deciding? What does it mean to her? How does she see this behavior in relation to her future?

Again, we need to emphasize that this will not be effective if you are using these questions as a manipulative way to get your points across. It is effective only when your teen feels you are really interested and will not ever use the information she give you against her. Many teens have decided, on their own, to change their behavior simply because they were invited to think about it in a supportive atmosphere instead of a threatening one.

Wendi is a case in point. As you read her story, notice how her mother was able to influence her in a positive direction, even though you may not agree with a teen staying out all night.

Wendi's mom, Erika, heard about rave parties from a friend, who explained that the kids were telling their parents they were sleeping at a friends house and then going to a rave where they took the drug ecstasy, danced all night, and often engaged in sexual behaviors with other party-goers. Erika was shocked to hear that her daughter had been lying to her. Erika did her homework, learned more about the drug and its side effects, and then asked Wendi to go out for coffee so they could talk about something.

Erika told Wendi that she wasn't in trouble, but that it was really important that they talk about the raves and the ecstasy. Wendi became defensive and explained that she was just doing what her friends did and having fun. She said that her mother was overreacting. Erika said that what Wendi said was entirely possible, but she wanted to run her concerns by her daughter without a fight. Erika talked about the damage to the central nervous system that might happen to people who take ecstasy. She shared information about guys who preyed on young girls at the raves, giving them drugs so they would have sex with them, without any concerns about feelings or safety. She stated her feelings about finding out that Wendi hadn't been forthright about where she went at night.

Although Wendi responded that Erika didn't really understand, the following week she came to her mom and said, "I'm going to a rave with my friends. I'm not going to lie to you and pretend I'm at a friend's house when that's not where I'm really going. I've decided not to use ecstasy, but I do intend to stay out all night and dance. And you don't need to worry about me being sexual with people I don't know, because that isn't something I want to do, ever."

Erika said, "I wish you weren't going to stay out all night, but I am very proud of you for being honest with me and for respecting yourself enough to choose not to use such a potentially dangerous drug." Wendi said, "I know you love me, Mom, and I appreciate that you are trying to help me. I love you, too."

Many parents who think Erika was permissive by "allowing" Wendi to stay out all night are in denial that their teens often do this without telling their parents. Teens often lie about where they will be (at a friend's). Other teens sneak out at night. Erika knew this occurred, but she knew she could not control her daughter. Instead of lecturing, she wanted to prepare Wendi for the dangers she might encounter.

The Challenge

YOU HAVE A challenge. You can decide whether to influence or to control your teens, whether to raise their self-confidence or to run their lives. You can focus either on building skills or on doing things for your teens to protect them. Parents often use the excuse that teens can make mistakes that could kill them or ruin their lives forever, but this is true at any age. Focusing on this fear invites you to try to control your teens' lives rather than letting go so they can live their own lives.

Ask yourself, "Am I coming from fear or trust?" Trust gives your teens room to make mistakes and to learn from them. As Rudolph Dreikurs said, "Better a bruised knee than bruised courage. A broken knee can mend, but broken courage lasts forever."

KIND AND FIRM PARENTING TOOLS TO REMEMBER

1. Use the skills of empowerment to help your teens build their inner resources, so they will be safe even when you aren't nearby.

2. Examine your priorities. Is your parenting aimed at helping your teens help themselves and be self-sufficient at some point in the future, or are you more interested in controlling the present?

3. Remind yourself that sometimes when it looks like you are doing something, you are making matters worse and when you think you are doing nothing, you may be practicing skills from the empowerment list. Because they are new to you and you are used to looking for the quick fix, you might forget that you are building character for the future.

4. Your teens really need your help to reverse discouraging situations, so be available with the skills of long-term parenting.

5. Instead of assuming how your teens think, ask questions and listen carefully to find out about their world. Don't be afraid to ask your teens to teach you about what it's like for them or for teens today.

6. It's comforting to remember that when you use your old, ineffective skills, you can realize it, reverse directions, and still have a positive effect on your teens.

7. Although it's true that teens can be risk takers and often don't think things through before trying out new activities, more often they will watch and wait before they jump into something that may be out of their comfort zones or over their heads. Don't panic and think it's a catastrophe until you really know what is going on. Even then, ask first for an explanation of what the activity looks like from their point of view.

Practical Application Activity

It is easy to get caught up in day-to-day living concerns and to forget about the big picture and long-term parenting. This activity will help you focus on your bigger priorities.

1. Pretend your teenager is ready to leave home to begin the adventure of life on his own.

2. Make a list of at least four things you would like your teen to have as a legacy of your parenting:
   a.
   b.
   c.
   d.

3. After each item you listed, write at least one thing you are doing to build this legacy for your teen. What could you stop doing to avoid detracting from the legacy you would like to leave? Repeat this activity once a month.

MY PLAN FOR THE WEEK

This week I will focus on

_____

_____

I will work on changing my attitude by thinking

_____

_____

_____

I will change my behavior by doing

_____

_____

_____

11

Is It Too Late to Teach Life Skills?

Building Character

Y OU HAVE MANY opportunities to encourage your children to develop the life skills they need to enjoy success and satisfaction when they go out into the world on their own. By now, we hope you see this as part of your job as their parent. We are sure that you would rather spend your parenting energy helping your teens be more capable, even though you may not always be sure how to do that. And we know that by now, you are aware that it's never too late to help your teens. The time you spend today pays off in the future—you are building character and skills in your young people. We've mentioned this before, but it's worth repeating—there is a delayed reaction with teens. Even though you often can't see the results of your efforts immediately, you can trust that within a week, a month, a year, or even two years, all the work you have put in will pay off dramatically.

Although our focus in this chapter is on strengthening your ability to invite and encourage competence, your teens might stumble upon other situations or people who will help them be more focused and responsible. Take Douglas, who refused to get good grades because he thought his parents were pressuring him, but changed his mind when he joined the golf team and his coach took him aside. Coach said, "If you don't get your grades up, you'll get kicked off the team. I'm willing to talk to your teachers and help you find out what you need to do to catch up. But if golf is important to you, you'll have to do the work."

Douglas went to all his teachers and found out exactly what he needed to do. Because golf *was* important to him, he brought all his grades up so he could stay on the team. It was the first time he could see any reason to do it for himself. We hope that like Douglas, your teens will stumble upon many life experiences that will help them grow up, but just in case they don't, we'll show you a myriad of opportunities you may have.

Although you can't make anyone change, you will be in a position to invite changes when you follow the advice and suggestions in this chapter. Your teens will make changes when they are ready, and you'll help them get ready faster when you practice the kind and firm parenting advice found here.

What Happened to the Natural Desire to Learn and Grow?

AS YOU HAVE read through the chapters, you may have discovered many of the ways you inadvertently discouraged your child's natural desire to learn and grow. Don't worry. Although the lessons take a little longer to learn as your children get older, it's not too late. All you have to do is reverse your discouragement and then you can reverse theirs. Even though you may find this hard to believe, your teens want you to think well of them and have faith in them. As you change some of your behavior, your teens will notice and respond in a positive way to your changes—especially if you release your expectations and refrain from pressuring your children for outcomes. Use the Essentials for Teaching Life Skills to be a mentor to your teen without taking over, rescuing, or criticizing.

> Even though you may find this hard to believe, your teens want you to think well of them and have faith in them.

ESSENTIALS FOR TEACHING LIFE SKILLS

1. Maintain a friendly attitude.

2. Know your teen's interests.

3. After getting permission from your teen, give information, not lectures.

4. Take time to train (work *with* your teen at first, rather than giving instructions).

5. Have faith in your teen.

6. Allow for mistakes and appreciate their value.

Maintain a Friendly Attitude

A friendly attitude invites closeness, trust, and cooperation, and is essential if you want to have a positive influence with your teens. When you have created closeness, your teens are more likely to listen and work on solutions. An unfriendly attitude creates distance, defensiveness, and resistance. You need to look at how often you create distance between yourself and your teenagers with your disapproval, criticism, and lectures. It's no wonder they don't want to work with you on improvement. If you are wondering how to create a friendly attitude, ask yourself how you would treat a friend.

One of our favorite exercises is to imagine inviting a friend for dinner and then talking to your friend the way you often speak to your teen. Ouch! We know you wouldn't reprimand your friend for elbows on the table, chewing with an open mouth, taking the last piece without asking if anyone else would like it, getting up from the table without clearing the plates, and on and on. We're not suggesting you wouldn't mention your wishes and feelings to a friend, but we're pretty sure that if you did, the tone of your voice and your intention would be conciliatory and kind. Try the same attitude with your teen. No more tight lips, raised voices, whining, or shaking fists (if, of course, you have been behaving that way).

Brainstorming is another way to maintain a friendly attitude, as well as developing the life skill of looking for options. Remind your teens that there are always many solutions to a problem, even though sometimes it seems that there are no good alternatives.

One mother brainstormed with her son, who hated emptying the dishwasher. They came up with the following ideas: buy a six-month supply of paper products at a warehouse store; eat with their fingers from the pans; save money to hire a full-time maid; do dishes by hand instead of using the dishwasher; rotate chores so each person would only have to empty the dishwasher

> Brainstorming is another way to maintain a friendly attitude, as well as developing the life skill of looking for options.

one week per month; and everyone fend for him- or herself. After considering all the options, her son said, "How about if you just ask me nicely when the dishwasher needs emptying and I'll do it?" Impossible? Not at all, when humor, friendliness, and goodwill are combined to work out issues.

Another mother tried brainstorming when her thirteen-year-old daughter said she wanted to go steady with a boy in her class. They came up with three suggestions: The mother could say, "Gee, this is exciting—your first opportunity to go steady"; the mother could meet the boy; and third, the mother could find out more from her daughter about what it means to go steady in seventh grade. This mother chose the last option, and the two continued the discussion until she had a better understanding of the situation. The mother learned that going steady meant having a boyfriend to hold hands with while walking in the hall, sitting together at lunch with a bunch of other kids, and talking on the phone a lot. She was relieved to learn that it didn't mean the couple would spend a lot of time alone.

In another family, Dianne thought her daughter Sunny was too tense. Sunny planned every minute and didn't seem to know how to relax. Dianne could see that her daughter would be less stressed if she could mellow out a bit, so Dianne decided to look for opportunities to teach Sunny the benefits of relaxing. When she tried talking about it directly, Sunny became defensive. It was obvious that Sunny felt attacked, unaccepted, and embarrassed. So, instead, Dianne thought of ways to model relaxing rather than to discuss how to do it. She said, "Sunny, you can do what you want, but I'm going to relax more. Since I really love to be with you, I'm going to ask you to join me. If you want to, terrific—if you don't, that's okay, too."

When Dianne planned outings—sunning at the swimming pool or going to movies, on shopping trips, or on picnics—she always invited Sunny. When Sunny chose to join in, Dianne said nothing—she simply focused on having a wonderful time with her daughter and letting her daughter experience for herself the joys of "mellowing out."

Know Your Teen's Interests

By being aware of what is going on in your teen's life, you can determine what he needs to learn. You can then become a resource for him. Two simple ways to know your teen's interests are to ask or to observe. Notice the following conversations in which the parent is curious and the teen is nondefensive. This could happen to you.

Conversation 1

PARENT: Why do you need more money?

TEEN: I've been broke lately, so I wrote down all the places I spend money and all the places I earn money or get money. I spend more than I earn. I was thinking about getting a job, but I'm not sure if I could keep my grades up.

PARENT: How about spending less?

TEEN: Look at my list and see if you can figure out where I could cut spending.

Conversation 2

PARENT: Why do you want to go out with Troy? You hardly know him.

TEEN: I know. That's why I'd like him to come over here and hang out and why I want to go for a ride with him after school. I'd like to get to know him.

PARENT: How do you know you can trust him when you're alone?

TEEN: I was thinking that Betsy would go with us till I get to know him better.

Conversation 3

PARENT: How will you afford to go skiing with Shannon? It's a pretty expensive sport.

TEEN: I know. Shannon's folks have discount lift tickets I can buy, and Shannon says I can borrow her ski clothes and old skis. I figured I could take some money out of my savings account and then replace it when I work for Grandma next month.

PARENT: Do you know for sure that Shannon's mom and dad have room for extra kids?

TEEN: I got their phone number from Shannon so you can call them and get more details.

If you are thinking these conversations are unrealistic, try being curious and tell your teens you'd really like to know more about what they enjoy doing or what they want. Your friendly tone of voice and your curiosity questions may help them think things through better, and, in turn, you may learn about what an interesting person your teen really is. (Refer to chapter 7 to refresh yourself about curiosity questions.)

Observing before reacting is another way to get to know your teen's interests. Candace was excited about the nice new clothes she bought for her daughter, Tyna. But Tyna slept in one of the outfits and threw the other two on the floor where the dog slept on them. Candace normally would become hysterical and berate her daughter, but this time she decided to observe what would happen without her intervention.

The next morning as Tyna was rushing around getting ready for school, Candace heard a wail and rushed into her room to see what happened. Tyna was holding up the outfit that had been doubling as the dog's bed with a look of horror on her face. "Mom, I was going to wear this today and look what Bailey did to it. There is dog hair everywhere. I was just too tired last night to hang up my clothes, and I love it when Bailey sleeps with me, but this is a disaster."

Candace sat down quietly and looked on sympathetically, resisting all urges to lecture or fix. To her amazement, Tyna pulled out a clothes brush and started brushing vigorously, laughing as she did. "Oh, Mom," she said, "aren't I being silly? Bailey is way more important than a few wrinkles and dog hairs. I hate it when I get so anal."

Candace gave Tyna a hug, walked out of the room, and realized, "I just learned something about my daughter today. Her priorities are really different from mine, but she sure is clear about them. And if I let her have her feelings and blow off some steam, she sure settles back down in a hurry."

Give Information

Every teenager in the world knows that when you say, "I want your cooperation," you mean, "Do as I say," and that "Let's make an agreement" means you will issue a new mandate without any input from your teen. How can you give information so that your teens will hear you instead of tuning you out and rebelling?

Many teens say they'd like to go to their parents for help, but they don't because they're afraid to face their parents' disappointment, disapproval, lectures, or punishment. Even if that's not the case, some teens will discard any information from their parents, regardless of how good it is, just because it is from their parents. How can they individuate if they do what their parents want? Other times, teens will hear the information, but will file it away until they're ready to use it—which is hardly ever as soon as their parents would like them to use it. Fortunately, there are several skills you can learn in order to diminish resistance and rebellion.

When you start a sentence with, "I've noticed," or, "Let's make a deal," or "Want to hear a thought I had?" you usually have a captive audience. If, in addition, you stress that listening to you doesn't mean agreeing and that your teen isn't in trouble, you double the likelihood for good communication. The following conversation demonstrates these skills.

> Every teenager in the world knows that when you say, "I want your cooperation," you mean, "Do as I say," and that "Let's make an agreement" means you will issue a new mandate without any input from your teen.

FATHER: I was thinking about something the other day. *Want to hear what it was?*

TEEN: Okay, Dad.

FATHER: When car insurance bills come, they're really expensive. So when you have a car, I have an idea about how you can deal with that. *Do you want to hear what it is?*

TEEN: Won't you be paying for the insurance?

FATHER: No, I'm not paying for your insurance. But Mom and I said we would help you buy a car, and of course, you can't drive a car without insurance.

TEEN: How am I going to pay for insurance?

FATHER: That's what I was thinking about. Here's my idea. First, we sit down and figure out how much the insurance will be. We'll probably have to call the insurance company to find out for sure. But suppose we find out it's about $600 every six months. How much would you have to save each month to pay that bill when it comes?

TEEN: Wow! That's $100 a month!

FATHER: Right. So how much would you have to put away each week from your paycheck?

TEEN: I only make fifty dollars a week. That means I have to save half just for insurance.

FATHER: Right. *And I've noticed that you like to have a lot of cash in your pocket to spend on fun.* What kinds of things will you have to sacrifice to do that?

TEEN: That really sucks! I'll have only twenty-five dollars a week for gas, hamburgers, dates, CDs, and everything.

FATHER: Maybe it isn't worth it to drive a car. What are your other options?

TEEN: Oh, I'll do it, but it sure sucks.

FATHER: I understand that feeling. I've had it many times.

In another conversation, Katharine gave information to her son Harrison in a way that invited cooperation. Harrison had volunteered to help Katharine with her new computer program. Katharine waited patiently throughout the day, watching Harrison move from activity to activity without seeming to remember his agreement. Finally Katharine said, "Harrison, I'm not trying to be a pest, and this isn't a criticism, but you know how I can get impatient. If you let me know when you are planning to work on my computer program, I can set my 'wait-o-meter.' If I know how long I have to wait, I can handle it much better. It's the wondering that I find difficult."

"Sorry, Mom," Harrison said, "I didn't know you were in a rush. I can do it right now if you like."

"Honey, it's not necessary to do it now; just let me know when you will do it so I'll know how long I have to wait."

"How about at 4:30?"

Harrison completed his work on Katharine's computer and was extremely helpful. The next day, seemingly out of nowhere he said to his mom, "I don't like not knowing how long I have to wait for things, either. That is the hard part, isn't it?"

Katharine, taken aback, remembered the conversation of the previous day and replied, "I guess we both do better when we can set our 'wait-o-meters.'"

Often, teenagers (like Douglas in the beginning of this chapter) are more willing to listen to someone else than they are to you. If this is the case with your teen, enlist the aid of a friend or relative to give the desired information. If you can keep your ego out of the way, you can be creative in helping your teens find other sources of learning.

Blythe was complaining about her parents to her friend's dad, Cal. She told Cal that her folks were way too strict and never listened. She said she hated the way they treated her like a baby, expecting her to come home by 9:00 P.M. when all her friends could come home at 10:00 P.M.

Cal listened as he always did and then said, "Blythe, I don't mean to sound trite, but being a parent of a teen isn't much easier than being a teen. Your folks are trying to do what they think is best and deal with their insecurities and fears."

"I know, I know, but I wish just once they could be reasonable."

"Well, Blythe," Cal said, "I'm sure you've already thought of this, but I wonder what would happen if you explained to them the reasons why it's important to you to stay out later and asked them to think about what you were saying before responding. Maybe you could even suggest they call some of your friends' parents to hear about how other families handle curfew. Do you think you might find them a more willing audience?"

Blythe looked doubtful but said, "Thanks, Cal, I'll give it a try." Even if her parents still won't listen, Cal helped Blythe by sharing a perspective she probably didn't have. And he expressed it in a way she could hear and understand.

Take Time to Train Your Teens

There are many opportunities for teaching life skills, such as those involving cars, money, clothing, shopping, family work, use of time, and attitudes toward learning and school. When teaching teens, look for these teaching moments rather than for more formal teaching situations.

Francine had been taking the responsibility to get her son Dan out of bed on Tuesday mornings for an early morning class. She would wake him up, he would go back to sleep. This scenario would continue, with increasing anger on both sides, until Francine would yank the covers off. Dan would then stumble out of bed, saying "Get off my back," and finally leave about half an hour late. Francine received a letter from the teacher saying that if Dan missed one more time, he would fail the class.

Later, as Dan and his mother were driving alone in the car, she said, "I got a letter from your teacher today saying that if you miss one more class, you'll fail first period. Do you want to go to class tomorrow or do you want to miss it and fail the class?" Dan was quiet for a few seconds before saying, "I guess I'll go." Then his mother said, "Do you want me to help you get up, or do you want me to leave you alone?" He said, "Leave me alone."

She agreed and Dan said, "Thanks, Mom." (Quite a difference from "get off my back.") The next morning, Dan showered early and left on time. Mom was sure he could feel the difference in her manner and intention and knew that she really was turning this responsibility over to him.

Some of the best teaching moments can be found when you piggyback on your teens' interests. For instance, most teenage girls are preoccupied with clothing. This preoccupation offers many opportunities to teach about budgeting, about earning money, and about planning ahead.

In Paula's family, the children received a clothing allowance twice a year. Paula decided to buy fewer but more expensive clothes. In her mind, she could always fill in her wardrobe by borrowing from friends and using her small monthly allowance.

Sylvia, Paula's mom, insisted that new clothes were absolutely not to be loaned out or left on the floor. She was trying to prevent Paula from making mistakes, but then she remembered that she wanted to help Paula learn from her experience. So, Sylvia told her daughter, "Paula, I made a mistake. I wanted to protect you from losing these expensive clothes, but I'm sure you can figure out whether or not you want to loan your clothes. I know it's up to you to decide how you want to treat the clothes you have."

A few months later, Paula came to her mother in a rage. One of her friends had borrowed her designer jacket and lost it at a party. Sylvia bit her lip and skipped the "I told you so" lecture. She gave Paula a big hug and said, "I can see how upset you are. I'm so sorry." Paula looked at her mother and said, "I'll never let her borrow my clothes again."

"Paula, would you be interested in an idea I have about loaning clothes?"

"Okay, Mom."

"You could tell them you want a deposit or something equally nice of theirs to hold until they return your clothing. This is called collateral."

"Thanks, Mom, but I don't think that would work with my friends. I'm just never going to let my friends borrow my nice stuff again. Their parents buy them whatever they want and they don't understand what it's like to be on a clothing allowance. I can't afford to lose my stuff."

"Good plan," replied Sylvia, as she hid her grin all the way into the other room.

Planning and scheduling together is an excellent training method. Life is filled with arrangements that need to be made around busy schedules. If you are making all the plans yourself and then informing your teen, you are missing out on an excellent way to help your teens learn life skills and build character. Your children will have no idea from one minute to the next what is planned for them, and they in turn will expect you to do things for them, take them places, and even intervene and rescue them if they get too busy.

> Life is filled with arrangements that need to be made around busy schedules. If you are making all the plans yourself and then informing your teen, you are missing out on an excellent way to help your teens learn life skills and build character.

You'll get better results, show respect, and teach skills when you involve your teens in planning ahead, even if it takes more time. Put a calendar in a centrally located place so that everyone in the family can easily refer to it. Schedule a family meeting at a time when everyone can give their full attention to discussing upcoming activities and appointments. Everyone can then take part in planning ahead by noting what is happening, when it's happening, who needs to be involved, and who is responsible for what.

Chaos, hurt feelings, resentment, anger, and other frustrations can be avoided by taking the time to formally plan ahead. Although many people complain they don't have the time, they don't seem to count the time spent in chaos and frustration! Good planning eliminates these problems—but it still takes time, plus attention to details and cooperation.

Antoinette was getting ready to go back to high school for her junior year. She had mentioned to her parents the things she needed to do to prepare for school. After dinner one day, they sat at the table and made a list of what needed to be done. They got out the family calendar to figure out when each thing could be accomplished and which parent would be available to assist if needed. Antoinette worked out a budget with her folks for school clothes and an allowance that would cover the rising costs for school activities and personal expenses.

The family also figured out ways that Antoinette could get to school each day, as the school was too far for walking and the bus didn't run at the right times. This allowed Antoinette plenty of time to get on the phone and arrange carpools for the days when her folks couldn't take her.

Contrast this picture with Rick and Stephanie's situations where chaos and frustration reigned. Rick wanted to go to a rock concert in a city fifty miles away. Because he didn't have a car or a license, he needed his parents' help to make the arrangements. Every time he asked them, they said they were busy and would talk about it later. Rick was frustrated—he wanted to know if he should save money to buy a ticket, and he wanted to have enough time to ask friends to go with him. Because Rick's parents didn't take him seriously, they didn't get back to him in time, and he missed the concert. His parents didn't realize they were being rude and disrespectful; they just didn't see his plan as important as all the other things they were dealing with in their lives.

Rick's story isn't unusual. When Stephanie wanted to go to a dance, her parents weren't comfortable with her going out with a boy, so they kept putting off answering her questions about the dance. Stephanie couldn't make the arrangements all her friends were making—buying their dresses, planning where they would go to eat, arranging transportation—because her parents wouldn't respond, and she didn't know how to get through to them.

Both Rick and Stephanie ended up as adults with very few skills for planning ahead. They didn't think their opinions or needs were very important, so both ended up in relationships with people who took control. Had their parents understood more about taking the time to plan ahead and schedule together, Rick and Stephanie might have grown up with a completely different adult experience.

Have Faith in Your Teen

Shawn wanted to tell his dad something he had never shared before because he was afraid of getting in trouble or meeting with disapproval. Dad could see that Shawn wanted to tell him something, but was having difficulty. Dad asked, "What's making you uncomfortable? What do you need from me?"

Shawn said, "I want your reassurance that you won't be disappointed in me if I tell you. And I have to work it out for myself before I'll tell you about it. Don't expect me to tell you first. I don't have the energy to deal with your stuff and mine. I'm not in touch with my own feelings. I can't be expected to be in touch with yours."

Dad listened without comment and then said, "I'm glad you shared that you are going through a lot right now, even though you can't tell me what it is. Whenever you're ready to tell me more, I'll be here. I can tell this was scary for you to tell me even this much. I hope you'll feel more comfortable next time. I have faith in you to figure out whatever you need, and I'll be here if you need me." Shawn's father demonstrated respect and trust. He was willing to accept where Shawn was without pushing for more and had faith in him to deal with it.

Another family showed faith in their son in a different way. On the morning of Tim's sixteenth birthday, he was first in line to get his driver's license. He passed his written test with a score of 97 and his driving test, which, in his mind, qualified him as an expert driver. He was ready to drive anything anywhere because the State of California said he could, and the state was bigger than his parents were!

When he came home, Tim asked his mother, Jane, if he could drive her car into San Francisco.

Jane later told her friend Marcia about Tim's request. "We live in a small, quiet town. San Francisco is full of steep, scary hills and heavy traffic. It's a very big city. I told Tim, 'No. You just got your license an hour ago.' He said, 'But I've been waiting and dreaming of this moment. How can you ruin my life? The State of California says I'm ready to drive anywhere. They gave me a license. I got a 97 on the test. What's wrong with you? Do you hate me?'"

Marcia asked, "What are you going to do?"

"I have to say this honestly," Jane continued. "My car was my first thought. It's a really nice car, and I didn't want to see it all banged up. I was also concerned for Tim. I wanted to protect him. I was worried about him having trouble just getting on the ramp to the freeway! I pictured all kinds of disasters for him—on the freeway and on the hills in the city. But I really could see what his issues were. He felt like a grown-up finally. He had a license, he had freedom, he had power, he had wheels. Also, he loves San Francisco; we've taken many trips there as a family. Now he wants to go on his own and take his friends. How exciting for him!"

"Do you think he can handle it this soon?" Marcia asked.

"We're going to find a way to do this in small steps. Although he hates waiting, he understands that we can't always move at the pace he wants. He knows we have faith in him, so he has faith in us to move forward. We're going to dedicate the next two weekends to Tim, so he can take the whole family to San Francisco. We'll have him go places he would never go on his own, just to give him our own personal San Francisco driver's test, with lots of opportunities to park. We'll let him drive us everywhere—up and down hills, to North Beach, Fisherman's Wharf, Chinatown. After spending four days driving around San Francisco with him, I'll feel better and know firsthand that he can do it. Then I'm going to give him the keys to my car, tell him to have fun, and when he drives off, I'll call you and panic and cry. He'll gain a lot of confidence, and I'll have a closet heart attack."

Marcia laughed and said, "You always have had a flair for high drama."

Contrast this story with Lindy, whose mother discouraged her from going on the senior-class trip. Lindy's mother described how awful the trip would be. She said no one would have any fun unless they got drunk and slept around, and since Lindy wasn't that kind of person, she'd be happier staying home. Because Lindy didn't want to get drunk and sleep around—and because she had no reason to doubt her mother—she felt she couldn't go.

When questioned, Lindy's mother said, "I've heard a lot of stories about this trip. I'm not sure if they're true, but if they are, I don't want my daughter to go. She can find some other way to celebrate graduation." But one thing she seemed to be ignoring was that in a few months Lindy would probably be living on her own at college. Not only would she lack the self-confidence that comes from handling difficult situations, she'd also lack the necessary skills—including decision making—because her mother made so many decisions for her. The more we talked about it, the more obvious it was that Lindy, unnerved by her mother's fear, was scared to go out on her own. She readily believed her mother's version of the senior-class trip because she herself was afraid of what might happen there.

Many teenagers want their parents to control them and to do things for them because they're afraid to grow up. If parents feed these teens' fears with fears of their own, their teenagers won't develop the skills necessary to become successful adults. Of course, there are also teens who refuse to be controlled and just plain rebel.

You can help your teens build courage by showing your enthusiasm for their growth process: "Won't it be exciting when you grow up and are old enough to leave home? Won't it be great when you get your first apartment? Aren't you looking forward to having a phone of your own, and a phone bill of your own? Isn't it going to be fun?" Your enthusiasm will be contagious and will help them look forward to being grown-ups out in the world. More importantly, you can help teens be courageous by giving them the chance to learn from you and then giving them the opportunity to use what they've learned.

> You can help teens be courageous by giving them the chance to learn from you and then giving them the opportunity to use what they've learned.

One mother, who had conscientiously tried to provide her son with life skills, asked him if he thought all the grocery shopping he had done as a teen helped him as an adult. He replied, "Are you kidding? I don't know how I would be able to live like I do if I hadn't had all that help. I know how to shop for bargains, how to stretch my money, how to plan ahead. I know how to do menus! I know a lot of stuff."

Allow for Mistakes and Appreciate Their Value

Justin, a seventeen-year-old boy with a penchant for living on the wild side, spent many weekends at his family's mountain retreat. He enjoyed the thrills of skiing and snowboarding and couldn't see why he shouldn't use the cabin even if his folks weren't along. He knew where the hidden key was, so he invited his friends to spend the weekend and they headed for the mountains. Naturally, things got a bit out of hand because some of his friends liked to party too much, but he fixed everything that got broken so his folks wouldn't figure out he had been there without permission.

Of course, his folks, Lydia and Wally, noticed the cigarette butts and beer cans in the yard. They lit into Justin, berating him, grounding him, and threatening everything they could think of so that he would never do this again. Justin was furious and told his folks how unappreciative they were of all his efforts to leave the place as clean as when he had arrived.

After talking with a friend who had gone to a parenting group, Lydia realized she had overreacted. After several discussions about other ways to handle the situation, Lydia approached Justin and said, "You're right, Justin. We focused on everything you did wrong and didn't tell you how responsible you were for leaving the cabin clean. We want you to know we appreciate your efforts to be that responsible."

Then Wally added, "Even though we appreciate your responsible behavior, we want to make it very clear that it is still not okay to use the cabin when we aren't there. We'd be happy to stay in the bedroom while you have friends there, but it is not okay to have parties when we aren't there."

Justin said, "Yeah, yeah."

A month later the Petersons discovered that Justin had used the cabin again. Lydia explained that she would be willing to accompany Justin and help him clean the place up, or he could pay $100 for the cleaning service. The job had to be done within the week because Wally and Lydia were renting the cabin to some skiers for the winter. After some arguing, Justin agreed to clean the cabin with help, and even thanked his mom for being willing to go with him.

Justin's parents realized that it was time for them to decide what they would do about the cabin, because it was obvious they couldn't control Justin's behavior about going there. They decided to rent the cabin until Justin was past the partying stage. You may feel critical of them or think they were too permissive. Their reply would be that they would prefer giving up the use of the cabin for a year or two if that was what it took to stop Justin from treating them disrespectfully. In their minds, the bigger picture was about building character. They wanted Justin to know that they would do whatever it took to stop making it easy for him to be disrespectful. Justin was the kind of teen who needed bigger help learning from his mistakes. Holding him accountable each time he messed up the cabin if he used it without permission was like water off a duck's back for him. But missing two ski seasons because of his behavior made a big impression on him.

Years later Justin was able to look back at his high school years and apologize to his folks for taking advantage of them, for lying to them, and for being an overall "jerk." His folks thanked him and said that those times were hard for them, too, but they had had faith that Justin would come out the other side a better person, and he did.

Unconventional Approaches (That Work) for Teaching Life Skills

KELLY'S GRADES WERE suffering. Her father, Pete, asked if she'd like to learn some tricks about studying. Kelly, feeling suspicious asked, "What kinds of tricks?"

Her father replied, "I could teach you the 'handy-dandy four-step system' if you'd like."

Kelly's interest was piqued, so she asked, "Where did you learn this system?"

Her father explained that his friend Lissie told him about it to help him work on his own procrastination. He continued, "Kelly, it really helped me. Would you like to hear about it?"

Kelly said, "Okay."

The Handy-Dandy Four-Step System

1. Decide what you want.

2. Make time for it.

3. Set up a deal or a trick to motivate yourself.

4. Use lists.

When Kelly asked how the four steps could help her, her father said that he would go through the steps with her if she would like. Kelly agreed.

First, Pete asked Kelly to think of some things that she really wanted to do each day. Kelly's list included spending time with friends, playing her guitar, studying, and watching TV.

For step two, Pete suggested that Kelly think of when she could make time for each of her choices. Kelly decided to be with her friends after school, and then come home and play her guitar, have dinner with the family, watch TV for 30 minutes, and then study.

Pete didn't point out that saving studying for last was doomed to fail. Instead, he went on to explain step three, making deals. He pointed out that people often don't do their least favorite things unless they first make deals with themselves. For example, "First I'll do what I don't like and get it over with," or, "First I'll do two things I like, then one thing I don't like, and save the best for last." He said another trick is to make dates with someone to do the things you don't like, explaining, "It can be more fun to study if you make a date to do it with someone else. And, you usually won't disappoint a friend, even if you might be willing to let yourself down."

Finally, Pete showed Kelly how to make a list of her four interests that included the amount of time for each and any deals she made with herself. They talked about how easy it could be to go back to old habits and forget new plans when the plans weren't written down. Pete suggested that Kelly use the list as a way to remember the decisions Kelly had made for herself.

Kelly wanted to know if her father planned to check up on her each day to see if she was following her list. Pete asked if that was what she wanted, and Kelly said, "No way!" So Pete said, "Good. My job is to help you learn. Your job is to decide if you want to use what you learn. I'll be happy to help if you ask me directly, but otherwise, it's up to you."

Friendly Bets vs. Bribery and Reward

A FRIENDLY CHALLENGE may help motivate teens to learn life skills. Deciding to try this method, Leilani said to her son, "I'll bet you can't get a B in that class."

Jon rose to the challenge, saying "How much?"

His mother challenged, "Ten dollars," and Jon agreed, "You're on!"

We don't believe in bribes, rewards, negative expectations, or discouraging statements. You may wonder how a bet is different.

According to Rudolf Dreikurs, a bet is like "spitting in the soup." Soup isn't very appetizing once someone has spit in it. A bet can be used when a teen has said, "I could do it if I wanted to." To be effective, the bet must be made with a friendly, respectful, playful attitude. "You're telling me you can, but I've got money that says you can't. Are you willing to put your money where your mouth is?"

You can make a bet with your teens without controlling them. But as soon as you hold out a bribe or reward, you are trying to control them. The trick is to learn how to be helpful while avoiding control.

Your Teens Can Teach You

ONE OF THE best ways to encourage and empower your teens is to let them teach you. They can teach you about their music, how to use digital watches, how to videotape a TV show, how to use a computer, and a million other things. If you're concerned about your teenager's driving habits, ask him or her to help you improve your own driving skills in as many ways as they can think of. Or ask them to share their hobbies with you, to show you how to sand a car, or to put on makeup so you can hardly see it's there. Your teens can be valuable resources if you give them the opportunity—and when you do, you not only demonstrate your respect for their abilities, you also model the joys of learning.

Other times when you can learn from your teens are when they are doing something you don't understand or might not approve of or when they answer you with obvious disdain for something you have said. Instead of jumping in and correcting or criticizing them, you could adopt an attitude of curiosity and let yourself be a learner. For example, when Jody got angry with her mother and said, "You just don't understand what I'm talking about." Her mom replied, "You are right. I don't understand, because I'm not your age. I'd really appreciate it if you would teach me, because I would like to learn." It worked! Jody then tried to explain to her mother what she meant (even if it was with a condescending tone). Mom was willing to take one step at a time and was excited that she had encouraged Jody to talk to her. When you're excited about learning new skills, you can help your teenagers see that learning benefits the learner. One teenager commented to her mother, "I just realized that the more I learn, the easier my life is." That's what raising teens is all about!

Creative Teaching

MAKING A GAME out of things can be a great way to teach skills. Buy a dictionary calendar and challenge your teens to learn new words and use them in sentences. Swap a joke a day with your teens. Play games like Scrabble or Pictionary.

Other fun ways to teach skills to your teens include asking them to survey other teens to find out how they and their families deal with money, curfews, allowances, and so on. Or help your teens plan a party or a picnic. Once you decide to be creative, you'll find there are many ways to teach skills.

We'd like to leave you with some choices that will help you continue in your efforts to be a kind and firm parent intent on teaching life skills. You may prefer small steps, or you may be ready to take a bigger leap. We will provide two options. The choice is yours. (Of course, there are other options. Our suggestions are here to invite your own creativity.) Your success will depend on the degree to which you stay in the present, focus on what you can do today, and give up worrying about how your teen will turn out. The life skills you teach today build character for tomorrow.

Parent/ Teen Issue	Small Steps	Bigger Steps
Cars	Make a list of all expenses involved in having a car. Be clear about what expenses you will cover (and then stick to it even when your teen gets into trouble). Make agreements about how to share the family car. Let your teen drive you around so you can research (with your mouth shut) your teen's skills and confidence. If you do have tips, ask if your teen would like to hear them. Involve your teen in caring for the family car. Share your teen's interest and excitement by looking through car magazines together.	Help your teens buy a car by teaching them how to take out a loan or by setting up a system to pay you back. Give your teen an old car to use and care for. Explain why your teen can manage without a car and help him or her learn how to use public transportation. Let your teens ride in cars with their friends so they don't need a car of their own. Research insurance rates together and look at the difference in rates with a "good student" discount. Expect your teen to help cover the deductible for any accidents and to be involved in setting up the repair process. Let your teen take you on a road trip.
Siblings	Talk with your teen about how he or she feels about siblings. Notice if you let one of your children get away with more than the other.	Schedule regular family meetings in which your teen learns to give and receive compliments. Stay out of siblings' fights.

Parent/ Teen Issue	Small Steps	Bigger Steps
Siblings, cont.	Read *Positive Discipline* or *Do-It-Yourself Therapy* to increase your understanding of sibling rivalry. Look at your own sibling issues and figure out how they might color your parenting Don't expect older siblings to parent younger siblings. Don't punish a sibling for the mistakes another sibling makes.	Suggest that siblings put problems on the family meeting agenda so the whole family can help brainstorm possible solutions. Let siblings create a plan together about who rides in the front seat or sits by the window, how to divide shared rooms, and a schedule for their favorite TV programs if they differ. Appreciate and encourage differences. Never compare one child with another.
Parties	Talk about your fears. Ask your teen to explain to you why kids like parties. Remember your teen years. Plan with your teen some parties at which you will make yourself scarce (in the house, but with your door shut). Read articles about what teens say about parties. Never leave your house without an adult over a weekend. Volunteer for "project graduation" nights. Take your teen to "First Nights" for New Year's Eve. Make a deal that if your teen drinks, you'll pick him or her up, no questions asked.	Ask your teen how he or she plans to behave at parties. Get real. Teens party. Their idea of a party is a place without parents and possibly with beer, wine, alcohol and other drugs. You don't have to like it, and you can try to stop it, but maybe it would be better to hold some honest discussions with your teen to keep the lines of communication open. That way, if your teen needs you, you will be someone to talk to without fear of judgment. Know your teen. Have faith in your teen. Teach your teen skills so he or she will know how to deal with situations and to have the self-confidence to do what is right for him- or herself. *(cont.)*

Parent/ Teen Issue	Small Steps	Bigger Steps
Clothing, hair, etc.	Sit in your car outside your teen's school and observe the other students. Go to the mall and observe what teens are wearing. Look at your own materialism. Set up a clothing allowance, and stick to it. Allow your teen to learn from mistakes if he or she goes over budget. Don't lecture or judge. Remind yourself that your teen won't carry the "teen look" into adulthood. Set up an appointment for your teen with a hairdresser or makeup specialist.	Enjoy the look; take pictures. If your teen pays no attention to hygiene, set up a routine *with* him or her and use follow-through. Let your teen choose his or her own look, but ask for give and take when you want him or her to dress specially for something important to you. Plan a shopping trip together (out of town so your teen's friends won't see you both at the mall together—God forbid!). Let your teen choose where to shop. Throw away your TV so your teen isn't so influenced by all the advertising.
Curfew	Set a curfew and let your teen know that it is open for discussion, as long as you both agree. Let your teen know you will be flexible as long as he or she respects your need to feel secure. Call other parents to find out what time they set curfew (instead of simply accepting, "All the other parents let their kids . . . "). Get a group of parents and teens together in your home for an open discussion about curfew and about what will work for everyone.	Let your teen tell you what time he or she will be home each night. Talk about curfew as a respect issue, the way you would with a roommate. Ask your teen to call if he or she will be late. Don't be afraid to say no if your teen needs a night home to regroup. Know your teen. Express your faith in your teens to think about what he or she is doing and how it will affect his or her life.

Parent/ Teen Issue	Small Steps	Bigger Steps
Money	Read *Chores Without Wars* or *Positive Discipline A–Z* for more information about setting up an allowance. Pay for work you would hire someone else to do. Pay only after the work is done. Start your teen on an allowance that is not connected to chores. Avoid bail outs. If you make loans, start with small amounts and keep a payment ledger to track repayment. Do not loan larger amounts until your teen establishes his or her credit worthiness with you.	Help your teen learn how to make a budget. Teach your teen, or have your teen show you, how to use computer-generated budgeting programs. Start your teen on a clothing allowance. Teach tricks for saving, such as one envelope for spending, one for long-term savings, and one for saving for a short-term goal.
Chores	Expect all your children to do chores. During a family meeting, get your teen's input as to how and when the chores should be done. Create routine chore charts together. Use follow-through to make sure the chores get done. Avoid excuses, even if there is a test the next day. Expect your teen to schedule time to help with chores. You can always offer to trade or help out on special occasions.	Get your teen involved in cooking, grocery shopping, doing laundry, making lunch, ironing, caring for the car, cleaning house, and anything else that will prepare your teen for being an adult. Respect your teen's busy schedule, but insist that he or she finds at lease one night to cook—no matter how simple the menu. *(cont.)*

Parent/ Teen Issue	Small Steps	Bigger Steps
Rooms	Go to a storage store with your teen to pick out hooks and other storage items. Let your teen decorate part of the rooms in the house. Expect your teen's room to be cleaned once a week. Offer a choice for your teen to clean alone or with your help.	Let your teen keep the bedroom the way he or she wants. Trust that your teen will clean the bedroom when ready. (Some of the messiest teens become the tidiest adults—and some stay messy.) Come up with a budget for painting, posters, and bedding. Let your teen redecorate the room.
Dating	Don't overreact, they'll probably break up within a week—if you stay out of it. Understand that "going steady" means different things for different ages. Find out what it means for your teen. With preteens, drive them to the movies or the mall and pick them up. Let your teen have pool parties or other coed gatherings with you as a chaperone. Promote group activities.	Educate your teen about date rape. Make sure you discuss your fears and thoughts about teenage sex and unprotected sex, and listen carefully to your teen's thoughts. If your teen feels ready to date, let it be, but stay involved and vigilant and be open to discussions. Include your teen's date in family activities. Make sure your teen feels loved. Otherwise your teen might feel the need to look for "love" in the wrong places.
School	Have a special time of day when the entire family does quiet work. Create routines *with* your teen instead of micromanaging. Read as a family. Take classes together. Take classes yourself. Read more of the Positive Discipline books for additional tips.	School isn't for everyone and some teens may work better with home schooling or by taking an equivalency test and returning to school later. Offer to help with schoolwork at certain times that fit your schedule, but let school be between your teen and the teachers. In other words, the teachers can allow your teen to experience the

Parent/ Teen Issue	Small Steps	Bigger Steps
School, *cont.*	Remember that the purpose of school is to learn and not to get the best grades and turn in the most papers. Let your teen know that he or she is more important to you than school grades. If grades go down, be a friend, look for the underlying reasons, and be realistic about your teen's capabilities. Do not withdraw the things your teen is good at as punishment.	logical consequences of not doing what is required—F's. Don't overreact when your son or daughter gets detention or a bad grade; wait and see what your teen does about it and be available and encouraging without taking over. Offer tutors when needed. Appreciate each child's efforts as a learner, regardless of how accomplished or far along he or she is. Encourage your teen to build on strengths. Don't harp on your teen to be good at everything.
Electronics (pagers, cell phones, computers, hand-held video games, TVs)	Limit time spent on computers, television, videos, and computer games. At a family meeting, thoughtfully schedule time for these activities *with* your teens. Use the parental controls on Internet servers. Talk with your teen about the danger and the value of chatting with people they don't know. Ask for ideas on how your teen can protect him- or herself from the potential dangers of online chats. Do *not* buy a television for your teen's bedroom. Remember that teens today see more explicit sex and violence on TV than ever before. You may not be able to protect your teen from this, but you can engage in	Eliminate all TVs, except for use with thoughtfully rented videos. (We know—this is a *very big* step.) If you aren't ready for the biggest step, at least watch your teen's favorite programs occasionally so you can be aware of what your teen is viewing. Ask how much your teen thinks the media influences what he or she thinks or does. Friendly discussions can help teens think about what they are seeing and verbalize it so they can come to some understanding of media's influence on them. Do not buy a cell phone for your teen (unless it is for emergency use only). If your teen can afford a phone, help him or her work out a budget for monthly bills. *(cont.)*

Parent/ Teen Issue	Small Steps	Bigger Steps
Electronics, cont.	friendly discussions about what your teen is watching and about what your teen thinks about it. Ask your teen to teach you computer skills. Do not eat meals while watching TV. Save this special mealtime for friendly conversation.	When your teen wants to buy products advertised on TV, help him or her think it through. "Why do you really want it? Can you pay for it? Are you being duped by consumerism?"
The mall, concerts, and other activities	Understand that, in terms of socialization, the mall and concerts are as important to your teen as barn dances were for your grandparents. Take your preteen to the mall; sit down by yourself with a soft drink or cup of coffee, and wait till he or she is ready to leave or meet at an agreed-upon time. Occasionally go to concerts with your teens and their friends. Agree to sit in the back row so they don't have to be seen with you. Take your teen to an audiologist (or research literature about audiology) for information about the danger to eardrums when exposed to excessively loud music. Ask for your teen's ideas on how to protect hearing.	Know your teens and have faith in them to use the skills you have helped them develop. They may rebel and make mistakes, but have faith in them to use the skills to decide what is right for them. Once you have provided opportunities for your teen to learn skills and to know that you love him or her unconditionally, be thankful that you don't know everything your teen knows—just as your parents didn't know everything you knew. Have faith in your teens to become fabulous adults (just as you did), even if you don't agree with their choice of music or current value system.
Friends	Look at why your teens might be choosing the friends they have. Do your teens feel insecure? Are they looking for friends who don't expect too much of them?	Let your teens hang out with their friends behind the closed door of their bedrooms. (It is very disrespectful to assume that because the door is closed they are having orgies or doing drugs.)

Parent/ Teen Issue	Small Steps	Bigger Steps
Friends, cont.	Provide many opportunities for your teen to develop perceptions of confidence and capability. This will translate into an ability to choose like-minded friends. Don't criticize your teen's friends. Instead, invite them into your home where you can be a good influence. If some of your teen's friends seem very scary to you, it is okay to trust your gut and let your teen know that these friends are welcome in your home, but only when you are there. Accept your teen's style. You may have a teen that prefers one close friend instead of being part of the popular crowd.	It is okay to knock on the door during the evening and ask if you can come in. Your teens will most likely say yes, and you will probably find them sprawled on the floor or the bed listening to music and talking. If your teens have trouble making friends, ask if they would like some hints. Otherwise, have faith in them to work it out.

KIND AND FIRM PARENTING TOOLS TO REMEMBER

1. Embrace your job of teaching life skills, knowing that you are helping your teen build character. The time you spend now will pay big dividends down the road.

2. Your teen is more likely to see you as a mentor when you maintain a friendly attitude.

3. Knowing your teen's interests is the doorway to teaching life skills. Use your teen's interests as a natural way to hold his or her attention.

4. For maximum effectiveness and respect, ask first before giving information.

5. No one can change overnight. It takes time to learn new habits, even when you and your teen are willing.

6. There's no better way to teach life skills than through a routine. Life is filled with routines, so why not work with your teen to set up some that work for both of you, instead of operating on the haphazard routines that may currently be running your family.

7. Your faith in your teen will go far in breaking down feelings of hopelessness.

8. Remember, even though your teen can learn from mistakes, some teens learn a lot from little mistakes and other teens need to make bigger or more frequent mistakes before learning anything.

9. Don't be afraid to be unconventional when teaching life skills. Maintain a sense of humor and playfulness with your teen.

10. There's not one right way for kind and firm parents to handle any given situation, so focus on our suggestions to find what works best for you and then create your own options.

Practical Application Activity

1. Using the parent/teen issue chart, look at the issues and the choices. Place a check beside the ones that make sense to you.

2. Add to the columns any other ideas you have, or create another column altogether.

3. Ask your teen, your spouse, your teen's friends, and your other children to do the same.

This activity should lead to a lively discussion, so sit back and enjoy the separate realities!

MY PLAN FOR THE WEEK

This week I will focus on

_____

_____

I will work on changing my attitude by thinking

_____

_____

_____

I will change my behavior by doing

_____

_____

_____

12

Is It Genetics?

Psychology 101
for Parents of Teens

THIRTEEN-YEAR-OLD Kevin's behavior was saying, "No one can make me do anything! I'm unlovable! I'm awful to be around! I hate everything and everybody!" His teachers tried to get him to comply by using rewards, punishments, removal from class, transfers, and calls to his parents. His parents tried to help him by using patience, anger, threats, praise, ignoring, and shaming. Nothing seemed to work. The adults were sure he had some kind of genetic, inherited problem—maybe one of those chemical imbalances the news was always talking about. Maybe he was depressed and needed to be put on antidepressants. Or maybe he had an obsessive-compulsive disorder. (What teen doesn't to one degree or another?) The family scheduled a visit to a local therapist.

Everyone was dealing with Kevin based on their perceptions of him, but no one thought to find out about Kevin's perceptions—how he thought and how he felt. There were many reasons that no one thought about Kevin's feelings: adults hardly ever think that children have different perceptions than they do; the conventional wisdom says that problems are genetic or inherited and are some sort of disease; most people don't have a true understanding of how personality is really formed. Fortunately for Kevin, the family had signed up with a therapist who explained problems in a way that ended up making a lot of sense to everyone and that helped Kevin immensely.

The therapist explained that genetics might be accounting for .00000001 percent of the problem. The discipline style of the parents and teachers also had a part. However, the main thing that was going on wasn't a disease or a chemical imbalance, didn't need drugs, and had more to do with how Kevin *saw* himself than with anything else. To help Kevin discover his perceptions of himself (which were formed at a subconscious level), the therapist asked Kevin to share some memories from his childhood.

Kevin related that when he was about four years old, he was playing with his sister, who was about ten at the time, and one of the kids in the neighborhood. The neighbor kid put some cleaning solution in a glass and tried to get Kevin to drink it. Kevin's sister knew the solution was poisonous and could hurt him, so she screamed and knocked the glass out of the kid's hand.

The therapist asked Kevin for a feeling word to describe how he felt when this happened and he replied, "Angry." Surprised, the therapist asked him why he was angry that his sister tried to save his life. Kevin responded that nothing ever happened to the kid who tried to kill him, so he decided (at age four) that nobody really cared about him and that he would be better off dead. This perception became the underlying theme in Kevin's life, motivating most of his behavior. Kevin didn't consciously know that this perception was driving his behavior, but the memory work helped surface a very powerful force that Kevin had created and that was now operating in the background of his relationships.

It is important to understand that when dealing with human behavior, the "truth" or commonsense logic of a situation does not matter. Rather, as with Kevin, all behavior is motivated by each individual's *perception* of what is true.

Adults often make the mistake of dealing exclusively with the behavior of teens and not with the underlying beliefs that inspire that behavior. Or worse yet, adults look for a cause—a disease that is causing the problem—and then they treat the so-called disease with a drug. Prescribing drugs does not make anything better; instead, it often makes the situation worse. The teen isn't really getting any help, so whatever feelings the teen has just get bigger. In addition, drugs not only make the situation worse, they also often have side effects. Current research indicates that there are many serious problems for many people who use drugs. When people take pills to control behavior, often their thinking becomes more distorted, their feelings become more extreme or numb, and their behaviors become more dangerous. Mix these reactions with adolescent hormones or drugs that the teen might be secretly using, and the result is a volatile situation just waiting to explode into some kind of personal or public tragedy.

> Adults often make the mistake of dealing exclusively with the behavior of teens and not with the underlying beliefs that inspire that behavior. Or worse yet, adults look for a cause—a disease that is causing the problem—and then they treat the so-called disease with a drug.

You may think our approach is over simplistic, but we are empirical researchers who look for solutions that work in real life and that make a difference in a positive way. Kevin's therapist, also an empirical scientist, wanted to find an approach that would help Kevin really know he was accepted and loved, encourage him to feel better, and show him ways he could change his behavior. Out of a myriad of possibilities, what worked especially well was asking Kevin what kind of animal he would like to be and why. He said, "I wish I were a dog, because everybody would like having me around and they'd pet me and play with me."

Surprisingly, this information had an immediate positive effect on Kevin's parents. Instead of feeling afraid of, angered at, challenged by, or disgusted with him, they were able to tap into his feelings of isolation, hurt, and abandonment—feelings that most of the 31 million children between the ages of 12 and 19 feel on a regular basis, according to a May 10, 1999 article in *Newsweek*. Kevin's parents began to cuddle him (yes, even though he was thirteen, Kevin still liked being hugged), to spend fun time with him, and to listen to his complaints of injustice. They didn't argue or try to change his mind. Although this certainly wasn't the end of the story, it was an important beginning for Kevin and his parents.

A Little Bit of Psychology Can Go a Long Way

ADLERIAN THERAPISTS USE early memories and other techniques to help them understand the private logic of their clients.[1] Their focus is on understanding the perceptions, beliefs, private logic, or separate reality that inspires the behavior or world view of each individual. As parents, you don't have to be trained psychologists, but it does help to know how to tap into the separate realities of your teens. In fact, without this information, all you have are assumptions about why your teens do what they do. When you act on those assumptions, they may have nothing to do with why your teens behave the way they do. Our goal in this chapter is to help you see that a little bit of psychological understanding can go a long way to help you parent your teens.

The following is another example of how understanding private logic helped parents deal more effectively with their teens.

Two Different Realities

Thirteen-year-old Monica decided to run away from home because all her friends had; she wanted to see what it was like. To do this, she created an elaborate plan, telling her parents: "I've never had a room of my own, and I've al-

---

1. The authors are students of the psychology of Alfred Adler and Rudolf Dreikurs. Alfred Adler and Rudolf Dreikurs were the fathers of modern psychology. Adler (1870–1937) had radically different thinking about human nature and motivation than his contemporaries. He and his student, Rudolf Dreikurs, embraced concepts of social equality, mutual respect, encouragement, holism, and human potential. They engineered ideas and techniques that are now familiar to practitioners everywhere, although they are rarely credited.

ways wondered what it would be like. I've talked with my teacher and the school counselor, and they thought it would be a good idea for me to experiment. What I would like to do is take some food and go into my room and close the door. I'd like my sister to spend time somewhere else and sleep somewhere else, too. Then, in the morning, I'll come out for breakfast, and I'll have had a chance to see what it's like to have my own room."

Often, parents wonder why teens concoct such outlandish tales, but imagine how it would sound if this teen had told the truth. The truth would have been the end of her experiment. Her parents, being encouraging, kind, and understanding, agreed to her plan. They arranged that no one disturb her, and off Monica went to her room with enough food to last a week.

At around 10:00 P.M., Mom noticed that Monica hadn't come out of her room even to go to the bathroom. Mom knocked on the door and got no answer. When she tried to open the door, she found it had been barricaded. Her daughter was gone!

When Mom called a friend of Monica's and found out what the girls were really doing, she panicked. "My daughter could be picked up, kidnapped, raped, even murdered." (Have you ever noticed how teens' behavior can invite feelings you didn't know you had in intensities you've probably never experienced before?) Monica had a completely different set of perceptions. All her friends had decided to try staying out all night, and she wanted to be cool and part of the group. Her dilemma was how to do what she wanted without hurting or upsetting her parents.

By the time Monica crawled back in through her window at 2:00 A.M, her mother, worried sick, said, "I'm so glad you're home! I'm so glad you're *alive!* I thought for sure you'd be dead by now."

Her daughter looked at her in complete disbelief and said, "Why? All we did was go to the school, but nobody was there. Usually kids go around stealing signs, T-P-ing houses, or throwing eggs, but we didn't feel like doing any of that. We couldn't find any other kids, so we walked to the doughnut shop. Then we went back to the school, but there still wasn't anyone there. We got bored and came home. We knew we were perfectly safe." In her mind, Monica had completed the experiment quite successfully and had learned something for herself.

At that point, Monica's mother could have lectured her daughter and then punished her—and Monica would gain nothing but resentment. Instead, Mom said, "Well, I can understand this was important to you. I just have to say—I don't even know what to say! I'm so upset I can't even speak." Monica's mom went into her bedroom and closed the door. She wasn't trying to teach her daughter a lesson or to punish her; she simply didn't know what to say, so she left. Later, Monica knocked on her mother's door and asked to come in to talk. Monica said, "I'm so sorry. I didn't mean to cause you any pain. I really didn't want to hurt you."

In this instance, both mother and daughter glimpsed the separate reality of the other. The mother realized that her daughter had only been thinking about being like her friends and having an adventure; not about intentionally hurting her mother. Monica saw that by "running away," she had really worried her mother—even though she had no intention of doing so. We often see our teens' behavior in terms of a power struggle or revenge, when in reality it has nothing to do with us. Understanding their private logic can help us quit taking everything personally.

> We often see our teens' behavior in terms of a power struggle or revenge, when in reality it has nothing to do with us. Understanding their private logic can help us quit taking everything personally.

Parents, Take Heart!

WHEN WE WORK with teens in the counseling office, we often ask them for four or five adjectives to describe their parents. Their choices are usually incredibly encouraging. Parents who have been convinced that their teens hate them hear themselves described as nice, friendly, helpful, and fair, even though their teens have been fighting with them morning, noon, and night. One stepparent, upon hearing her stepson list her as part of the family, said, "Oops, I don't think your supposed to put *me* in." He said, "Why not? *You're* part of the family." Although she thought of him that way, she had no idea he felt the same about her.

Thoughts, Feelings, and Actions

UNCONSCIOUS THOUGHTS DRIVE actions by creating feelings that provide the fuel for movement. The following, from interviews with a group of teens, show teens' separate realities and resulting feelings and actions of those realities.

Sixteen-Year-Old Boy

Event: Parents' sudden divorce

Teen's Decision or Thought: My parents aren't the perfect people I thought they were. I had them on a pedestal, and they both disappointed me. I can't count on them now. I can only count on myself.

Teen's Feelings: Anger, betrayal, loss, fear

Teen's Behavior: To stop living like a beer-drinking airhead and to take charge of his life

Thirteen-Year-Old Girl

Event: Parents' attempt to set up a financial reward system for good grades to motivate daughter to improve on D's and F's

Teen's Decision or Thought: All my parents care about is whether I go to college. They don't like me unless I'm how they want me to be. They don't even know or care about the things that are important to me.

Teen's Feelings: Anger, hurt

Teen's Behavior: To get revenge on parents by running away or by doing other things to hurt them, including hurting herself by cutting into her arms with a knife

Fifteen-Year-Old Boy

Event: Childhood friend's death from illness

Teen's Decision or Thought: I'll never make another friend because I don't ever want to feel this kind of pain again.

Teen's Feelings: Grief, despair, hopelessness

Teen's Behavior: When his family moved to a new community shortly after the death of his friend, he decided the only way to his commitment to himself was not to make any new friends and to flunk out of school.

Thirteen-Year-Old Girl

Event: Parents' constant fighting and cold war

Teen's Decision or Thought: My parents are probably going to get a divorce because they're so mean to one another. If they do divorce, they'll probably split up the family, and one parent will take me and the other will keep my brother. They'll probably move far away from each other, and I'll never get to see my brother again.

Teen's Feelings: Hurt, fear

Teen's Behavior: Noticing that her brother could make his mother really angry by refusing to do chores, she decided to copy him so her mother would let both kids live with their father. That way, at least she wouldn't be separated from her brother. Therefore, she refused to do any of the chores she had agreed to do.

Fourteen-Year-Old Girl

Event: Attempt by brother-in-law to molest her

Teen's Decision or Thought: My brother did this to me when I was little. This must be how I have to be to get boys to love me. This must be how boys know you love them and how you show them they are important members of the family.

Teen's Feelings: Shame, guilt, fear

Teen's Behavior: In order not to lose the "close family" she always wanted, she let her brother-in-law molest her and kept it a secret.

Behavior always makes sense when you understand your teen's perceptions and private logic. For this reason, it was impossible to work effectively with these teens before understanding the beliefs and feelings motivating their behavior.

Understanding how your teens really think and feel takes a nonjudgmental attitude and the ability to keep your own perceptions separate. Teenagers place a tremendous amount of trust in the people to whom they confide their private thoughts and feelings. Sometimes the help of a therapist is the only way to get at a teen's innermost beliefs. But whoever elicits a teen's confidence must treat it with the utmost respect and seriousness; otherwise the teens will feel betrayed as a result of sharing their private world.

> Behavior always makes sense when you understand your teen's perceptions and private logic.

The Family Pie

THE PRIMARY GOAL of every human being is to find belonging and significance. Children in a family use their own private logic to decide what they need to do to achieve this goal. When you were growing up, your personality was most influenced by the sibling you saw as your chief competitor—although you didn't consciously realize this.[2] Children seem to believe that only one sibling can be special in a certain way; if one sibling has already decided to find belonging and significance by being the "good" child, another

---

2. For information on the importance of birth order, see chapter 3 in *Positive Discipline* by Jane Nelsen or chapter 4 in *Do-It-Yourself Therapy: How to Think, Feel and Act Like a New Person in Just 8 Weeks* by Lynn Lott, Riki Intner, and Barbara Mendenhall.

may decide to be the "social" child, the "athletic" child, the "shy" child, or the "rebel." We call these choices "slices of the family pie."

The family pie is composed of the children in the family, but not the parents. If a child is an only child, he or she gets the whole family pie, but may compare him- or herself with the same-sex parent, a kid in the neighborhood, a cousin, or a sibling who has died. When asked who their chief competitor was, most only children are quick to name a specific person.

Many oldest children feel they must always be first; they become competitive overachievers. Second children often become the "we try harder" kids, peacemakers, or the rebels. The youngest become the adorable ones, used to having things done for them; they often develop skills for manipulating others to take care of them. Other youngest children become competitive, wanting everything their older siblings have; often these youngest feel they aren't good enough or smart enough because they can't do what the big kids can do. Only children like to be special and often compare themselves with adults; sometimes this leads to feelings of inadequacy, because everyone else seems more capable than they are.

Many of the problems that parents deal with during their children's teen years have their origin in the family pie. You can better understand the private logic of your teenagers when you know what slice of the family pie they have chosen.

The No-Problem Kid

Two parents came to a therapist because one of their children constantly created problems, driving the mother crazy. At each session, the therapist asked if anyone had anything he or she wanted help with. The eldest boy consistently stated that he didn't have any problems; he never lost the opportunity to point out that his sister was the problem child in their family. The slice of the family pie he had chosen was to be perfect. He was trying to find his way of being special and different in the family by "having no problems." Convinced that if he revealed a problem, it would make him the "bad, sick" boy, he found it hard to get help with anything. He was also trapped in the cycle of trying to be perfect at all times. If he couldn't be perfect all the time, at the least he would find a way to show everyone how imperfect his sister was.

The Good Kid/Bad Kid Scenario

In many families, one of the children has the label (or slice of the family pie) of being "good" and another "bad." In one family, the oldest boy played out the role of the bad kid. His teenage individuation process was painful and rebellious. His younger, "good-kid" sibling did all her rebelling behind her parents' backs so she could keep her "good" place in the family pie.

Mom's Favorite/Dad's Favorite

In another family, the pie was divided into Mom's favorite and Dad's favorite. When the family split up, the children went to live with the parent who they thought liked them best and then worked overtime—unconsciously, of course—to point out their sibling's negative qualities. This was their insurance policy on their special place in the family.

The Mistaken Goals

AS WE HAVE said before, the primary goals of every person are to belong and to feel significant. Separate realities (perceptions) can motivate teens (or anyone else) to choose ways to achieve belonging and significance that are not in their best interests. In fact, the behaviors they choose often result in attaining the opposite of what they really want. Negative self-perceptions often lead children to negative activities, especially when children mistakenly believe that the only way to find belonging and significance is through what Rudolf Dreikurs called the mistaken goals. Whenever kids feel discouraged or insecure, they choose a mistaken goal—a goal that never takes them where they want to go—as a vehicle to belonging and significance. Instead of achieving their goal, they find alienation from those closest to them, as well as deeper discouragement. Their mistaken goal becomes a vicious cycle: the more discouraged they become, the more they escalate their efforts through the mistaken goal.

> Becoming aware of mistaken goals can help you understand your teens, improve your relationship with them, and help them see options for their behavior.

Behind every mistaken goal is a mistaken private logic. When you deal with your teen's behavior without understanding and addressing the underlying beliefs, you will be frustrated in your efforts to effect change. Becoming aware of mistaken goals can help you understand your teens, improve your relationship with them, and help them see options for their behavior. There are four mistaken goals, each with a corresponding mistaken belief.

Mistaken Goals and Their Underlying Beliefs

1. *Undue Attention:* "I am significant when you notice me and treat me special."

   Everyone wants recognition and attention. The problem occurs when attention and recognition are sought through behaviors that are annoying ("Look at me, look at me") instead of respectful ("I feel special when I am making a contribution or helping others feel special"). Another key to healthy recognition is when teens think, "It is nice to be recognized, but it isn't mandatory."

2. *Misguided Power:* "I am significant when I do what I want—or at least don't do what you want."

   Everyone wants power and will use their power, either in contributing ways or in destructive ways. When parents try to control teens, teens are likely to respond by using their power in rebellious ways. What teens need are guidance and the skills to learn how to use their power in constructive ways.

3. *Revenge:* "I feel hurt when you treat me as though I am insignificant. I believe my only choice is to hurt you back."

   When teens feel hurt or believe that things are unfair, they often strike back with hurtful behavior. Then parents feel hurt and strike back, which hurts their teens. Thus, a revenge cycle is created. It is the adult's responsibility to understand what is happening and to break the cycle. The "T-shirts" described on page 273 will help you do this.

4. *Assumed inadequacy:* "I feel like giving up because I don't know what to do. I don't feel significant at all."

   It would be very rare to find a teen who truly is inadequate. However, teens can become so discouraged that they believe and act as though they are. They give up instead of trying, or they look for perfection in their behavior and beings. When they find flaws (which every human has), they decide they are worthless and stop trying. Telling teens that they are not inadequate does not help. Instead, parents need to find ways to help teens change their perceptions of inadequacy. All of the strategies proposed in this book are designed to help teens feel capable, competent, and confident. More ideas follow.

> Understanding mistaken goals can help you see that whatever your teens do, they do because it makes sense to them.

Understanding mistaken goals can help you see that whatever your teens do, they do because it makes sense to them. Just because you aren't aware of their logic doesn't mean it isn't there. Except in the sense of the mistaken goal of revenge, when your teens might be trying to even the score or hurt you because you have hurt them, your teens aren't doing things to you or against you. Even with the mistaken goal of revenge, your teens may feel hurt by others and take their feelings out on you.

It takes two to fuel mistaken-goal behavior. We have never seen a power-drunk teen without a power-drunk adult close by. If your teen hurts you, then he or she probably feels hurt by you. Awareness of mistaken goals is the first step toward change. The second step is to change your behavior in a positive way. But more about this later in the chapter.

Identifying a Mistaken Goal

The easiest way to understand which mistaken goal your teen operates from is to tap into your own feelings. If you're irritated, annoyed, feeling sorry for your child, worried, or exhausted from giving undue attention or special service, the teen's goal is probably a need for undue recognition. Feelings of anger, challenge, or defeat let you know the mistaken goal is misguided power. If you are hurt, disgusted, or disbelieving, the mistaken goal is probably revenge. And, finally, if you feel a sense of despair and hopelessness and think nothing will ever change, your teen's mistaken goal is assumed inadequacy (your child assumes his or her skills are inadequate or nonexistent).

You can find detailed information about mistaken goals in any of the Positive Discipline books or in *Do-It-Yourself Therapy*. What we'd like to offer here is a very simple way to start using this information to help you change your behavior with your teens in a positive way, with the possibility of inviting growth and healing. The method was inspired by one of our colleagues[3] who first came up with the concept.

Look at the following chart and find the feelings in the "If You Feel" column that most closely resemble how you feel when your teen's behavior is problematic for you. Now look at the corresponding information in the "Picture Your Teen Wearing a T-Shirt That Says." Ask yourself what you would do if you pictured your teen wearing that T-shirt. Put what you would do into practice. We bet your reaction is something different from what your first instincts would be without benefit of the chart.

The T-Shirt Chart

If You Feel:	Picture Your Teen Wearing a T-Shirt That Says:	What Would You Do?
Irritated Annoyed Sorry for Worried Exhausted	Notice me Involve me	
Angry Challenged Defeated	Let me help Give me choices	
Hurt Disgusted Disbelieving	Help me I'm hurting	
Despairing Hopeless	Believe in me Don't give up on me	

---

3. *Positive Discipline for Preschoolers* and the facilitator's supplement for *Positive Discipline for Preschoolers* contain an activity called "Hat Messages," created by Roslyn Duffy, a Seattle parent educator and family therapist and coauthor of *Positive Discipline for Preschoolers*.

Four Parents Use Their Understanding of Mistaken Goals to Reverse Their Teens' Discouragement

Undue Attention

As a single parent, Rachel was exhausted; she felt she could never do enough for her two children. One was constantly in trouble, and the other was constantly demanding special help and time to talk about her feelings. No matter how much time she put in, nothing changed. Rachel was convinced that the problems were caused by her working outside the home and by the divorce. She looked up her feelings in the T-Shirt Chart. When she pictured her teens wearing T-shirts that said, "Notice me. Involve me," she thought, "Well, what's new about that?" After pondering the information further, she realized that she spent a great deal of her time trying to escape her children and that when she did notice them, it was with irritation and impatience in her voice. She realized that perhaps her two children were keeping her busy as a way of being assured that she loved them. She could see that the competition between them to be her favorite was fierce and destructive.

One of Rachel's first improvements was to stop siding with her youngest. She decided to listen carefully and without impatience. Then she assured the youngest that the two siblings could work it out together, without her help, or that they could put the problem on the family meeting agenda so they could all work together on a solution after a cooling-off period. Rachel expressed her love for her youngest and planned special time for doing things they both enjoyed. With her older daughter, Rachel found ways to listen to her when her younger sister wasn't around. Mother and daughter found that they really enjoyed each other's company. With Rachel's new attitude, her two children were getting attention, but in much more positive, productive ways. And Rachel was enjoying their company more.

Another improvement was Rachel's refusal to get involved in the fights between her two children, even when the fights got physical. This was very frightening at first, because the older girl was quite a bit larger than the younger. At one point, out of desperation and fear for the safety of her younger daughter, Rachel decided that the two girls couldn't be left alone together. She then decided what she would do to avoid this situation (an excellent kind and firm parenting skill). Every time she went somewhere, one of her daughters had to go with her. Of course, this soon wore thin, and the children decided they could stay home together, even when their mother wasn't around. Over time, they fought less and less.

Misguided Power

Gary, a father of a teenaged girl, said, "I can see that my issues with my daughter involve misguided power, because I'm always feeling angry, challenged, and overpowered. I can't open my mouth without her walking away or yelling at me. I don't feel I have a chance."

> One day, I decided that I'd been pushed around long enough. The next time my daughter became angry, yelling hysterically and throwing things, I didn't wimp out. In the past when she did that, I've said, "You've got to get out of here." If she refused to leave, I'd lock myself in the den, go to my room, or get in the car and drive away. But by doing that I realized I was treating her like an out-of-control criminal. This time, I sat in the chair and said, "Honey, you're out of control. You're really angry. I want to hear everything you're angry about, but I can't hear you when you scream at me and throw things. Sit down and tell me. I'll listen to every single thing you have to say." She kept screaming and throwing things. Again I said, "Honey, I'm here. I care about you. I want to hear what you have to say. It's obvious that you're angry. It's okay that you're angry. But I can't hear anything when you scream at me."
>
> Finally, she stood still and began talking. Two minutes later, she sat down and we talked for more than half an hour.
>
> Later, I realized that I'd switched from the power struggle to wanting to find out what was going on for her. It was a switch, on my part, from blame and defense to support and interest.

In a similar situation, Dirk was in a serious power struggle with his mother over school grades. Even though his poor school performance was jeopardizing his participation in sports, he would neither study nor do any homework. Although he didn't really want to fail in school, it was more important to him to show his mother that she couldn't make him do the things she thought were important. When he did things that were important to him, his mother would step in and take over. Dirk would then go on total shutdown, copying his father's passive-aggressive method of dealing with anger and frustration.

Luckily, with help from a friend and his parents, Dirk was able to turn his life around. He became an important athlete at his school and raised his grades from F's to B's. What caused these dramatic changes? First, his parents began to validate his feelings by saying, "We can tell you're angry, and you have a right to be. What we're doing is inappropriate because you aren't involved in deciding what to do and you have no choices." (His parents had seen the T-shirt message, "Let me help. Give me choices," and it made a lot of sense.) His parents continued, "We'd like to get your help in creating a way to deal with school and your input in what you think would work best. We're willing to try out a new plan for awhile to see if we can't reverse this trend."

Revenge

Cherylyn was in terrible pain because her parents refused to acknowledge who she really was. Instead, they focused on who they wanted her to be. They wanted so desperately for her to be an athlete that they were willing to bribe her to get her to comply. They had good intentions: they honestly believed that if she were successful in a sport it would raise her self-confidence, which would be to her greater good and happiness. In reality, Cherylyn—who wanted to be a rock star—would have felt better about herself if she felt validated for who she was and who she wanted to be.

Cherylyn felt that her parents didn't love her for herself. They never bothered to find out what really interested her and what she wanted to do with her life. Their lack of interest hurt Cherylyn so badly that she became caught in a revenge cycle, wanting her folks to hurt as much as she did.

Fortunately, Cherylyn's parents became aware—by tuning into their own hurt feelings—that Cherylyn's mistaken goal was revenge. They were able to picture their daughter wearing the "Help me. I'm hurting" T-shirt and put their plans for her aside while showing genuine interest in hers. By supportively listening to their daughter, they were able to break the revenge cycle and promote her feelings of self-worth.

When teens get into a revenge cycle, they usually hurt themselves in the process of trying to hurt their parents. Some will even destroy their lives through drug abuse or suicide just to get even. Many parents have no idea how upset their children are, because the teens do not—or cannot—tell their parents. Instead the teens employ destructive behavior.

It doesn't do any good to tell teens that they are in a revenge cycle and are hurting themselves in the process. What helps is to find out *why* they are in pain by showing loving interest and support, so that they can reveal their true feelings.

> When teens get into a revenge cycle, they usually hurt themselves in the process of trying to hurt their parents.

Assumed Inadequacy

Adam was feeling depressed and kept telling his parents how unhappy he was because he didn't have a girlfriend. He was the only kid in his circle of friends who hadn't invited someone to homecoming. No matter what his parents said to help cheer him up or empathize with him, Adam insisted that no matter what he did, no girl would ever go out with him. Adam's folks were so concerned about him that they suggested he talk to the family counselor.

When Adam came in to share his story, the counselor realized that Adam had a mistaken idea that no matter what he did, he would fail. Therefore he believed it was better not to try at all. Adam was convinced that girls didn't like him because he was shy. He believed that if he even attempted to talk to a girl, she would be bored and tell all her friends what a jerk he was. When the counselor asked where he got this idea, Adam mentioned that he had overheard some of the girls at school talking about a guy who had called them the night before. The girls laughed and shared stories of how they would get rid of this guy if he called any of them. Adam knew he didn't want to make a fool of himself like this guy.

When teens are that discouraged, the job of the parent or counselor is to help them get their courage back. By telling teens who have the mistaken goal of assumed inadequacy, "I have faith in you," "I won't give up on you," and "Here's a small step you could take if you like," adults help them work through the issue.

Adam's counselor asked him if he would be willing to look at the situation another way. Adam agreed. The counselor then asked Adam if he had ever purchased any clothing for himself? With a puzzled look he replied that he had just purchased a new ski jacket. "Did you just grab the first jacket you saw on the rack?" asked the counselor.

Adam said, "Of course not! I must have tried on about twenty to thirty jackets before I found the right one."

"Well, Adam," said the counselor, "do you think picking a girl to go to homecoming should be any easier?"

"I never thought of it that way," said Adam. "But what if I call someone and she tells her friends what a jerk I am?"

"You could tell yourself how grateful you are that a girl that rude decided not to go out with you."

Adam thought about all this and said, "It makes a lot of sense, but I still feel scared to talk to a girl. What if I can't think of anything to say?"

Adam and the counselor role-played calling girls, with different reactions to Adam's introduction. Adam realized that if a girl answered the phone with a little bit of enthusiasm, he would find it easier to think of things to talk about. If a girl was quiet and uncomfortable, Adam realized she might not be the right person for him to spend his first date with.

Adam was almost ready to go home and call someone, but he got cold feet one more time. The counselor noticed how scared he was and asked Adam if he had ever pushed through his fear anywhere in his life. Adam thought for a few minutes and then replied, "I used to be afraid to ski down really steep hills that had moguls on them, but now I love to."

"How did you manage to overcome your fear?"

"I stood at the top of the hill with my knees shaking and said to myself, 'Go for it!,' and I did. It was wonderful."

"Well, Adam," said the counselor, "go for it!"

Adam grinned.

Adam was able to take steps toward correcting his perception of inadequacy because no one said to him, "It's silly to feel that way." Instead his parents listened well enough to know he needed help. His counselor listened, empathized, and explored the basis for his perception. She then helped him work on skills, based on his own experiences with success, to help him overcome his fears.

Once you understand the mistaken goal, you'll find there are many ways to encourage your teen and improve a situation. Then you can actively attempt to make things better, rather than merely reacting to your child's behavior.

This chapter introduced several tools for helping you understand your teen's perceptions. Even if you don't feel completely comfortable using these tools, it's helpful to know that they exist and that there are reasons, not always easily understood, why teenagers behave the way they do. The purpose of this chapter is not to turn you into amateur therapists. However, introducing some of the tools of the therapist provides you with an opportunity to widen your perspective and look a little deeper into your teens' behaviors. This in turn helps you be less judgmental, less reactive, and more able to have faith in the growth process.

> Remember that the perceptions teens have and the decisions they make about their experiences color their pictures of themselves and help explain some of their behavior.

Remember that the perceptions teens have and the decisions they make about their experiences color their pictures of themselves and help explain some of their behavior. It's also helpful to remember that your teen's reality may be different from your own. In addition, keep in mind that teenagers have not yet become adults—their current values, which many of you find disturbing, are not necessarily those they will hold as grown-ups.

KIND AND FIRM PARENTING TOOLS TO REMEMBER

1. Remind yourself that your teen's behavior is more a result of unconscious perceptions than of anything else. Stop looking for causes and diseases and start looking for your teen's separate reality.

2. Imagine how your teen would describe you to a friend. Talk with your teens to find out if how you think they see you is really how they see you. You might be surprised at how encouraged you could feel by their answers.

3. Remind yourself that you *are* doing something when you use the methods described in this chapter. You don't have to punish or control to be effective at reversing extremely negative patterns with your teen.

4. You can never be sure of what your teens really think about anything unless you ask them and then listen very carefully. Assuming they think like you do is a very faulty, and even potentially dangerous, assumption.

5. Your teens have opinions about themselves based on their place in the family pie. Reviewing the information about birth order can be extremely helpful to you for understanding your teens better.

6. All behavior has a purpose, even if your child (and you) aren't aware of what the purpose is. When you notice your feelings, you get valuable information about what the purpose of your teen's behavior might be.

7. Instead of reacting to behavior, use the T-Shirt Chart for inspiration.

Practical Application Activity

BREAKING THE MISTAKEN GOAL CYCLE
Find out how you might be part of the problem.

1. Talk with an objective friend or therapist.

2. Write in a journal. You often gain insight when you review in writing what actually has happened between you and your teen.

3. Ask your teen. Let your teenager know you are not a mind reader. Admit that you might not have been a good listener in the past, but you want to listen now. You may suggest that you contributed to the problem. (Even little kids, when told "I think I did something to hurt your feelings," can tell you what you did.)

4. Look at the T-Shirt Chart for ideas and inspiration.

Make some guesses out loud to your teen about what you are thinking might be going on. If your guess is correct, you'll hit a responsive chord; your child will feel understood and will acknowledge the accurateness of the guess. On the other hand, it's okay if your guess is not correct. Your aim is not to be right but to get information. If you're wrong, you've still learned something.

When you understand your teen's perception, validate him or her. Let your child know that you can see how he or she might have come to that conclusion. Then, plan together to make changes that are supportive of both of you.

MY PLAN FOR THE WEEK

This week I will focus on

_____

_____

I will work on changing my attitude by thinking

_____

_____

_____

I will change my behavior by doing

_____

_____

_____

13

Are Your Own Unresolved Teen Issues Getting in Your Way?

Raising a teenager brings up a lot of unresolved issues from your own adolescence. Anything that didn't get worked out when you were a teen still lurks in the shadows of your unconscious, waiting for another chance. Even though these issues are below the surface, they influence how you parent your teen. Not only does the old baggage you carry around with you from your teen years get in the way of living a full, rich life, but also it often creates stumbling blocks when dealing with your teens.

Going through your teen's adolescence gives you another chance to work through some of these issues. In doing so, you will experience countless benefits. You'll be a more effective parent, have more compassion, understand your teen better, heal the teen within you, and feel better.

If you think about the issues your teens are dealing with, you won't be far from identifying the unresolved issues you still may need to work out for yourself: power, self-image, body image, intimate

> If you think about the issues your teens are dealing with, you won't be far from identifying the unresolved issues you still may need to work out for yourself.

relationships, friendships, relationships with your parents, and independence. Consider the following examples and see if you can relate to any of them.

A Vicious Cycle Repeats Itself

AS A YOUNG MAN, Preston wanted to please his parents, but to do so meant he had to give up what was important to him. He tried, but soon found that to be impossible. What seemed to work better was to do what he wanted in secret and lie to his parents. His plan worked well until he came to his parents announcing that he planned to marry a girl "from the wrong side of the tracks." His parents were hysterical and told Preston that he would be disowned if he didn't give up the girl immediately. Preston gave up the girl, married someone suitable to his family and buried the pain deep inside.

When Preston's son became a teenager and started dating, Preston was so determined not to make his son suffer by being controlling and telling him what to do, that he went to the other extreme. He had such a hands-off attitude, his son thought he didn't even care about him. Feeling unloved, his son looked for love in all the wrong places, got a girl pregnant and then found himself in the same position as his father. He wanted to do the right thing by marrying her, even though he didn't love her, thus perpetuating the cycle. As Preston watched his son struggle and suffer, he was aware of how important it was to take another look at his unresolved issues so that he could help his son.

His first step was to see a therapist who helped him deal with his old issues. Next he told his son, "I can see that I have acted in ways that could give you the impression that I didn't care. I made a mistake. I thought I was just giving you lots of freedom to make your own decisions. I still have faith in you to do that, and I want to be here for you if there is anything you want to talk about. I can be a good sounding board because I really do love you."

It is interesting that kids often want the opposite of what they get. When parents give too much advice, kids wish their parents would leave them alone. When parents leave them alone, they wish they had a parent who cared enough to get involved. So now you know: Parenting is like a high-wire balancing act that is successful when you can let your teens know you care without taking over their lives.

A Poor Self-Image Gets in the Way of Parenting a Teen

FRANK SHARED THE following with his friend Neil as they rode together to their weekly men's group. "Whenever I schedule an activity with Nate, he backs out at the last minute. The chance of us doing a planned activity together is about 2 percent. I feel sad because I don't get to spend the time with him, and I feel angry because he says yes but acts no. Then I get mad at myself because I say, 'No problem. We can try again another time,' even though I really want to give him a piece of my mind."

"What does Nate say when you tell him it's okay?" Neil asked.

"He says, 'I'm really sorry, but something else came up and I just can't keep our date.'"

"Why do you let him get away with that when it really bothers you? I thought we were working on being more honest in our relationships," Neil countered.

"You're right, Neil," Frank responded, "but I feel torn because I think it's my job to be there for my son."

Later at the men's group Frank shared some information about when he was a teen. In his senior year, he didn't have a date for the prom. He finally asked a friend if he could get him a date. He felt embarrassed and inadequate, but he couldn't bear missing his high school prom. One of the group members asked if his folks knew how he felt. Frank laughed and said, "There were no adults involved. I didn't share anything with the adults, and I never thought of doing that. My mother was my only parent, and we didn't have that kind of relationship. I would have been embarrassed for her to find out I wasn't capable of attracting female companionship. I felt unloved and unattractive."

"Isn't feeling unloved a theme running through your whole life?" Neil asked. "I wonder how you'd handle the situation you were telling me about with your son if you didn't feel that way."

"That's easy," Frank said. "I'd confront my son and tell him that if we're going to schedule something, let's do it; and that if it falls through after we've planned it, I'm going to be upset. I guess I'm still worrying about being loved, so I'm not honest with my son for fear of him disliking me. I'll bet Nate would be more respectful if I had the courage to tell him what was really going on inside me. He probably doesn't even think of talking to me when he changes his plans, because he doesn't think it's a problem for me. How could he, when I always say, 'No problem'?"

How Your Fears Can Reveal Unresolved Issues

WHAT ARE YOUR fears? How many of your parenting methods are based on fear—fear of what the neighbors will think, fear that your kids will ruin their lives with their choices, fear that you aren't being a good enough parent?

A mother in one of our classes decided to explore her fears to find out what some of her unresolved issues were. She began by using the activity found at the end of this chapter in the activity section. The problem she described with her teenage son was that she wanted her son to be home more, saying that she missed him even though he wasn't very pleasant when he was there.

> How many of your parenting methods are based on fear—fear of what the neighbors will think, fear that your kids will ruin their lives with their choices, fear that you aren't being a good enough parent?

"Maybe I want him home so he can do his chores. I feel used when he wants to receive but not to give. And I'm afraid he won't be a responsible person and won't be happy later if he doesn't show responsibility now. Mostly, I'm afraid I'm not being a good mother if he doesn't do his chores.

"First, I need to take care of my issues about being a good enough mother. What would happen if I accepted that I'm good enough, just by being who I am, and worked on feeling better about who I am? The trouble is, I can't convince myself I'm a good mother if my son isn't responsible and considerate."

As she continued with the activity, she revealed that she was raised in a strict religious home where all behavior was gauged by what the church and the neighbors would think. As a teen, she wasn't allowed to do many activities considered by most to be normal for a developing girl, including dating, because the church forbade them. When it came to dating, she was rebellious and sneaky. Her need to individuate and to honor her biological clock was stronger than her need to comply with the church.

The guilt, shame, and fear she felt at getting caught are the very issues that get in her way today when parenting her teenage son, especially because he is doing things society disapproves of out in the open. She, at least, tried to hide her rebellion.

"I can't stop worrying about my son's drinking and smoking and stealing. Not only am I worried about how it will affect his life, but also I'm worried about what people will say about me. And I'm worried that he'll want me to support him when he should be supporting himself. I'm afraid that some of his habits might cause him unhappiness later in life—and that it will be my fault. So, what can I do about all my worries?"

With help from her parenting group and with insights gained from the activity, Mom was able to get some new perspectives on the situation. She came up with the following alternatives to her previous behavior:

1. "I can offer my son information about smoking and drinking. I can become a source of information for him. I will first ask if he would be interested to hear what I have to say so it doesn't sound like a lecture. If he doesn't want to hear it from me, I'll find a friend or a mentor he will be willing to listen to."

2. "I can quit providing him with unnecessary material things. I need to decide what I'm willing to provide—what makes sense to me—that I can give willingly, without any resentment or strings. I can prepare myself for the temper tantrums that will probably come when I quit indulging him—because I've been the biggest perpetrator of the belief that he should be indulged. I can help him plan to get things he wants—when he wants my help."

3. "I can realize that the habits that will cause him unhappiness are no worse than the habits that have caused me unhappiness; and that I can't rob him of the opportunity to learn what he needs to learn in this life. I've been a perfectionist, feared rejection, had an inordinate need to please, feared what others would think, been a workaholic, been judgmental, had unrealistic expectations, held grudges for supposed wrongs to myself and others, and felt

> It can be more difficult to eliminate ineffective teen behaviors when you don't have an understanding of your own unresolved issues and how they are the basis of your ineffective behaviors.

dissatisfied because I hadn't accomplished all that I felt I should. What right do I have to worry about his habits when I still have so many of my own?"

4. "I can let go of my fear that his habits might kill him. True, adolescence is a dangerous time. But my cousin was killed when he was a teenager by a hay baler in the course of doing his normal chores. In other words, there are no guarantees. I'm quite sure my habits have caused just as much damage to my body as his have to his body. So the key is to work on my own healing."

It can be more difficult to eliminate ineffective teen behaviors when you don't have an understanding of your own unresolved issues and how they are the basis of your ineffective behaviors.

How Your Unresolved Issues Obstruct Parenting

A MOTHER TOLD us that her sixteen-year-old son's economics teacher called to say her son had been tardy or absent six days out of ten. The teacher wanted to know what Mom was going to do. Without a second thought, Mom said she would come in for a parent-teacher-student conference.

When asked why she responded that way, Mom said she wanted to look good to the teacher. Upon further exploration, she realized she was automatically intimidated upon hearing the teacher's voice and immediately felt she had done something wrong. Immobilized, she turned her power over to the teacher.

Mom also realized, with help from her parenting group, that she felt disappointment. When she thought she had done something wrong, she was sure she had disappointed the other person and was thus disappointed in herself. Mom also believed that to be worthy of love or friendships, she could never be wrong, otherwise no one would like her. So when she thought she'd made a mistake she immediately tried to fix the situation to the other person's satisfaction. So intent on doing what was "right" in the eyes of others, she couldn't see what was "right" for her son—and herself. In this case, she was more intent in staying out of trouble with the teacher than in helping her son.

Deal with the Needs of the Situation Instead of Reacting to Your Fears

RATHER THAN ACCEPTING what the teacher had said at face value, it would have been more helpful for Mom to talk to her son to find out what he felt was going on and what he wanted to do about it. Or Mom could ask the teacher if he had discussed the problem with her son. Mom could also let the teacher know that although she didn't approve of her son's behavior, she felt it was up to him to work it out with the teacher. She could ask her son if he wanted her to go to school with him to discuss the situation with the teacher or if he would like to handle it on his own.

Many parents think that their kids won't talk to them because of something the parent has done. But teenagers often don't confide in their parents because they need to figure things out for themselves, which is part of the individuation process. Teens also sometimes won't talk to their parents because they think of themselves as already being adults. They interpret their parents' help as being treated like little kids.

Once you get your personal issues out of the way, including the feeling that your teen is trying to hurt you, you can stop feeling guilty about your teen's problems. You can also be available to help your teens when they need you, instead of interfering to save face for yourself.

Use a Magic Wand to Deal with Your Unresolved Teen Issues

JANA, A MARRIED woman with two teens, shared with her parenting group that when she was thirteen, her mother had read her diary and found out all about her first "going steady" experience. After reading that Jana had kissed her boyfriend twelve times, Jana's mother wouldn't speak to her for several days. Not only didn't her mother respect her privacy, but also when Jana tried to say she was sorry, her mother replied scornfully, "You should be."

Jana imagined how she would change that memory if she had a magic wand and could redo it any way she liked. She said, "My mother wouldn't read my diary. However, if she did find out about my boyfriend, she would sit down and talk to me. She might tell me she is scared and why. She might tell me what it was like for her at my age. And she would ask me if I would like to tell her what is going on for me. Then she would encourage me to use my best judgment and tell me that even if I made a mistake, she was sure I could handle it. She'd let me know that if I ever wanted to talk to her, I could do that without being judged, and that if she ever did seem critical, it was just because she was bothered by her own issues."

In addition to healing the old hurt, rewriting your teenage memories with the help of a "magic wand" can also provide information for how you can handle the situation with your own teen. Jana decided she would do for her daughter what her mother couldn't do for her.

Exploring Your Memories

Dealing with a child who is addicted to or abusing drugs can bring up a lot of unresolved past issues. The following conversation took place with Kay, who came to therapy to deal with her own issues around her daughter's drug use.

KAY: I don't want my child to be a drug addict.

THERAPIST: I know you've done a lot to help your daughter get treatment and that she's still deciding to use chemicals. You can't make her stop using drugs, but you can help yourself let go. Let's explore some of your issues about letting go by going back to an early memory from your teenage years.

KAY: The one that comes to me is when I was a little older.

THERAPIST: How old?

KAY: Twenty-one.

THERAPIST: That's interesting. It's close to your daughter's age now.

KAY: I was divorced. I had custody of my two young children. Their father had the kids every Wednesday night and every weekend, but the kids were constantly upset about being shifted back and forth. One Wednesday night when their father hadn't brought them back on time, I was so upset that I called my father and asked if he could come help me get the kids. Well, my Dad got real upset. All the time we were out looking for the kids, my dad was griping and complaining. I said to him, "You never did love me." He said, "What do you mean? I always loved you more than all the rest put together." But I totally could not believe that.

THERAPIST: What were you thinking?

KAY: I was thinking, "I have created this total mess of my life. My kids don't have a father. My Dad is mad at me. My kids are always upset."

THERAPIST: What were your feelings?

KAY: I was feeling hurt, inadequate, stupid, defensive.

THERAPIST: What were you doing?

KAY: I was crying, lashing out at my Dad, accusing him of never loving me. I was depending on him to help me and paying a big price for it.

THERAPIST: What is the price you were paying?

KAY: I had to listen to him yell at me and put me down.

THERAPIST: So when he was griping and complaining, you interpreted that to mean he was yelling at you, scolding you, and putting you down. Anything else?

KAY: The kids' father was angry with me. That's why he wasn't bringing the kids home on time—not keeping his commitments. And when I picked up my father to look for the kids, my mother met me at the door with a disapproving look.

THERAPIST: You certainly seem convinced that everyone was mad at you or disapproved of you. Now let's return to the situation with your daughter and see if there are any parallels.

KAY: Good grief! She's messed up her life, and I'm scolding her and putting her down and giving her self-righteous, disapproving looks and messages.

THERAPIST: What are you telling yourself?

KAY: That she's messed up her life. That she's not doing the things that will make her happy. She's hurting me. She's not keeping her commitments.

THERAPIST: How are you feeling?

KAY: Unappreciated. Guilty. Self-righteous. Good grief, I'm feeling every one of those feelings from my own memory. I'm feeling disapproving, guilty, and blaming—and inadequate about how to handle it. I wonder if that's how it was for my parents, or for that matter, for my ex-husband?

THERAPIST: What are you doing with your daughter?

KAY: Lecturing and putting her down. Disapproving. Trying to fix it and take care of it. Trying to control her and make her do the right thing—just like everyone did to me.

THERAPIST: Do you realize that in addition to all those things, you're also seeking help and learning about your codependency? Part of your struggle is that you are half in and half out of being a codependent. Even though you are doing many of the things to her that made you feel worse, you are also working on changing old patterns. That takes time and practice. Just the awareness of some of your discouraging behaviors can help you stop doing them when you catch yourself in the act.

This session was life changing for Kay and for her teen. She stopped doing to her daughter all the things her father had done to her, and started doing the things she wished her father had done for her. She became a kind and firm parent.

Kay spoke with her daughter. She told her that although she thought her daughter was making a mistake by using drugs, she had a right to make her own mistakes in life. Kay shared with her daughter, "I have made so many mistakes that I can hardly sit in judgment of yours. . . . I will no longer try to control your life, but I will control my own. I will love you no matter what, but I will not let you take advantage of me or treat me disrespectfully. I will not support your drug habit, but I will support you. You cannot stay in our home, even for one night, while you are doing drugs, but I will support you getting into treatment if you ever decide to do that."

The daughter was almost speechless as she felt her mother's confidence and strength. After getting her bearings, however, she sneered, "Fine," and walked away. For a week afterward, Kay had no idea where her daughter was. Then her daughter called and asked to have lunch with her mother.

Kay said, "I would love that."

To her amazement, her daughter asked if she would go with her to a treatment center because she really wanted to change her life. As soon as they finished eating, they went to the treatment center and her daughter signed herself in.

Letting Go Brings Up Issues of Past Loss

THE MORE YOUR teens struggle for independence and freedom, the more you realize that the teen years are just the beginning of a new kind of relationship with your children, possibly one in which you don't see much of them. If you are like many parents, this thought can bring up feelings of loss. On top of dealing with whatever losses you may experience with your teen, you end up dealing with all the past losses that still hurt you even though they are buried under the surface.

When Anya's daughter, Mariah, complained that her parents were stricter than any of her friends' folks were, her mother dismissed what Mariah said as the normal grumblings of a teenager. But Anya then started thinking about whether there was any truth to Mariah's words. She realized that in many ways she and her husband were trying to keep Mariah young. She wondered why would they would want to do that. Then it hit her like a ton of bricks. She had experienced so many losses in the past five years. Her friend had died of breast cancer, both of her parents had died, and one of her classmates had died in a car crash just a few weeks ago. As she thought more about her losses, she remembered back to her teen years when her best friend was orphaned because her parents' plane went down in a storm. For Anya, losses were forever. It was no wonder she feared "losing" her daughter.

> The more your teens struggle for independence and freedom, the more you realize that the teen years are just the beginning of a new kind of relationship with your children, possibly one in which you don't see much of them.

Then Anya remembered a conversation she'd had with her friend, who was explaining how often one of her kids came home for a short time. Her friend said that when her first child went off to college she had been worried that it was the beginning of the end. However, instead she soon had to put a sign on the guest bedroom door that said, "The In-Between Room:"

Now that all the kids have moved away, we need at least one room where they can stay when they are in between school semesters, jobs, relationships, training programs, or whatever else. The agreement is that the kids can stay with us while they are "in-between," but they can't move back home permanently. There are times they might want to, because it's a challenge to be out in the real world, but they know they need to regroup and then go out and try again. So far it seems to be working really well. Our kids have a place to crash when they need it. We almost always have one of the kids at home. I thought we were going to have an empty nest. I certainly was wrong.

If you feel stuck in your old issues, we recommend reviewing this chapter often. Try the activity at the end of the chapter to help identify your unresolved teen issues and put them to rest. What you learn from the experience will enrich both your life and your teen's.

KIND AND FIRM PARENTING TOOLS TO REMEMBER

1. Look at having a teenager as a wonderful opportunity to get rid of old baggage from your teen years, instead of dragging it along with you or dumping it on your kids.

2. If you have issues about your self-image, your teen is sure to bring them to the surface. It's time to separate your issues from your teen's issues.

3. Paying attention to your fears can be an excellent way to zero in on past problems. As you understand what your fears are, you can let them go and deal with the real needs of the situation, not just those you imagine.

4. With new perspective, options appear, as if by magic.

5. Sometimes the simplest way to get unstuck is to imagine that you have a magic wand. "Wave" it over your situation, think about how you'd like to change it, and see what new options you can create for yourself.

6. Remember back to your own teen years to look for parallels between your memories and your current situation with your teen.

7. Don't forget that the pain of most losses you experience is short-lived and that your teens will constantly be moving in and out of your life.

Practical Application Activity

Use the following activity to identify unresolved issues from your teenage years and to put you in touch with your teen's world. Instead of thinking like a parent "should" think, you will be able to recall how you thought, felt, and behaved when you were a teen. You will begin to remember what it was like to be a teenager, which gives you a better understanding of your teen's perceptions and shows you may be taking some of your teen's behavior much too personally.

DISCOVERING YOUR UNRESOLVED TEEN ISSUES

1. Think of a situation that occurs with you and your teen that you wish were different. Describe the specifics of the situation in writing.

2. How do you feel when the situation occurs? Be sure to use feeling words and not words such as *that, as if,* or *like.* A feeling can be described with one word. If you use more than one word, you are describing what you think. For example, "I felt as if my teenager hated me" is a thought. "I felt hurt," on the other hand, describes feelings. (You can be experiencing more than one feeling and can use as many single words as it takes to describe them, but they won't be in complete sentences: mad, sad, helpless, and so forth.)

3. What is it that you are doing in the problem situation?

4. What is your teen's response to your behavior?

5. What is your decision about your teen's response?

REMEMBER A TIME FROM YOUR OWN TEEN YEARS

1. Think of a time when you were a teen and things weren't working out the way you wanted them to. Describe the specifics of the situation in writing.

2. How did you feel about the situation?

3. How did you behave in the situation?

4. How did the adults around you or your parents behave in the situation?

5. What was your response to their behavior?

6. What did you decide about the situation?

USE INSIGHTS FROM YOUR PAST TO HELP YOUR PRESENT

1. Review what you wrote about the previous two situations. Describe an issue that remains unresolved from your own teenage years.

2. What information, if any, did you get from your teen memory that can help you deal more effectively with your current problem situation?

MY PLAN FOR THE WEEK

This week I will focus on

_____

_____

I will work on changing my attitude by thinking

_____

_____

_____

I will change my behavior by doing

_____

_____

_____

14

What Do You Do When Your Teen's Behavior Scares You?

W E HAVE BEEN told by hundreds of teens that they love our ideas and our book because we really understand them. They wish their parents would read it so they could get along better. Your teens want to get along with you, even if it doesn't seem like it at times. They just aren't willing to give up who they are to be loved by you.

Even more parents have told us that the first edition of this book saved their relationships with their teens, as well as their sanity, so keep the faith as you read this chapter. We know you want to have good relationships with your teens, yet often their behavior really scares you. When it does, you don't always use your best parenting skills and your relationships suffer.

What you may interpret as a potential problem might simply be perfectly normal teen behavior that looks dysfunctional to you. We've noticed that a behavior that scares one parent doesn't necessarily scare another. Have you ever wondered why that is? We certainly have, and our conclusion is this: parents are different, just like kids are different. For some parents, what is most frightening are events that *trigger their unresolved issues;* for other parents their fears are based on their *lack of personal experience;* and for still others, their fear is based on *having the personal experience.*

There are certain subjects that we have noticed come up time and again in our parenting classes and workshops. Those subjects are the focus of this chapter. (We've already talked about some of the subjects elsewhere in the book, so the information here is an addendum to what you have already read.) The subjects include music, movies, and videos; gangs and bullies; drugs and other addictive behaviors; sexual activity and AIDS; sexual abuse; suicidal behaviors; eating problems; and young adults who won't or can't leave home. Let's start with the least scary, but one that's scary nonetheless.

Videos, Music, Video Games, and Movies

YOUR TEENS MAY be listening to music, watching videos, playing video games, or going to movies that promote death, destruction, violence, disrespect for men and women, and worse. They may have hard-core porn hidden under the mattress or sexist posters hanging in their rooms. They may visit Web sites that show explicit sexual activities. What's a parent to do?

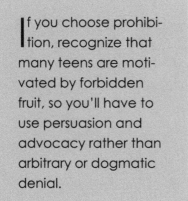

If you choose prohibition, recognize that many teens are motivated by forbidden fruit, so you'll have to use persuasion and advocacy rather than arbitrary or dogmatic denial.

Within the boundaries of your values, you may wish to allow your children to experience some of these or you may wish to prohibit them from doing so. If you choose prohibition, recognize that many teens are motivated by forbidden fruit, so you'll have to use persuasion and advocacy rather than arbitrary or dogmatic denial. You may choose to use their entertainment medium of choice as a way of teaching values and discussing ideas and attitudes. Or you could tell your teens it's not okay with you for them to listen to, play, or watch them because they promote violence, degradation, exploitation, or stereotyping. However, it is important to remember that your teens may just go underground to do what they know you don't want them to do. You will have better results if you respectfully involve your teen in some way.

One of our favorite ways to involve teens (discussed in chapter 7) is to ask your teens to teach you more about why young people are interested in these particular forms of entertainment. Accompany your teens to concerts, go to movies (even though you may have to sit in the back row so their friends don't know their parents tagged along), or play games with them so you can engage in discussions armed with knowledge. When your teen asks to take part in a potentially iffy situation, it is okay to say "no" until the activity can be discussed at a family meeting. By now you know that taking away privileges, cars, computers, and allowances is not the answer to dealing effectively with your teens. Nor is secretly searching their rooms for contraband.

Keep in mind that the activity is not the culprit. The culprit is what your teen decides about the activity. For example, music doesn't drive teens to violent despair or anger. However, negative decisions are more likely in negative environments, so it's still up to you to use your judgment about how to handle your teens' choices.

We think doing nothing is the worst choice. At the least, hold a friendly discussion with curiosity. Words found in songs aren't evil. When your teen chooses to indulge in what you consider to be negative activities by listening to music you don't approve of, look at the purpose of the behavior. Focus on the deeper issues of identity, power, fairness, and competence. (See chapter 12 for a review of the mistaken goals and what to do as a proactive parent.) Provide a friendly atmosphere in which your teens can tell you what they think about what they are hearing. But remember that there still may be times when you feel the need to bring the railings of the bridge a little closer by providing limits.

Keep in mind that with many teens, if they understand your reason for your requests and if they feel they have some choice, they'll work with you. Some of the choices might be: "You can listen to your music elsewhere, but not in our home. You can go to concerts when you are a certain age. Never do this around younger siblings whose judgment is not as mature as yours is."

Friends, or Lack Thereof

ANOTHER SCARY, BUT not so scary, behavior is having a teen who can't seem to get along with peers or who isolates him- or herself beyond what seems like a reasonable amount of time. If your teen is willing to hear some tips, we recommend the following:

Instead of gossiping behind someone's back, talk to that person directly.
Don't start or spread rumors.
Practice smiling when you walk through the halls at school.
Ask other kids questions about themselves.

You might want to encourage or set up opportunities for your teen to get involved in activities in which he or she can meet teenagers with similar interests. Sometimes you have to take a heavy hand and insist that your teen must try something four times before quitting. We are often amazed at the number of young people who need just this kind of help from their parents.

You can also help your teens explore, through a friendly conversation, what they think the long-range results of their relationship behaviors might be. If they are critical of everyone or afraid to ask to join in and instead wait at home to be called, they might have few friends. If they do all the talking and forget to listen to their friends, or if they are selfish and refuse to share the limelight or experiences, they may be driving others away. You could also watch your own behavior. If you tell your teens how to behave, you'll probably have very little influence. But, remember, your teens do watch how you act, and they often mimic your worse habits. For example, do you yell at people on the freeway or talk about a person's "stupid" behavior? Do you talk down to salespeople or service providers? Don't be surprised if your negative child has taken a page out of your book. Sometimes the best approach for helping a teen with peer relations is to butt out and let him or her work it through. This is an especially good idea when teens make a situation much worse than it really is. Your teen may turn a row with a friend into a situation in which they don't have a friend in the entire world. Usually after a day or two, all is well again. However, if you butt in to this situation, it may get dragged out and made worse than it really was.

When You Dislike Your Teens' Friends

Many battles are fought when teens choose friends that their parents do not approve of. This is a reasonable concern for many parents, because friends do have an influence on each other's choices and behaviors. However, the way that most parents handle this problem only intensifies the battle, driving teens to be even more loyal to one another. We know of very few (actually none, but we imagine there must be some) parents who have been successful at forbidding their teens to have certain friends. Instead, parents who do so often end up widening the gap in their relationship with their teens. Because parents can't monitor every moment of their teens' day, it is impossible to control who the teens have as friends.

Instead of controlling your teen's friends, try the opposite. Welcome them into your home. Be friendly and joke around with them. You have more influence when you create a welcoming home environment where your teen feels more comfortable. When you give your teens this kind of space, they often tire of the friend on their own. Also, the bad behavior of some teens could be an indication that this friend does not have an encouraging home environment. Hanging out in your home could be the opportunity for him or her to experience encouragement.

If you are worried about the influence that other teens have on your own, be honest about your fears. Use all the methods discussed in this book—role-play, family meetings, joint problem solving, and curiosity questions—so your teen will be equipped with more skills for dealing with potentially dangerous situations. Doing so not only helps to discuss your feelings, but also provides your teen with skills to think and prepare ahead. Of course, this doesn't guarantee that mistakes won't be made, but it does decrease the chances.

Keep in mind that just as your own teens' behaviors aren't forever, their friends' behaviors aren't forever either. Many parents, after learning what fine people some of their teens' friends have turned out to be, have been embarrassed that they had treated them so poorly.

Gangs and Bullies

NOW TO SOME of the scarier problems that teens and their parents face. You and your teens may worry about dealing with gangs, bullies, and other out-of-control teens. If so, your teens need your help, as well as the school's help, to follow an aggressive zero-tolerance policy for violence or weapons on or near the school grounds.

Young people must be taken very seriously when they ask for your help or the school's help to deal with prejudice, violence, hazing, or other safety issues. We have heard stories of both parents and teens asking authorities for assistance in dealing with violence only to be ignored or put off. There are many programs that school employees can research and put into effect to get help with peer counseling, mediation, conflict management, and positive discipline in the classrooms. Schools that use methods of reaching out with love and respect to help kids deal positively with differences have considerably less, if any, violence on campus.

One thing we have seen is that most people focus on the wrong solutions for violence in schools. They talk about gun control, uniforms, corporal punishment, guards, and holding parents accountable. What very few discuss is the value of teaching kids self-discipline, responsibility, respect for self and others, and problem-solving skills—all of which teens learn when they participate in regular and effective class meetings.[1] Schools tend to encounter very few problems when they use class meetings to help every student feel a sense of belonging and to teach students how to use their power in constructive ways.

Research shows that the three main reasons kids join gangs are for a sense of belonging, a sense of power or security, and for protection. Young people are less likely to join gangs if they believe they are respected and accepted at home and in classrooms for who they are, and if they experience authority as some-

---

1. See *Positive Discipline in the Classroom,* by Jane Nelsen, Lynn Lott, and H. Stephen Glenn, Revised 3rd Edition. Roseville, CA: Prima Publishing, 2000.

thing designed to help them do better rather than to hurt, punish, shame, or rescue them.

An extreme solution that isn't always an option would be to move to a neighborhood where gangs aren't prevalent. In some neighborhoods, parents have dealt with the gang problem by forming groups of volunteers to walk the streets and talk to teens in a friendly manner. In other places, teens have been trained to walk the streets in uniform, talking to other teens and reporting on walkie-talkies about events that need adult supervision. Many cities have created teen centers to provide other options for feeling belonging and significance and for dealing with boredom.

As your children get older, they are probably going to be confronted by a bully who threatens, intimidates, or steals from them. The best defense to teach your teens is a good offense. Teach or give permission for your son or daughter to let a bully know, in no uncertain terms, to leave their stuff alone. Using the same voice he or she uses when a sibling invades his or her space is most effective. You may also choose to send your teen to self-defense classes, which greatly changes the way your child thinks of and carries him- or herself. You're not training your teens to become lethal weapons or to meet violence with violence; rather, you are providing your teens with self-confidence and the ability to defend themselves, which usually makes the actual defending unnecessary.

Although there are many ways to help young people with their difficulties, we find that sending the teen off for help without parental involvement or putting the teen on prescription drugs to cure complex problems can result in worse problems. The better option would be to talk with the teen and deal with the deeper issues. For example, if you notice your teen stockpiling weapons or reading books on how to make bombs, get help from a professional who can assist all of you without prescribing drugs. In our experience, prescription drugs have the opposite effect from what is expected, often making teens more depressed and more violent.

Drug Use and Other Addictive Behaviors

THE FEAR OF drug abuse is the number one problem plaguing parents of teens today. You've heard the stories of ruined teenage lives and teenage deaths from drug overdoses or drug- and alcohol-related accidents. You know that someone could slip something into a drink at a party and your teen could take a "trip" she never intended, possibly ending in rape or worse. Just like most other parents, you are probably struggling with what to do about all this information.

Many parents fear drug abuse because they had used or abused drugs themselves when they were younger. Many of these parents worry that their teens will do what they did but won't recover. Other parents never used drugs but have many fears and judgments about drug use. Some parents don't even realize that drugs are a potential problem until they find out their teen is using alcohol or pot. These parents usually stumble on the information by discovering a bong, roller, or cigarette papers while putting away the laundry; a thermos filled with something that doesn't smell like coffee or water; or maybe empty beer cans in the family car.

There are other signs, such as dramatic changes in behavior, aggressiveness, depression, alteration in sleep or eating habits, weight loss, spaciness, and lack of concern for activities that used to be important, that are often misinterpreted by well-meaning professionals as mental illness. We are amazed that many parents prefer dealing with a mental illness rather than thinking their son or daughter has a drug problem or is an addict.

There's a lot of denial about drug use and abuse, which we think of as misinformation and misunderstanding. We've come across professionals who have said that marijuana isn't addictive and is probably even good for your teen. Other misinformation includes overlooking certain substances, such as tobacco, alcohol, sugar, and prescription or over-the-counter drugs, and not realizing they are drugs. Then there are the substances that you may not know about, such as GHB and "roofies," not to mention the ones you probably do know about, including cocaine, inhalants, ecstasy, heroin, amphetamines, barbiturates, and hallucinogens. But abuse can also happen with "substances" or behaviors you may not even know are potentially addictive, such as television, video games, computers and the Internet, shopping, spending money, gambling, and more. Although we focus on drugs in this section, you can substitute any of the behaviors/substances we mentioned to learn more about what is happening with your teen and what to do about it.

If drugs are so scary to parents and potentially damaging to teens, why are they so popular? Some teens say they want to experiment and find out what effect the substance has; others say they like to be part of the group; still others say they think using substances makes them less shy, less boring, freer, faster, sexier, more fun, and happier. Many youths use drugs to emulate their idols in the entertainment world or famous writers who have glorified drug use. Some enjoy the escape to a different reality or "feeling place." Young people will use speed to lose weight or stay awake to study for finals, or a date may give a sedative to a girl to make her out of it and forgetful so he can force sex on her without getting caught. Some teens use drugs because they think it makes them more grown-up. Others say someone they thought was cool introduced them to drugs, and they wanted to be just like that person, so they started using.

In spite of the side effects of damaged relationships with parents and old friends, hangovers, nausea, vomiting, black outs, mood swings, rapid heart beats, reduced inhibitions, breathing difficulties, or even the possibility of death, teens continue to use substances until they decide not to. Teens have grown up in a culture that stresses the "short-term feel good" and the "quick fix." Therefore, using drugs fits in with the cultural norm. Many teens lack a feeling words vocabulary. They don't have a person with whom they feel safe talking or a place where it is safe to express feelings. For these teens, drugs provide a way to numb feelings and make problems seem to disappear. Overcontrolled or overprotected young people will use drugs as a way to rebel against parental controls.

> Teens have grown up in a culture that stresses the "short-term feel good" and the "quick fix." Therefore, using drugs fits in with the cultural norm.

Parental Fear Is a Natural Response to Information About Teen Drug Use

No wonder you are frightened. Maybe you're remembering some of your own drug experiences or recalling a friend or family member who has struggled with addiction. Much of the current literature suggests that you should know what is going on in your teens' lives at all times. You are told to monitor your teens' friendships, supervise their relationships, communicate with other parents, supervise teen parties, and refuse to let teens go anywhere that they might encounter drugs. You are told that these methods will protect your kids from using or abusing drugs. This is an overly simplistic and unrealistic statement when you consider what is really going on and how ineffective those methods really are.

The best way to help your kids make intelligent decisions about drugs is to empower them in all the ways we've been suggesting in this book. When your teens have opportunities to contribute, when they feel listened to and taken seriously and know they can talk to you about what is really going on, and when you provide opportunities for them to learn skills and experience success, they are less likely to abuse drugs. Notice we say *abuse* drugs, not *use* drugs. Your teens may chose to use drugs whether you like it or not, whether you remain vigilant or not. This is reality. Teens who have the self-confidence and skills we have been discussing are likely to experiment with alcohol and drugs, but are less likely to abuse them.

Suggestions for Dealing with Teens and Drugs

Given all this information about drug use, you're still probably asking, "What can I do?" We like the advice from the Office of National Drug Control Policy found in the September 8, 1999, issue of the *San Francisco Chronicle*. Some of their suggestions include the following:

"The best thing about this subject is that you don't have to do it well. You simply have to try. If you try, your kids will get the message that you care about them, that you understand something about the conflicts they face and that you're there when they need you."

"Start anywhere. (Ask) 'Have you heard about any kids using drugs? How do you feel about that? Why do you think kids get involved with drugs?'"

"In matter-of-fact, unmistakably clear language say, 'Drugs are a way of hurting yourself. I love you too much to see you throw your life down the drain.'"

"It's okay if you don't know much about drugs. Your kids do. But they need to know how you feel about the subject. And whether you care."

Some teens won't use drugs if you tell them you don't want them to, so go ahead and say it if it's how you feel. Some of you may show your concern about drug problems by getting involved with drug-free dances, safe parties, safe-ride programs, and the just-say-no program. Even though it's unrealistic to think that these activities by themselves can tackle the drug problem, all efforts are important—and these programs *have* made a difference. If anything, you will probably feel better knowing you are doing something, *anything,* to make a difference.

OTHER HELPFUL SUGGESTIONS

1. Get and give information, using statements like, "We feel ____. What are your ideas?"

2. Share your values.

3. Give teens a safe space to learn from their mistakes, encouraging them to talk with you when they are ready.

4. Don't remove or minimize consequences of your teen's behavior.

5. Know when to get help, for all of you.

The Continuum of Use

There are different kinds of drug use. People without information think of drug abuse as the only alternative to abstinence. The continuum of drug use moves from abstinence (no use) at one end to chemical dependency at the other, with experimentation, social use, regular use, and problem use in between. Being aware that there are differences can be helpful to you, and your response to the problem needs to match the type of use.

There are many teens who, for reasons of their own, have chosen abstinence and who lead a drug-free life. Some of them are always the designated driver at social gatherings, while others hang out with young people who have made the same choice as they have.

Experimental use means: "I heard about it. I want to try it out. I want to know what it feels like. A bunch of us are going to get together and find out what happens when we get drunk, or what happens when we take pills." A teen experimenting may try a drug once and never again. This may not make drug use any less scary for you, but we suggest you don't over-react. Encourage a friendly discussion and share your fears that your teen may be getting into something that could become dangerous, and you wish he or she would stop now. Some of you may be reassured to know that teens who party have often seen what happens when someone has a "bad trip"; these kids have their own limits and methods for trying out only what they feel safe doing.

Social use involves using drugs for social occasions without letting the drug take control. A social user can stop after a small amount of a drug, whereas an addict can't do just a little or stop. You may still be concerned, because whatever people practice, they get better at, and there are plenty of addicts out there who started using socially and ended up with a full-blown addiction. Say what you think, how you feel, and what you want, and make sure you are clear with your child.

Regular use is drug use that has become ritualized and is thus potentially more dangerous because it could turn into an addiction. We have worked with many teens who get stoned every day or drink regularly and still are able to maintain their relationships, school work, and their self-respect and dignity. However, many have moved into the next point on the continuum—problem use.

Problem use happens when teens' drug use leads to them having problems with managing their lives. They have problems with school, family, and work.

With teens especially, the more they use, the less they develop their skills to meet challenges and become competent. They use chemicals to repress their feelings instead of expressing them. They may even cause serious physical damage to themselves from prolonged use. If you think your teen's use is problematic, tell your child you love him and say that you want to help or get help with the problem. Don't accept promises for change. Although your teen may be sincere, he or she may not realize the hold the chemical has on the body. Also, when you talk with a person who has become addicted, you are not talking with a rational person. Don't expect reason. It won't happen. However, if you do get help at the problem use stage, you may be able to avoid the next stage. The line between problem use and chemical dependency is different for every person. Some people will never cross the line, others will. Some people become chemically dependent without going through all phases of the continuum. Chemical dependency occurs when the drug is running your teen's life. The following poem was written by a pot addict who started using pot regularly at age fourteen and hasn't been able to stop yet. He is now in his early thirties.

Awakening
I have poisoned my body
for so many years
it's time to get real
it's time to think clear.
Life is passing me by
year after year—
I long to love myself
when I look in the mirror
Please God, help me
be strong and sincere;
I want to find true love
I can't in this cloud.
I'll say it again,
I'll say it out loud,
"Let's do it this time, Buddy,
don't let me down."

When you and your teens understand the continuum of drug use, you are both in a better place to evaluate what is going on and what to do about it. There are still too many stereotypes about what makes a real addict. If you or your teen is looking for the extreme behaviors like the addicts you may see on the streets, you could be minimizing the seriousness of your teen's relationship with drugs. The previous poem so aptly describes the hopelessness and helplessness of addiction. If you met the poet on the street, you'd never know he was an addict; if you read his poem, you can't help but hear his cry for help. He wants to be "caught" and helped because the drugs have taken control away from him. If your teens are in this place, do whatever it takes to get them into treatment.

> When you and your teens understand the continuum of drug use, you are both in a better place to evaluate what is going on and what to do about it.

Whether you believe that drug abuse is a disease or a decision, every problem user and addict knows that the behaviors stop when the user decides it will stop—and not before. Your job as a parent is to help your child make that decision, if you can. Chemical dependency is like being on an elevator going down. People don't need to hit bottom before getting off—they can get off on any floor. With very few exceptions, however, once a person is chemically dependent, the only choice for breaking the cycle is abstinence along with interventions and with help (treatment, therapy, group help like Alcoholics Anonymous).

Choosing a Therapist

If you need professional help, the most important criterion to consider in choosing a therapist is finding one your teen can relate to. Even though it is important for you to feel comfortable, you need to keep shopping until your teen is comfortable. Stay away from therapists who recommend a punitive, restrictive approach for parenting teens. It will just make things worse. We also recommend being very careful about a therapist who recommends prescription drugs. Usually this is similar to putting duct tape over the engine-trouble light on your dashboard. Is it really helping to mask the problem with drugs instead of finding a good therapist who will help you deal with the problem?

If possible, ask people you know to refer a therapist with whom they have felt satisfied. If no one you know has been to a therapist, ask Al-Anon groups or church groups for referrals. When you find a therapist, don't hesitate to ask for a get-acquainted interview, so you can learn about his or her basic philosophy and you can tell the therapist about your perspectives on your teen.

Remember, when teenagers are chemically dependent, they will not want to see a therapist because they will want to protect their drug use. Find an Al-Anon group for yourself and work towards intervention.

Interventions Can Happen at Any Time

Another way you can help your teen with drug problems is to use an intervention. Interventions are also on a continuum from informal to formal, with formal interventions occurring with the help of a trained interventionist. An intervention is a way for you to get out of denial and start dealing with what is really happening. Doing an intervention means you stop rescuing, overprotecting, controlling, or in any way taking responsibility for your teen's life. You begin treating your teen as an adult-in-training and start saying only what you mean and following through with actions you can take. Interventions require you to be gut-level honest and to stop playing games.

Some informal interventions happen when you begin to look at some of the messages you've inadvertently been giving your teen about drugs. Do you use over-the-counter or prescription drugs to deal with all of your feelings? Do you suggest a pill to make the pain go away whenever your teen is complaining? Do you zone out at the computer or in front of the TV, shop, read, or eat to avoid dealing with your feelings? If you answer yes to these questions, don't be afraid to open a dialogue with your teen about your awareness.

There is a wonderful intervention story about Gandhi. A mother came to him and said, "Please tell my child to stop eating sugar." Gandhi said, "Would you come back in three days?" The mother came back in three days with her child, and Gandhi said to the child, "Stop eating sugar." The mother asked, "Why did you have to wait three days to tell him that?" Gandhi said, "Well, I had to stop myself before I could tell him to stop."

More Informal Interventions

Addison told his teenage son, "I'm concerned about your drinking. I notice that you drink a lot and drink fast. Your grandfather is an alcoholic, and research has shown that kids who have one or more relatives who are chemically dependent have an increased risk of becoming chemically dependent themselves. I hope you'll think about what I'm saying. I love you, and I wouldn't want you to go through the pain of addiction."

Clara told her teenagers, "I know there will be times you may decide to use drugs. It's not okay with me to have drugs in our house or at any parties here. I realize that may create some problems for you, but I'm happy to help in any way to plan parties with you that can be fun without drugs. If you do decide to use drugs, I want you to know that even though I prefer that you don't, I love you and I'm here to listen and not judge you if you'd like my help or want to talk to me about it."

Bob told his twin boys, who insisted that pot wasn't a problem and that he was just uptight and didn't understand, "I'm not into this. You're right, I don't really know much about it, but I don't really like it. I don't even approve of using pot. But I want to know what it's like for you. I want you to tell me more about it. I want you to help me understand what it means to you."

Michael, father of a fourteen-year-old boy, was very clear with his son about having parties at their house. "I know you kids use alcohol and drugs at parties, and I know you don't have the same values I have; but I don't want you having a party here with people using marijuana or alcohol. If I see anyone using them, I'll ask them to go home. If that will embarrass you, you need to work it out to have a party without drugs, or you can boot out your friends who are using before I boot them out. I know you feel differently about it, and I understand that. I know you think I'm old-fashioned, but that's how I plan to handle it in this house. I'm concerned and scared about the possible short- and long-range effects of teens using drugs, and, although I know I can't stop you from using, I prefer that it doesn't happen in our home."

Sometimes interventions have to be accompanied by hard choices on your part. When Thomas was twenty-one years old, he was heavily into cocaine and marijuana. He went to a treatment center and did well for awhile. Then he started using drugs again. His mother minimized the situation for a long time before she finally got the courage to tell Thomas that he could no longer live at home as long as he chose to abuse drugs. Thomas left, vowing never, ever to forgive his mother. One month later, Thomas wanted to come home and sleep on the couch for "just a few days" until he could find another place to live. Although Mom knew on one level that Thomas was conning and manipulating, she still found it very difficult to refuse such a reasonable request—for just a few days.

Addicts lie and manipulate, so it would be entirely predictable for Thomas to say things like, "Can I sleep on the couch tonight? I will be moving into an apartment real soon," or "I'm going to look for a job tomorrow," or "I can't believe you can just write me out of your life forever," and on and on.

Mom, remembering that Thomas was better at being the "look good guy" instead of the "do good guy," finally used an intervention when she said, "Thomas, I want to stop trying to control what you do, but I also plan to stop rescuing you when you get into trouble. I have faith in you to make decisions for yourself, to learn from your mistakes, and to figure out how to solve problems that come to you or that you create. Specifically, this means that I'll no longer provide a place for you to stay. It also means I won't badger you about getting back into a recovery program, but I will know when you are helping yourself. You know that I am always willing to help you when you are willing to help yourself."

Mom certainly found a way to get the message of love across without jumping in and rescuing her addicted son. In so many words, she was telling Thomas, "Be just the way you are; feel just the way you feel; do just what you think you want. I love you because you're you. I may not always like or agree with some of your decisions, and I'll probably let you know my thoughts and feelings, but it won't change my love for you."

There is a lot of help out in the world for you if you are struggling with a teenager abusing drugs. Getting help means you are wise enough to make use of all the support that is available through friends, therapists, support groups such as Al-Anon, parenting books, drug-information books, and treatment programs that have intervention specialists.

We often explain to our clients who seek therapy that they are now in the league of champions who are wise enough to know they need a coach. Olympic champions or championship ball teams would not even consider trying to function without a good coach. The champions still have to do all the work, but the coach can stand back far enough to see with perspective and objectivity. The coach teaches the necessary skills, but the champion still has to practice to apply the skills. Just look for a coach who can help you fight drug abuse using drug-free methods, who understands abuse and isn't trying to convince you that your teen has a mental illness.

Alcoholics Anonymous has some of the best suggestions for helping you keep the faith when dealing with an addicted son or daughter. You may have seen the bumper sticker that reads, "Let go and let God," or maybe you've heard the serenity prayer: "God grant me the serenity to accept the things I cannot change, the courage to change the things I can, and the wisdom to know the difference." Use these and other inspirational quotes to help you remember that most teenagers grow up. The teenage years are not forever. You were once a teen yourself, and you made it and so will your teen.

Teen Sexual Activity, Pregnancy, and AIDS

AS PARENTS, YOU may want to think your teens are asexual, just waiting until they are older for you to give them the "big talk." Guess again. Your teen may have a very different value about sexual activity than you do. Many teens are not only sexually active at a very young age, but also experience multiple partners. It is important to discuss your concerns about AIDS and the spread of sexually transmitted diseases, as well as sharing your values and being open to hearing your child's values. Because many young people feel embarrassed to talk openly with their parents about sex, you might find another place where your child feels safe to discuss concerns and issues.

Never label your child or disrespect him or her by calling names like "whore," "slut," or "pervert." It is not unusual for some young people to experiment with bisexuality and to question their sexual preferences. These issues can be gut wrenching for both you and your child, so find a safe place to discuss your struggles.

The greatest contributor to teen pregnancy is the lack of sex education and a failure on the part of the significant adults in teens' lives to acknowledge and cope with teen sexual activity. You really can't avoid sex education, because even refusing to talk about sex is a form of sex education that could invite damaging conclusions such as "sex is secret, bad, and not to be discussed with your parents." In most cases, these conclusions don't prevent sexual experimentation. They just invite guilt, shame, and silence after it has already taken place. We suggest that both parents talk about sex with their children, discussing the difference between sex and love. Make discussion, not agreement, the goal of conversations on sex education.

As parents, you may want to think your teens are asexual, just waiting until they are older for you to give them the "big talk." Guess again.

Even when you are open and willing to discuss sex with your kids, they may feel too embarrassed to talk to you. Teens have a need for privacy, and this is one area where that need is strongly felt. To save their lives and to prevent your children from having children, you need to have birth-control and safe-sex information readily available. Prevention of AIDS is best accomplished by using condoms, and yet most teens are not likely to have the nerve, the money, or the desire to go to a store to buy them. Teens are certain they are invincible and may even think they are immune to AIDS. For this reason, some parents have decided to keep a supply of condoms next to the extra soap, toothpaste, and toilet paper in the linen closet, even if they themselves feel uncomfortable talking with their kids about sex or their kids feel uncomfortable talking with them. Yet these parents notice the supply has to be replenished from time to time, and they feel it is the least they can do if their teens or some of their friends have decided to be sexually active.

Parents who buy condoms for their teens may or may not approve of their kids having sex, but they don't want to see their children die from AIDS or bring children into the world before their teen is ready to parent and love them. One out of four female teenagers will be pregnant before the age of twenty. Therefore, within the bounds of your religious, moral, and ethical beliefs, it is important that you develop a strategy for dealing with your adolescent's sexuality.

Sexual Abuse and Incest

Sexual abuse is one of the most painful dysfunctional systems for anyone to deal with. The following poem says it all:

Pain

Pain is so sad to see
It hurts so much inside you
But no one cares to see
The pain that is inside you
Hurts like no other
It hurts so much more
That you wish you could die
You know the pain won't last
Not forever at least
As you cry yourself to sleep
No matter how hard you try
To make it cease
But the pain keeps growing
Growing forever deep
This kind of pain leaves deep scars
You feel you can't go on
You know you must so you try
Every day you live like this
Hurts you even more
Your pains are so true and deep
You feel no one understands
You see my friend
I understand because I too
Hurt the same as you
Someday soon you too
Will no longer be feeling blue
Everything will get better
Maybe not so soon
Don't forget though

That happiness is waiting for you
To come and take its hand.

Emily, a thirteen-year-old survivor of incest, wrote "Pain." Emily's experience wasn't uncovered until her mother went to a therapist to deal with some other issues. Mom was feeling a lot of pressure in the family, but she couldn't put her finger on any one thing. She simply knew it just didn't feel right around her house anymore, so she decided to go in for counseling. As a result, she became more open and emotionally honest. Her improved communication skills started rubbing off on her thirteen-year-old daughter. One day, her daughter told her that one of her relatives was molesting her. It ultimately came out that there had been sexual abuse in this relative's home for years, and nobody had known. This is not unusual in a dysfunctional system. Because denial is such a big part of dysfunction, many people won't admit there is a problem until it slips out.

Emily's upbringing had been very strict, and her parents had overprotected her. Emily's family taught her to do as she was told and to listen to grown-ups. Because her siblings had been rebellious, Emily took the "good, compliant child" role in the family. She focused on doing what others wanted. In some ways, Emily's molestation was an extension of her thinking—she couldn't see an alternative to doing what older people wanted her to do. When the perpetrators asked her to cooperate, she worried that she wouldn't be loved if she said no. Luckily for Emily, when she told about the abuse, her mother never questioned the truth of her statements.

We cannot emphasize how important it is to take your kids seriously when they tell you something of this nature. They have already experienced a great deal of shame, guilt, and degradation. They have felt isolated and thought of themselves as "bad." The last thing they need is for you to question or blame them.

Once again, this is an area where outside help is essential through therapy or group support. Many communities have Parents United programs and other similar services to help you deal with sexual abuse and incest.

Most often, the perpetrator of incest or sexual abuse will deny that it happened and accuse the victim of lying. Their denial is similar to the addict who is protecting his use. In this case, the perpetrator may also be saving face. Nevertheless, they, too, need help. Perpetrators' healings begin when they find out they are still worthwhile human beings with certain behaviors that must stop immediately. They need to hear that help is available to deal with the feelings, thoughts, and behaviors that brought them to this situation in the first place.

The healing process for someone who has been molested is a long one, but it is much easier if your child can be helped before he or she represses the information. Otherwise, it can take years and years of pain for the information to surface again so that it can be dealt with. Repression never makes the pain go away. Only talking about the problem and dealing with the feelings can do that.

Just as in chemical dependency, the healing process involves the entire family, as all of you have a reaction and are affected by the problem. Those family members who are unwilling to participate in therapy and self-help groups continue to suffer until they do get help.

Teen Suicide

SUICIDE IS A choice. When your teens lose self-confidence, suicide becomes one of their choices. A loss of self-confidence coupled with the belief that control is out of their hands may lead to teen suicide. Many teen suicides are also drug related. If your kids haven't been learning how to cope with life's difficulties themselves, or how to solve their problems and stand on their own feet, suicide may look like the only choice left to them. Many kids haven't learned that making a mistake is just an opportunity to try again, and not the end of the world. Unfortunately, because teens can be so intense and dramatic, they may choose a final solution to a temporary problem without a lot of forethought.

> Many kids haven't learned that making a mistake is just an opportunity to try again, and not the end of the world.

Losing a child has got to be one of the most difficult experiences that parents could ever face, and losing a child to suicide may be doubly hard. We wish we could give a formula to make sure no one ever had to go through this kind of pain, but that isn't possible. All we can really say is that it's vital to heed warning signs and get help immediately.

Take your teens seriously if they exhibit signs of suicide. Encourage them to talk to you or help them find someone they can talk to. Show concern and really listen, even if they have threatened suicide in the past without following through with action. They need a ray of hope to let them know that, however bad it may seem now, there is a tomorrow when "this too shall pass." One mother who suspected her daughter might be thinking of suicide told her, "Honey, I remember a couple of times when I felt like committing suicide. I felt so bad; I couldn't imagine things getting any better. But they did. I hate to think of how much I would have missed if I had killed myself. For one thing, I would have missed you."

When talking to your child about suicide, it's important to use words such as *suicide* and *death*. Don't shy away from these terms for fear of introducing an idea that you think your teen doesn't already have. Ask if they have a plan or if they've tried already. Finding out their plan shows you how far along they are in their thinking—a teen with a plan is like a loose cannon.

You can ask your child how his life would be different if he killed himself. By doing so, you'll probably find out what is really troubling him. The following conversation shows the wrong way to react. We include it here because, unfortunately, it is more typical of parental responses than doing what needs to be done. It shows a lack of compassion, a judgmental attitude, and no listening.

CLIFF: No one cares if I live or die.

DAD: You always feel so sorry for yourself.

CLIFF: Well, you and Mom split up and you expect me to live with that disgusting person who calls herself my stepmother.

DAD: How dare you talk like that around me! Your stepmother is doing the best she can.

CLIFF: Oh, yeah? Then why does she hit me and put me down in front of my friends?

DAD: Cliff, I know your stepmother, and I know that just isn't true. Why do you tell such lies?

CLIFF: Nobody believes me. I hate you all, and I wish I were dead! A lot you guys would care!

DAD: Cliff, there you go exaggerating again. You know you don't mean what you say. Now settle down and think about how you can get along better with your stepmother.

In this family, Cliff didn't kill himself, but he did run away at the age of fourteen and no one knows where or how he is.

If Cliff's father had taken Cliff seriously, he would have used the listening skills described in chapter 7. He also would have reassured Cliff that he was concerned and that he would like to go with Cliff to see a counselor so they both could get some help with this problem. When you operate in these ways with your kids—when you see your mistakes—you need to bury the hatchet, admit your mistakes, and try again.

Don't hesitate to seek professional help if there are any indications of suicide. Stella felt helpless to deal with the discouragement of her daughter, Traci, who was acting more and more depressed. Stella asked Traci if she would see a therapist. Traci agreed but wanted her mother to go with her. The therapist asked Traci to fill out a different kind of "pie" chart than the one described under sibling rivalry. This chart listed four slices of life: family, friends, school, and love. Traci was asked to rate each slice of the pie with a one to ten, with a ten representing the best. Traci marked a two in family slice (her parents were talking divorce, but she loved both parents very much), a zero in the friend slice (she had just had a huge fight with her best friend and thought there was no hope of a resolution), a one in the school slice (she was failing—probably because of all the other problems), and a 10 in the love slice (she felt the only good thing in her life was her supportive boyfriend).

The counselor said, "No wonder you are feeling so discouraged. Three out of four areas of your life seem very dismal. However, did you know that suicide is a permanent solution to a temporary problem?"

Traci thought about that, and then asked, "Do you really think these other problems are temporary?"

The counselor asked, "What do you think?"

Traci said, "I guess they are, but I don't see any solutions now."

The counselor asked, "Would you like some help with solutions?"

Traci said yes, and the counselor suggested they tackle one at a time. Traci chose the friend slice. The counselor role-played with her on ways to talk with her friend to solve their problem. Traci left feeling very encouraged and hopeful. She said, "I know things will get better. I certainly wouldn't want to try a permanent solution to a temporary problem." That statement had obviously made a deep impact. It is a good quote to share with teens once in awhile—even if they aren't feeling discouraged—so they will have it for future reference.

Eating Disorders

WHEN SOME SCARY behaviors, such as sex or suicide or sexual abuse, are involved, you may have a tendency to ignore the topic and hope that it will take care of itself. But when diet is concerned, like most parents, you probably take the opposite approach and become overly involved in an area that is often none of your business.

Parental concern for the health of their children can get out of proportion around the subject of food, especially because many of you have your own hang-ups about weight, looks, and diet. You try to be good parents by making sure your kids eat properly. Quite often, instead of providing healthy choices and trusting your kids to eat when they are hungry and stop when they are not, you interfere in this natural process and, without knowing it, plant the seeds for eating disorders.

Most eating disorders start in childhood. For many different reasons, some children stop regulating their eating internally, stop listening to their bodies' cues, and no longer trust themselves to eat what is right for them. Because everything can be intense and extreme when kids are teens, problem eating in the younger years can take on serious and even life-threatening proportions in the teen years.

Teens with eating disorders have become dependent on external processes to control their weight. In the most extreme cases, they have completely stopped listening to their bodies' cues to the point of near death.

Just like chemically dependent people, teens experiencing eating disorders come to a point where they can't stop their damaging behavior without help. Their eating patterns are no longer voluntary but compulsive.

Some of the most common eating disorders we see in teens are extreme obesity; anorexia or near starvation by a restricted amount of food intake; and bulimia, a condition in which people binge on food and then induce vomiting or use laxatives as a means to stay thin. The last two patterns are found mostly, but not exclusively, in females.

Eating Disorders and Control Issues

Most eating disorders have to do with control issues that the teen has. At some point, teens with eating disorders lost their own sense of power over their bodies and either eat out of control (obesity) or use starvation (anorexia) or vomiting (bulimia) to overcompensate for their lack of power. In other cases, they decided they were bad or undeserving and punished themselves through food or a lack of food.

To say that a teen with an eating disorder is discouraged is an understatement. Why they would chose to act out their discouragement through food, though, is usually a function of the atmosphere created by society or the parent or by the parental style of nurturing.

This is one of those places where changing your behavior a little can make huge differences to your teen, who can then change his or her behavior a lot. One of the best ways to prevent or stop potentially damaging patterns from getting out of hand is to stop interfering with your kids' food intake. That includes putting kids on diets, nagging, criticizing, taking them to clinics and doctors without being asked, controlling what foods or how much they are allowed to eat, or taking away allowances so they can't buy food. You can also look at your own attitudes about weight and the modeling you're doing with your eating patterns. However, if your child is overweight, you can stop bringing junk food into the house yourself, and you can provide healthy meals.

As frightening as some of these eating disorders can be, most of them can be prevented if you just turn eating over to the child. One mother learned that whenever her teen says she's going on a diet, it's better to say, "That's nice," and see what happens than to lecture, panic, or even help. Usually, her already trim daughter diets for a few days and then goes back to her normally balanced and healthy eating patterns (which include a certain amount of junk food). And if your child decides to become a vegetarian, ask how you can be supportive. On the other hand, if you are a vegetarian and your child insists on eating meat, the same advice applies.

Express your concerns, if you must, in nonjudgmental ways, such as, "I'm concerned about your excessive dieting because you're already so thin." Then ask your teen to describe the way she is eating. Let your teen know that secrets make people sick, so if you suspect she is throwing up or starving herself, you say it first. Let your child know that you saw her make herself throw up, if that happened, and that you have scheduled help as this is a very serious condition.

We believe the very best way to help your kids be fit is regular exercise. Set up opportunities for them to exercise, and maybe go with them. Normal weight is a function of both internal regulation and exercise. Joining a health club, skiing, buying a set of weights and a bench are simply a few suggestions out of many possibilities. Making these available without control may be much appreciated by teenagers.

Never insist your child eat everything on his or her plate or eat only when you are hungry. Your job is to encourage your child to listen to his or her body rhythms and to take them seriously. We know you would never call your child names like "fatty," "skinny," or "tubby," so we don't have to mention it, but you might make more subtle comments about how cute she would look if she lost a few pounds or dressed differently. Most teens are already so self-conscious about appearance that your comments along those lines only make matters worse. When you hear the stories of people who have anorexia or bulimia, it often started when they heard someone call them fat.

Because any discouraging behavior tends to be a mistaken way of dealing with thoughts and feelings, it is also important to listen to your kids and not to discount or ignore their feelings. Through the communication skills taught in chapter 7, you can also help your kids learn to express their feelings in words rather than through discouraged behaviors. If you find yourselves focusing on achievement rather than on building competence, you need to back off, because such pressure gives the message that you only love your kids if they are "perfect."

Many teens who have been physically, sexually, or verbally abused, or who have grown up in families where a parent is chemically dependent, have made the mistaken decision that there is something wrong with them, that they are different, and that they are worthless. Not only can they find comfort in eating, but also being overweight is an unconscious way of proving their lack of self-worth.

If your kids' eating disorders have moved into the extreme, get professional help, which includes a trip to the doctor to check out your teen's physical condition, a series of appointments with a therapist, and help from a dietician if needed. In an extreme case, your teen may first need to be stabilized medically before he or she can learn to change the symptoms and deal with the deeper issues in therapy. Once again, the greater the involvement of the family in the therapy process, the faster the healing for the teen.

Young Adults Who Won't or Can't Leave Home

TODAY WE HAVE a new phenomenon—kids who won't leave home. These are people in their twenties who have still not become responsible adults with good judgment.

In view of the problems we've been exploring, it may be surprising to think of children who won't leave home as exhibiting dysfunctional behavior; but we think children who lack the courage or the drive to start their own lives away from their families have serious problems. We are also concerned about the changes in our culture that leave many parents thinking it is their job to provide room and board, advice, cars, money, and maid service to their young adults. There was a time when mothers dreaded the day of the empty nest, when their children had all left home and left them feeling no longer needed. Today, many parents long for an empty nest, wondering if their grown children will ever leave home and be on their own.

Why are thousands of adult children still living at home with their parents? Many kids want to live at home because they can't live anywhere else in the style to which their parents helped them become accustomed with so little effort of their own. Other kids stay home because their overprotective parents have completely convinced them that they'll never make it on their own and there's no point in trying. They've lost faith in themselves. Some stay home be-

cause they have an alcoholic or severely discouraged parent who they are convinced will die without them.

If your adult kids are living at home, the kindest thing that you can do is
move them out. You can give them a deadline and offer to help them find a
job, make a budget, or find a place to live. If you would have helped a child fi-
nancially who went to college, consider helping the non-college bound young
adult with a small monthly stipend until he or she gets started. The best rule of
thumb is to help those who are helping themselves.

Summary

WE KNOW WE have said it a gazillion times. You can probably even guess
what we are going to say. That is good. You got it. But, just in case you can't
guess, here it is: Know your teen. Love your teen unconditionally. Spend
time that counts with your teen. Provide opportunities for your teen to learn
skills. Have faith in your teen. These are the ingredients that provide the best
prevention for most problems. And, most of all, enjoy your teen—whenever
you can.

KIND AND FIRM PARENTING TOOLS TO REMEMBER

1. When your teens do something that scares you, tell them that it scares you.
    Ask them to stop doing the scary behavior, letting them know that what
    they are doing may not be a problem for them but that the thought of los-
    ing them is a problem for you. If they understand your reasons, they just
    might comply, especially if they respect your opinion.

2. Don't expect your kids to deal with gangs, bullies, and violence alone. Find
    ways to help them through whatever difficulties they encounter.

3. Remind yourself about the continuum of drug use if you start panicking.
    Review the different parent behaviors for each stop on the continuum.

4. No matter how worried you are about the right way to say things, let go of your fears of making a mistake and make an effort to talk with your teen, to say what you think and feel. Not talking is worse.

5. If an intervention is in order, give it a try. You'll get many chances to try again even if the first, second, or third ones don't work.

6. Most teens today are sexual beings whether you approve or not, so start talking with your teen and creating a dialogue rather than trying to get promises that probably won't be kept.

7. If you think that sexual or physical abuse is occurring in your house, get help quickly. You won't be judged; you and the rest of your family will get a release from the pain.

8. Take all threats of suicide seriously enough to talk with your teen either by yourself or with the help of a counselor. Even if your teen uses the expression, "I could kill myself," as a way of making a point and not as a threat, you need to explain why that particular comment isn't helpful and suggest some other ways to express feelings.

9. Stop trying to control what your teens eat or how they look, and watch many eating disorders disappear as if by magic.

Practical Application Activity

TEEN SECRETS

It's easy to "catastrophize" the outcome of normal teenage behavior and believe that how your teens are now is how they will be forever. Remembering your teen years can relieve your worries and restore your faith in your teens.

1. List at least three things you did as a teenager that you didn't want your parents to know about.

2. Are there any entries on your list that you still have never told anyone?

3. What relationship, if any, do you see between your own teen secrets and your fears or judgments about your teen?

4. Your teens love it when you share some of your secrets with them so they don't feel like they're the only "bad" people in the family. It makes you seem more human, too, which is a real asset at this time.

MY PLAN FOR THE WEEK

This week I will focus on

_____

_____

I will work on changing my attitude by thinking

_____

_____

_____

I will change my behavior by doing

_____

_____

_____

15

Conclusion

Can I Change?
Is It Worth It?

CHANGE ISN'T EASY, but of course you can do it—if you know it is worth it. Is it worth it for you to have a good relationship with your teen now and a truly fabulous relationship when the teen years are over? Is it worth it for you to provide opportunities for your teens to develop beliefs and skills that will help them become happy contributing members of society? Is it worth it for you to enjoy parenting and to find it a rewarding experience instead of a frustrating and discouraging experience?

If you answer yes to any or all of these questions, then change is worth the effort it takes—and it does take effort.

The Lazy Parent

WE KNOW YOU are not a lazy parent, but did you know that some of your neighbors are? They will try some of the methods we have suggested, and will probably even experience some success. However, at the first hurdle, they will forget their long-term goals, give up, and go back to their old, disrespectful methods.

Your lazy neighbors don't care if they ever deal with their unresolved issues. They would rather live in denial and space out in front of the TV, or become workaholics or "activiti-aholics."

Your lazy neighbors will wallow in guilt the first time they make a mistake, instead of getting excited about the possibilities of what they can learn from the mistake—and how they can model for their teens that mistakes are wonderful opportunities to learn.

Your lazy neighbors prefer the quick fix they obtain when they use control or permissiveness. They will not bother to think about the long-term effects—about what their teens are feeling, thinking, learning, and deciding about what they will do in the future.

Because you are not a lazy parent, you will deal with your unresolved issues (which can take a lifetime of exciting discovery); you will learn from your mistakes; you will keep your long-term goals (for yourself and for your teens) in mind; and you will truly enjoy your teens—most of the time. And, you will keep up with the times.

Society Changes and Grows

IT WASN'T TOO long ago that the word *teenager* could not be found in the dictionary. In those days adolescents served an apprenticeship to learn a skill, got married, and as adults often did not live past the age of thirty-six.

Although political, economic, and health standards have changed dramatically in our society, it seems to be more difficult to catch up with emotional and social changes. In one of our workshops, we invited participants to look at the different characteristics of teens in the 1920s, the 1960s, and the 1980s. Participants were amazed to see tremendous differences, and then more amazed to see how little parenting had changed. Parenting skills had obviously not kept up with the times. The only major change the workshop participants could see was the importance currently placed on helping children develop healthy self-esteem. However, they concluded this is largely an intellectual understanding, because parents still use the old methods of overcontrol or overprotection, which makes it difficult for children to feel good about themselves.

> Your challenge as a parent is to grow and change as fast as the times do and as fast as your teenagers do.

Your challenge as a parent is to grow and change as fast as the times do and as fast as your teenagers do. The first step is to stop treating your children like babies, especially your teens. You need to treat them like people who are worthy of respect and who are capable of learning, contributing, and growing.

I've Already Made So Many Mistakes! Is It Too Late?

MANY PARENTS WONDER if it's too late to repair a severely damaged relationship with their teenage sons or daughters. It's never too late. Relationships can be repaired and redeemed. Beth told of repairing an extremely dysfunctional relationship with her son after learning some of the principles we teach in this book:

> *My oldest son left home at the age of fourteen to hitchhike across the country. As I look back on the situation now, I can see how wise and capable he was to leave a situation where I vacillated between overcontrol and overpermissiveness and then always berated him for not cooperating.*
>
> *I had just learned about the principles for empowering teens and was able to empower him at a time when it was very scary for me to do so. He*

was getting involved with drugs. I wondered about his sudden interest in weeding the garden and discovered he was growing pot in our backyard. When I told him this wasn't acceptable, he threatened to leave home. He had run away from home before when we had arguments. I could see that something had to be done to stop the destructive patterns of argument and manipulation we were following.

I sat down with him one day and decided to be totally honest. I started by telling him I loved him unconditionally. I then told him I didn't agree that using drugs was right, but admitted, "Who am I to talk? I do stuff that isn't making me happy. I'm a pleaser and a workaholic. All the stuff I do is accepted by society, but it isn't healthy. I don't think drugs are the answer, and I don't understand drug use, but I don't know. I know I'm not willing to let you grow pot in my backyard because it's against the law, and I'm not willing to risk the consequences of breaking the law. If you choose to do that you can't live here. If you choose to leave, I hope you'll remember that I love you unconditionally. I hope you'll keep in touch and even feel free to tell me your feelings and experiences with drugs. I hope some day you'll stop using drugs because I know they aren't the answer, anymore than what I do is the answer."

He chose to leave saying, "I guess you would rather have me grow pot out in the open where I can get caught than in the safety of my backyard." I didn't let that guilt trip hook me. I said, "I wish you wouldn't leave, but I know you'll do what you want to do and that I can't stop you."

When he'd run away before, the police would stop him a lot and hassle him. He asked if I would give him a note saying he had permission to hitchhike. I knew a lot of people would think I was crazy, but I knew he was going to go. I knew I couldn't control him. I decided to follow my gut-level desire to let go and support him in what he was going to do anyway.

Sure enough, I got calls from sheriffs in several states who thought I was an extremely neglectful parent. I was sure most people would agree and often was afraid they might be right. To back off and give nothing but unconditional love was scary, but the long-range results speak for themselves.

At fourteen, my son found jobs so he could survive. He found friends and set up apartments. He became a carpenter's helper, eventually became a very skilled carpenter, and built his own house. It took him eight years to decide drugs did not fit into his life. I may be deluding myself, but I think one reason he was able to come to that conclusion eventually was because I removed one reason for him to continue—rebellion against me.

He is now an adult, married and has two children. We've developed a wonderful relationship. A highlight of my life was when he called one day and said, "Mom, you're one of my best friends. No, you are my best friend." And that's the way I feel about him. He's one of my favorite people to be around. We share things with each other now that only best friends would feel free to share. He knows I'll never judge him for anything, and I know he'll never judge me for anything.

Okay! Okay! But Why Is Change So Hard?

IT CAN BE very difficult to let go and believe in the basic capability of your teenagers to learn without being controlled or overprotected by you. A basic reason for this difficulty is not understanding the difference between fearful parenting and courageous parenting.

Fearful Parenting

Fearful parenting is not letting go because it is too hard. You're scared and you fear permanent damage. You think control works. You take the easy way out rather than facing your fears, seeing your own issues, and growing past them. Fearful parenting happens when you don't see small-step alternatives, so you think your only choice is to do nothing, and that isn't okay with you. After all, you were probably raised by parents who were controlling or permissive (or both) and you turned out okay—didn't you?

Fearful parenting is worrying more about what others might think or say than doing what is best for your teenagers, including allowing them to learn from their mistakes. It means being more interested in perfection than in the growth of your teenagers. You think it's your job to "overparent." Maybe you don't have anything better to do. Fearful parenting is reactive because you are sure that you only have one chance to deal with any given situation and you don't dare make a mistake or your child will suffer irreparable damage.

Fearful parents don't mean to hurt their children, but there are many things they do unknowingly that stunt their teens' growth and development. Overprotection, control, rigid rules, and a lack of communication are but a few of the methods that contribute to stealing strength and capability from teens. You can't control what other parents do, but you can stop doing that to your teenagers.

> Fearful parenting is worrying more about what others might think or say than doing what is best for your teenagers, including allowing them to learn from their mistakes.

Courageous Parenting

Courageous parenting means facing the fear (yes, it is scary to let go and allow your children to make mistakes) and doing what needs to be done anyway because of the greater good. Courageous parenting means taking the time to teach skills even though it's easier to criticize or rescue.

1. Surround yourself with other people who have the same goals.

    (This may mean starting your own parenting support group.)

2. Read this book again and again. You will learn something new with every reading.

3. Do the activities at the end of each chapter.

Courageous parenting is having faith in the basic capabilities of your teenagers and knowing they can learn when given the room and support they need.

When you think of your teens as competent and capable people who have the ability to learn what is good for them through experience, it's easier to be courageous.

Ruth exemplifies the capabilities of a teenager. At fifteen, she was able to plan the menu, shop for groceries, cook, do her laundry, get herself to school, figure out her homework, get to the library to research projects, get good grades in school, bake and wrap cookies for all her friends at school, and buy presents for all her friends with money she had earned, saved, and managed.

Ruth figured out how to pay for part of a car and the insurance on that car. By sixteen, she had a car and at seventeen took her first solo long-distance trip to Los Angeles, where she lived on her own for a month while attending dance classes. These capabilities and accomplishments weren't accidental.

In Ruth's family, kids participated in family meetings, did chores, had allowances to manage themselves, handled their own homework without parental interference, and were allowed to pursue whatever they felt ready to do with support and help from their parents. No one forced Ruth to be independent, but she was given encouragement and taught the life skills necessary to succeed.

Accidental Empowerment

SOMETIMES TEENS ARE allowed to work things out for themselves simply because their parents don't know what their teens are doing so they don't interfere. Roy shared an example of accidental empowerment:

I'm so glad I didn't know Ian was cutting classes to go surfing for most of the school year. He had a friend in the attendance office who was covering for him, and his grades were A's and B's, so I never found out. When Ian finally told me about his escapades, I said, "How could I have missed all that?" He said, "Aren't you glad you did? We would have been fighting constantly and it wouldn't have changed anything except our relationship. I learned what I needed to learn, too, when I couldn't get into the university because of my grades and had to start off in the state college. But you know what, Dad, I'd probably do the same thing all over again. I've made tons of great friends both surfing and at the college, and it cost a lot less for me to figure out what I wanted to major in."

Perspective Helps

DURING INDIVIDUATION, YOUR teenagers, like Ian, may seem to get all topsy-turvy. So do you when you let your fears run rampant based on the horror stories you've heard about the few teenagers who ended up badly. But if you keep your perspective, you'll know that most teens usually end up on their feet.

Part of helping your teens come back to themselves is giving them the room to travel experimental roads and try out different roles. Adolescence is a time for tremendous growth and change. Teens need all the support they can get from you. You can be their copilots until they are ready to fly solo.

As parents you have a choice—to control or empower, to protect or empower, to feel pity or empower. The choice is yours, and when you choose to stop stealing their confidence and initiative away from them, your teens strengthen their wings so they can fly on their own.

BIBLIOGRAPHY

Adler, Alfred. *Cooperation Between the Sexes.* New York: Anchor Books, 1978.

———. *Social Interest.* New York: Capricorn Books, 1964.

———. *Superiority and Social Interest.* Evanston, IL: Northwestern University Press, 1964.

———. *What Life Should Mean to You.* New York: Capricorn Books, 1958.

Albert, Linda. *Coping with Kids.* New York: E. P. Dutton, 1982.

Ansbacher, Heinz, and Rowena Ansbacher. *The Individual Psychology of Alfred Adler.* New York: Harper Torchbooks, 1964.

Bayard, Robert, and Jean Bayard. *How to Deal with Your Acting-Up Teenager.* San Jose, CA: The Accord Press, 1981.

Beecher, Willard, and Marguerite Beecher. *Beyond Success and Failure.* New York: Pocket Books, 1966.

Christianson, Oscar. *Adlerian Family Counseling.* Minneapolis, MN: Educational Media, 1983.

Corsini, Raymond, and Genevieve Painter. *The Practical Parent.* New York: Harper and Row, 1975.

Corsini, Raymond, and Clinton Phillips. *Give In or Give Up.* Chicago: Nelson Hall, 1982.

Deline, John. *Who's Raising the Family?* Madison, WI: Wisconsin Clearing House, 1981.

Dinkmeyer, Don, and Rudolf Dreikurs. *Encouraging Children to Learn: The Encouragement Process.* Englewood Cliffs, NJ: Prentice-Hall, 1963.

Dinkmeyer, Don, and Gary McKay. *Parents Handbook: Systematic Training for Effective Parenting,* 3rd edition. Circle Pines, MN: American Guidance Service, 1989.

———. *Raising a Responsible Child.* New York: Simon & Schuster, 1978.

Dinkmeyer, Don, and W. L. Pew. *Adlerian Counseling and Psychotherapy.* Monterey, CA: Brooks/Cole, 1979.

Dreikurs, Rudolf. *Psychology in the Classroom.* New York: Harper and Row, 1966.

————. *Social Equality: The Challenge of Today.* Chicago: Contemporary Books, 1971.

Dreikurs, Rudolf, Raymond Corsini, and S. Gould. *Family Council.* Chicago: Henry Regnery, 1974.

Dreikurs, Rudolf, Bernice Grunwald, and Floyd Pepper. *Maintaining Sanity in the Classroom,* 2nd edition. Accelerated Development, 1998.

Dreikurs, Rudolf, and V. Soltz. *Children: The Challenge.* New York: E. P. Dutton, 1987.

Glenn, H. Stephen. *Developing Capable People* (audiotape set). Orem, UT: Empowering People, Books, Tapes and Videos (1-800-456-7770).

————. *Developing Healthy Self-Esteem* (audiotape/videotape). Orem, UT: Empowering People, Books, Tapes and Videos (1-800-456-7770).

————. *Empowering Others: Ten Keys to Affirming and Validating People* (videotape). Orem, UT: Empowering People, Books, Tapes and Videos (1-800-456-7770).

————. *The Greatest Human Need* (videotape). Orem, UT: Empowering People, Books, Tapes and Videos (1-800-456-7770).

————. *Introduction to Developing Capable People* (videotape). Orem, UT: Empowering People, Books, Tapes and Videos (1-800-456-7770).

————. *Six Steps to Developing Responsibility* (videotape). Orem, UT: Empowering People, Books, Tapes and Videos (1-800-456-7770).

————. *Teachers Who Make a Difference* (videotape). Orem, UT: Empowering People, Books, Tapes and Videos (1-800-456-7770).

Glenn, H. Stephen, and Jane Nelsen. *Raising Self-Reliant Children in a Self-Indulgent World.* Rocklin, CA: Prima Publishing, 1988.

Janoe, Ed, and Barbara Janoe. *About Anger.* Vancouver, WA: Arco Press, 1973.

————. *Dealing with Feelings.* Vancouver, WA: Arco Press, 1973.

Kvols, Kathy. *Redirecting Children's Misbehavior.* Seattle: Parenting Press, 1997.

Lott, Lynn, and Jane Nelsen. *Teaching Parenting Manual.* Orem, UT: Empowering People, Books, Tapes and Videos (1-800-456-7770).

Lott, Lynn, and Riki Intner. *Chores Without Wars.* Rocklin, CA: Prima Publishing, 1997.

Lott, Lynn, Riki Intner, and Barbara Mendenhall. *Do-It-Yourself Therapy: How to Think, Feel, and Act Like a New Person in Just 8 Weeks.* Franklin Lakes, NJ: Career Press, 1999.

Manaster, Guy J., and Raymond Corsini. *Individual Psychology.* Itasca, IL: F. E. Peacock Publishers, 1982.

Nelsen, Jane. *From Here to Serenity: Four Principles for Understanding Who You Really Are.* Roseville, CA: Prima Publishing, 2000

————. *Positive Discipline.* New York: Ballantine Books, 1996.

————. *Positive Discipline* (audiotape). Orem, UT: Empowering People, Books, Tapes and Videos (1-800-456-7770).

————. *Positive Discipline* (videotape set). Orem, UT: Empowering People, Books, Tapes and Videos (1-800-456-7770).

————. *Positive Time-Out and 50 Other Ways to Avoid Power Struggles in Homes and Schools.* Rocklin, CA: Prima Publishing, 1999.

Nelsen, Jane, Cheryl Erwin, and Carol Delzer. *Positive Discipline for Single Parents.* Rocklin, CA: Prima Publishing, 1999.

Nelsen, Jane, Riki Intner, and Lynn Lott. *Positive Discipline for Parenting in Recovery.* Rocklin, CA: Prima Publishing, 1996.

Nelsen, Jane, Lynn Lott, and H. Stephen Glenn. *Positive Discipline: A–Z.* Rocklin, CA: Prima Publishing, 1999.

————. *Positive Discipline in the Classroom.* Roseville, CA: Prima Publishing, 2000.

Pew, W. L., and J. Terner. *Courage to Be Imperfect.* New York: Hawthorn Books, 1978.

Smith, Manuel J. *When I Say No I Feel Guilty.* New York: The Dial Press, 1975.

Walton, F. X. *Winning Teenagers Over.* Columbia, SC: Adlerian Child Care Books.

Information on Special Problems

Al-Anon Family Group. *Al-Anon: Is It for You?* New York: Al-Anon Family Group Headquarters, 1983.

Alcoholics Anonymous World Services. *Alcoholics Anonymous "The Big Book,"* 3rd edition. New York: Author, 1976.

Beattie, Melody. *Co-Dependent No More: How to Stop Controlling Others and Start Caring for Yourself.* San Francisco: Harper/Hazelden, 1987.

Black, Claudia. *It's Never Too Late to Have a Happy Childhood.* New York: Ballantine Books, 1989.

————. *My Dad Loves Me, My Dad Has a Disease.* Center City, NJ: Hazelden Educational Materials,1989.

Hafen, Brent Q., with Kathryn J. Frandsen. *The Crisis Intervention Handbook.* Englewood Cliffs, NJ: Prentice-Hall, 1982.

Hollis, Judi. *Fat Is a Family Affair.* San Francisco: Harper/Hazelden, 1986.

Kimball, Bonnie-Jean. *The Alcoholic Woman's Mad, Mad World of Denial and Mind Games.* Center City, NJ: Hazelden Educational Materials, 1978.

McCabe, Thomas R. *Victims No More.* Center City, NJ: Hazelden Educational Materials, 1978.

Pickens, Roy W., and Dace S. Svikis. *Alcoholic Family Disorders: More Than Statistics.* Center City, NJ: Hazelden Educational Materials, Minneapolis, MN, 1985.

Powell, John S. *Why Am I Afraid to Tell You Who I Am?* Allen, TX: Argus Communications, 1969.

Wholey, Dennis. *The Courage to Change.* Boston: Houghton Mifflin, 1984.

Woititz, Janet Geringer. *Adult Children of Alcoholics.* Hollywood, FL: Health Communications, 1983.

————. Co-Dependency: The Insidious Invader of Intimacy. In *Co-Dependency, An Emerging Issue.* Hollywood, FL: Health Communications, 1984.

INDEX

ABOUT THE AUTHORS

 **Jane Nelsen** is a popular lecturer and coauthor of the entire POSITIVE DISCIPLINE series. She also wrote *From Here to Serenity: Four Principles for Understanding Who You Really Are.* She has appeared on *Oprah* and *Sally Jesse Raphael* and was the featured parent expert on the "National Parent Quiz," hosted by Ben Vereen. Jane is the mother of seven children and the grandmother of seventeen.

 **Lynn Lott,** family therapist, author, and speaker, has been helping people create more loving and healthy relationships since the early 1970s. She is coauthor of more than a dozen books, including many in the POSITIVE DISCIPLINE series and her latest, *Do-It-Yourself Therapy: How to Think, Feel, and Act Like a New Person in Just 8 Weeks.* Lynn divides her time among Point Richmond, Truckee, and Santa Rosa, California, where she works as a marriage and family therapist.

FOR MORE INFORMATION

THE AUTHORS ARE available for lectures, workshops, and seminars for parents, parent educators, therapists, psychologists, social workers, nurses, counselors, school administrators, teachers, and corporations. (Lectures can be tailored to fit your needs.)

Workshops include:

Positive Discipline in the Classroom (a two-day workshop or a one-day inservice)
Teaching Parenting the Positive Discipline Way (a two-day workshop)
Empowering Teens and Yourself in the Process
How to Think, Feel, and Act Like a New Person

Workshops, seminars, and facilitator training are scheduled throughout the United States each year. To find a location near you or to bring a workshop to your area, contact:

Jane Nelsen
Positive Discipline Associates
4984 Arboleda Drive
Fair Oaks, CA 95628
1-800-456-7770

Lynn Lott
Lynn Lott Enterprises
1201 Brickyard Way, #314
Point Richmond, CA 94801
maxlynski@aol.com
1-707-526-3141, ext. 3#

View www.positivediscipline.com for featured articles, answers to parent and teacher questions, and workshop and research information.

ORDER FORM

To: Empowering People, P.O. Box 1926, Orem, UT 84059
Phone: 1-800-456-7770 (credit card orders only)
Fax: 801-762-0022
Web Site: www.positivediscipline.com for discount prices

BOOKS

	Price	Quantity	Amount
Positive Discipline in the Classroom, by Nelsen, Lott, & Glenn	$16.95	_____	_____
Positive Discipline: A Teacher's A–Z Guide, by Nelsen, Duffy, Escobar, Ortolano, & Owen-Sohocki	$14.95	_____	_____
Positive Discipline for Preschoolers, by Nelsen, Erwin, & Duffy	$16.00	_____	_____
Positive Discipline: The First Three Years, by Nelsen, Erwin, & Duffy	$16.00	_____	_____
Positive Discipline, by Nelsen	$11.00	_____	_____
Positive Discipline A–Z, by Nelsen, Lott, & Glenn	$16.00	_____	_____
Positive Discipline for Teenagers, by Nelsen & Lott	$16.95	_____	_____
Positive Discipline for Your Step Family, by Nelsen, Erwin, & Glenn	$16.00	_____	_____
Positive Discipline for Single Parents, by Nelsen, Erwin, & Delzer	$16.00	_____	_____
Positive Discipline for Parenting in Recovery, by Nelsen, Intner, & Lott	$12.95	_____	_____
Raising Self-Reliant Children in a Self-Indulgent World, by Glenn & Nelsen	$12.95	_____	_____
Positive Time-Out, Nelsen	$12.00	_____	_____
From Here to Serenity, by Nelsen	$14.00	_____	_____
Chores Without Wars, by Lott & Intner	$9.95	_____	_____
7 Strategies for Developing Capable Students, by Glenn & Brock	$12.95	_____	_____
Do-It-Yourself Therapy, by Lott, Intner, & Mendenhall	$15.00	_____	_____

MANUALS

	Price	Quantity	Amount
Teaching Parenting the Positive Discipline Way, by Lott & Nelsen	$49.95	_____	_____
Positive Discipline in the Classroom, by Nelsen & Lott	$49.95	_____	_____

TAPES AND VIDEOS

	Price	Quantity	Amount
Positive Discipline audiotape	$10.00	_____	_____
Positive Discipline videotape	$49.95	_____	_____
Building Healthy Self-Esteem Through Positive Discipline audiotape	$10.00	_____	_____

SUBTOTAL _____

Sales tax: UT add 6.25%; CA add 7.25% _____

Shipping & handling: $3.00 plus $0.50 each item _____

(Prices subject to change without notice.) **TOTAL** _____

METHOD OF PAYMENT (check one):
_____ Check made payable to Empowering People Books, Tapes, & Videos
_____ MasterCard, Visa, Discover Card, American Express

Card # _____ Expiration _____/_____
Ship to _____
Address _____
City/State/Zip _____
Daytime phone (_____)_____